THE PROBLEM OF THE HOUSE

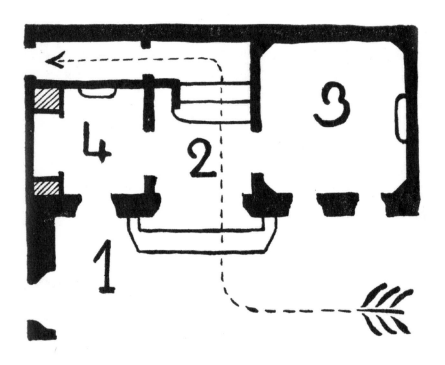

A MCLELLAN BOOK

UNIVERSITY OF WASHINGTON PRESS   *SEATTLE & LONDON*

THE
PROBLEM

FRENCH DOMESTIC LIFE

AND THE RISE OF

MODERN ARCHITECTURE

OF
THE
HOUSE

ALEX T. ANDERSON

The Problem of the House: French Domestic Life and the Rise of Modern Architecture is published with the assistance of grants from the McLellan Endowed Series Fund, established through the generosity of Martha McCleary McLellan and Mary McLellan Williams, and from the University of Washington Architecture Publications Fund.

UNIVERSITY OF WASHINGTON PRESS
PO Box 50096, Seattle, WA 98145
www.washington.edu/uwpress

The paper used in this publication meets the minimum requirements of American National Standard for Information Sciences–Permanence of Paper for Printed Library Materials, ANSI Z39.48-1984. ♾

LIBRARY OF CONGRESS
CATALOGING-IN-PUBLICATION DATA

Anderson, Alex Thomas.
The problem of the house :
French domestic life and the
rise of modern architecture /
Alex T. Anderson.
p. cm.
Includes bibliographical references
and index.
ISBN 0-295-98632-8 (hardback : alk.
paper)
ISBN 13: 978-0-295-98632-6
1. Architecture, Domestic—France.
2. Architecture—France—19th
century. 3. Architecture—France—
20th century. 4. Decorative arts—
France—History—19th century.
5. Decorative arts—France—
History—20th century. 6. Interior
decoration—France—Influence.
I. Title.

NA7346.A65   2006
728.0944'09041—dc22
2006004914

Front cover: Eileen Gray and Jean Badovici, E. 1027, 1926–29; *back cover, top:* Le Corbusier, immeubles-villas, 1922; *back cover, bottom:* Auguste Perret, Chana Orloff studio, 1926–29

FOR MAUREEN

CONTENTS

ACKNOWLEDGMENTS *ix*

INTRODUCTION *3*

1 RAISING UP THE BOURGEOIS HOME *23*

*The Ordinary Supersedes the Extraordinary
    at the Expositions Universelles 25*
Structural Rationalism and the New French House 32
The Liberalization of the Bourgeois French Interior 48
Domestic Themes in the Fine Arts 59

**2 DESIGN AND DOMESTIC SETTINGS:
THE SALONS D'AUTOMNE OF 1910 TO 1913** *68*

1910—The German Challenge 72
1911—Constructeur/Coloriste 77
1912—Un Salon Bourgeois 83
1913—The Good and Well-Made Thing 92

**3 THE WAR, HOUSE RECONSTRUCTION,
AND FURNITURE PRODUCTION** *107*

**4 THE END OF DECORATIVE ART,
THE HOUR OF ARCHITECTURE** *120*

Toward a Union of Modern Designers 128
The End of Decorative Art 133
The Hour of Architecture in France 136
The Architectes-Décorateurs 143
French Modern Architecture 161

AFTERWORD *163*

NOTES *169*

BIBLIOGRAPHY *195*

INDEX *207*

ILLUSTRATION CREDITS *219*

ACKNOWLEDGMENTS

Although its cover bears my name, this book results in large part from collaborative effort with friends and colleagues. Over the years of writing and producing this book I have had the privilege of receiving many people's ideas, support, encouragement, and advice. First among all of these collaborators is my wife, Maureen, whose friendship, unfailing enthusiasm, and myriad behind-the-scenes efforts exceed by far whatever thanks I can offer here. David Leatherbarrow helped me shape my first thoughts on the subjects covered in this book and deftly guided me to the right sources and better ways of looking at them. I am grateful for his continued friendship and well-considered advice. Joseph Rykwert and Marco Frascari read drafts of the manuscript in its earliest form as a dissertation at the University of Pennsylvania. Although that document underwent substantial changes on its way to becoming this book, their efforts are still a part of it. Vikram Prakash provided advice and enthusiastic support at a crucial moment when a less-defined manuscript began to take its current shape, and I gratefully acknowledge his continued support. Grant Hildebrand offered characteristically insightful feedback and thoughtful advice about the text and illustrations, and has been a ready source for good counsel on this project. I would also like to thank Jeffrey Ochsner for his encouragement and advice about the intricacies of producing a book of this sort and, more generally, for his kindness and mentorship over the years.

Many other friends and colleagues have read all or part of this book at various stages. I would especially like to thank two of them here. Claus Seligmann lent his critical eye to the text and helped me sort out some of its early shortcomings. Meredith Clausen provided prudent advice along the way, and I am grateful for her warm support of my efforts.

Many students in my seminars on early modern architecture at University of North Carolina at Charlotte and University of Washington have contributed to this book, perhaps unknowingly, but significantly nevertheless. Whether they accepted or challenged my views on the vital period of architectural history covered in this book, their work has served to deepen my understanding.

In the production of this book Michael Duckworth has been continually helpful in guiding me through the process. Although the people he selected to review the manuscript must remain anonymous, I am grateful for their critical feedback, and I hope that, in revising the manuscript, I have managed to do their efforts justice. Mary Ribesky has been a ready source of advice throughout the late stages of revisions and production. To Laura Iwasaki I offer special thanks for the great care she took in editing the manuscript and for her cheerful responses to my many queries about subtle points of grammar and style. Thanks to Breffni Whelan for preparing the index. I would also like to thank Nan Ching Tai, who generously produced the plans of Auguste Perret's rue Franklin apartment and Mela Muter studio.

Staff at libraries and archives in the United States and Europe have been a great help in locating source material and images for the book. I am grateful, in particular, for assistance I received at the libraries of the University of Washington, the University of North Carolina at Charlotte, and the University of Pennsylvania. I would also like to acknowledge with thanks the many people who assisted me at the Bibliothèque de la Ville in La Chaux-de-Fonds, Switzerland, the Fondacion Le Corbusier in Paris, the Musée des Arts Décoratifs in Paris, and the Bibliothèque Nationale in Paris. For their help tracking down images and securing permission to use them, Marcus Bugbee in Stuttgart, Frank Cruise in Dublin, Katherine

Danalakis in New York, Scott Gilchrist in Montreal, Nicole Heck in New York, Ingred Kastel in Vienna, Stéphanie Lemache near Caen, Anastasia Mikliaeva in St. Petersburg, Alexandre Ragois in Paris, Shelby Spaulding in San Antonio, and many others are all assured of my gratitude.

I received generous financial support for this project from the College of Architecture and Urban Planning and the Department of Architecture at the University of Washington, and from the College of Architecture at the University of North Carolina at Charlotte.

Finally, I would like to acknowledge a few people who have been a big part of this undertaking because they have been a big part of my life. My parents, Mary Pat and Tom Anderson, have never wavered in their enthusiasm for this, or any other project I have chosen to undertake. Their support from afar has been a source of great comfort. Closer to home, George, Maeve, and Gerald, my three bright and much-loved children, have grown up with this book. And they, more than anyone else, have wondered when it will be finished. That has been encouragement enough to keep the project moving. They each receive my heartfelt thanks—and a book on their shelves to remember what it was that kept their father up late too many nights while they slept and dreamed nearby.

THE PROBLEM OF THE HOUSE

INTRODUCTION

The problem of the house is a problem of the epoch. The equilibrium of society to-day depends upon it. Architecture has for its first duty, in this period of renewal, that of bringing about a revision of values, a revision of the constituent elements of the house.

—LE CORBUSIER, *TOWARDS A NEW ARCHITECTURE*

P aris, July 1925. Visible, but unobtrusive in a corner behind the Grand Palais, shaded by high elm trees, stands a single-family dwelling. The high stockade, erected by cautious exhibition administrators to obscure it from view, came down only a day or so ago. Its lines are straight and <u>unfettered</u>; its broad planes show shades of white and pastel. The lofty, prismatic volume opens on one side to form a porch and garden in which potted plants and ordinary steel café chairs repose (fig. 1.1). A tree passes through the floor of the porch and continues up through a broad circular opening in the flat roof above. Inside, a few pieces of carefully chosen furniture, a globe, several paintings, and a sculpture constitute the decor of a spacious living room (fig. 1.2). Pushed against the high white wall, a small table flanked by bentwood chairs supports a heavy glass bowl (an ashtray?) and a white ceramic vase with flowers. There are also a pen, ink, a notebook, a ledger, and a small stack of books. The notebook is open, and a chair has been pushed back (see fig. 74). Someone has just left the room. A steel stair climbs to the dressing rooms and bedrooms above.

This model dwelling is one of the great essays of modern architecture. Its designers envisioned it as "a house for everybody," one of a multitude of similar dwellings constructed in series and inhabited by ordinary people, who would furnish and equip them with inexpensive, standardized products of manufacturing industries.[1] Each dwelling unit thereby acts as the unobtrusive backdrop to a tale about individuality, about specific needs, about personal sentiments. Collected together in large apartment blocks, called *immeubles-villas*, the backdrop multiplies and stages many simultaneous stories (fig. 1.3).

These dwellings encompass the equipment and spaces of everyday living. They also demonstrate the advanced state of civilization. They show, in their selection of furnishings, that modern industry, through systematic refinement of ordinary, useful objects, has contributed a sense of purity to the things people use. They also "affirm the value of the pure work of art" by giving art the space in which to live unconstrained by the stultifying atmosphere of great public museums. And finally, they "demonstrate the radical transformations and new freedoms granted by reinforced concrete and steel in the conception of urban living."[2]

The Pavillon de l'Esprit Nouveau, by Le Corbusier and his cousin, Pierre Jeanneret, suggested a refuge for everyday existence and brought together the great advances in modern urban planning and the astounding innovations of engineering. But it did so under the unlikely "banner of decorative art." Le Corbusier extolled these developments in *The Decorative Art of Today* (L'art décoratif d'aujourd'hui): "The spirit which is awakening, springing up full of wonder, fighting against suffocation, winning its place and, as the days dawn, affirming itself in the clarity of an ideal precisely formulated, because precisely conceived—this spirit was first enlisted under the banner of decorative art."[3] Decorative art comprises popular art: ceramics, jewelry, glassware, furniture, printed papers, woven textiles, murals, metalwork, lithographs, embroidery. These are the unlikely vanguards of architectural revolution. But they are popular, widespread, and, in many ways, the material constituents of every household. They constitute its decor, adjust its functions, and express the histories, tastes, and aspirations of its inhabitants.

Change, revolutionary change at least, develops and gains strength not so much in the expression of revolutionary ideas but in their increasingly broad acceptance. The designers of the Pavillon de l'Esprit Nouveau saw hope for change in the reformation of public tastes, incrementally

I.1 Le Corbusier and Pierre Jeanneret, Pavillon de l'Esprit Nouveau, Exposition Internationale des Arts Décoratifs et Industriels Modernes, Paris, 1925, exterior view

I.2 Le Corbusier and Pierre Jeanneret, Pavillon de l'Esprit Nouveau, Exposition Internationale des Arts Décoratifs et Industriels Modernes, 1925, interior view

1.3   Le Corbusier,
immeubles-villas, 1922

adjusted in the things people like to buy and live with, in their sensible and coherent aggregation, in the architecture that frames them. The house, then, was the fulcrum on which the great architectural revolution would turn. Le Corbusier proclaimed that it was propelled by change in the decorative arts—in all those things that, assembled, constitute the habitable environment of a house. "The problem of the house," he said, "is a problem of the epoch. The equilibrium of society to-day depends upon it. Architecture has for its first duty, in this period of renewal, that of bringing about a revision of values, a revision of the constituent elements of the house."[4] This passage suggests that modernization of architecture follows, rather than propels, social change. But everyday life and everyday values are imbricated with everyday objects, with the "constituent elements of the house." Architecture often conducts its affairs with people through these elements.

There are many ironies associated with the Pavillon de l'Esprit Nouveau. Not the least is its venue at the great Exposition Internationale des Arts Décoratifs et Industriels Modernes in Paris. Hidden away on one of the worst sites at the exhibition, and that only begrudgingly provided by the organizers, it has by now come to light as perhaps the best-known exhibit of the whole fair. It was also one of the most clearly built manifestations of early modern architecture up to that time. In another twist, Auguste Perret—who was president of the design jury, a former employer of Le Corbusier, and a famous "modern" architect whom Le Corbusier greatly admired—roundly criticized the pavilion, saying "there is no architecture in it!"[5] He might have said "there is no decorative art in it" and been closer to the mark. Perhaps the greatest irony of the pavilion was intentional. Its designers set out, at this great exposition of decorative art, to supersede decorative art and the decorative ensemble that had become so popular among the most successful French designers. Le Corbusier and Jeanneret aimed to replace these with "equipment" assembled in architecture. The pavilion repudiated the decorative arts as they had come to be practiced; it showed that "modern decorative art is not decorated."[6] The austere ceramic vases, glassware, and furniture placed alongside sculptures and paintings, framed by the unadorned walls of the pavilion, proclaimed hopefully that society no longer required decorative art—domestic equipment and works of art, yes, but not decorative art.

As an artist trained in the decorative arts, with already more than a decade of experience in the design of furniture, interior finishings, and houses as well as extensive and highly specialized knowledge of various decorative arts movements in Europe, Le Corbusier considered the transfer of authority over the house and its furnishings—from the decorative artist to the architect—to be both monumentally significant and deeply personal. This was not merely an architect laying claim to new territory. Le Corbusier was a decorative artist and painter who recognized that circumstances were propelling him toward more encompassing tasks: because buildings, especially dwellings, are so deeply intertwined with the lives of people that they must open themselves up to the problems of human existence. In particular, the house must help people fill and profit from the sixteen hours of repose that follow the eight-hour workday. At the most basic level, the house must frame these hours of rest. Household equipment (the product of modern "decorative arts") accommodates physiological needs; paintings address the sentiments; architecture encompasses them both. Le Corbusier meant for the pavilion "to affirm that architecture opens itself to the most insignificant, practical furnishings for the house, to the street, to the city, and to the world beyond."[7] The Pavillon de l'Esprit Nouveau represented the first tolling of what Le Corbusier called "the hour of architecture."[8]

It also lay at the nexus of Le Corbusier's extraordinarily influential design production and polemical work of the 1920s. By his own count, he wrote nearly a dozen essays for the journal *L'esprit nouveau* that reflected on the upcoming pavilion project, which he published in 1925 in *The Dec-orative Art of Today*.[9] Two years earlier, he had published a similar collec-tion, *Towards a New Architecture* (Vers une architecture), a central purpose of which was to inquire into "the problem of the house."[10] In *Towards a New Architecture*, Le Corbusier reached this definitive, if seemingly self-evident, conclusion: *"A house is made for living in,"* not for looking at. *"Pictures are made to be looked at."*[11] The Pavillon de l'Esprit Nouveau aimed to demonstrate this. In 1927, he published the third book in the series, *The City of Tomorrow and Its Planning* (originally published under the title *Urban-isme*), whose primary purpose was to expand on the issues posed in the Pavillon de l'Esprit Nouveau.

Although Le Corbusier probably articulated it most forcefully, the pre-sumption that modern architecture must commit itself seriously to the con-ditions of everyday life and to the design and equipment of the modern house was on the minds of many of his contemporaries. It was a central concern of a small group of modernist designers in France who called them-selves *architectes-décorateurs:* Pierre Chareau, Eileen Gray, Pierre Jeanneret, Francis Jourdain, Le Corbusier, and Robert Mallet-Stevens. They began their careers as decorative artists and interior designers, but their inter-ests expanded into architecture in the 1920s.[12] The work of these designers— especially their domestic interiors, houses, and housing proj-ects—and their position as originators of the modern movement in archi-tecture in France are the major subject of this book. Although this book concentrates on France, it is important to note that the broader subject of the house and its modernization also motivated many of the most inno-vative designers and architects throughout Europe. Designers who came to exercise considerable sway over modern architecture and urban design in Austria, England, Germany, and the Netherlands during the late 1920s and 1930s had been doing important work in the decorative arts, product design, the configuration of domestic interiors, and the construction of houses since before the First World War.

When Ludwig Mies van der Rohe called together a host of European architects to contribute to the 1927 Deutscher Werkbund exhibition The Dwelling (Die Wohnung), the theme was the contemporary house. "Life is for us the decisive factor," Mies declared at the time. "In all its fullness, in its spiritual and real commitments."[13] Spread out on a hillside above Stuttgart, Germany, more than thirty houses and apartment buildings demonstrated architects' efforts to develop artistic solutions to the design of dwellings for working-class people (fig. 1.4).[14] The interiors of these build-ings showed the results of experiments undertaken with the functional

I.4 Weissenhof housing settlement at The Dwelling, Werkbund exhibition, Stuttgart, Germany, 1927

I.5   J. J. P. Oud,
kitchen, Weissenhof
housing settlement,
Stuttgart, Germany,
1927

layout of rooms and the design of inexpensive, mass-produced furniture (fig. 1.5); Sigfried Giedion asserts, for example, that "The Weissenhof settlement . . . solved the organization of the kitchen."[15] Although often considered to be the first real manifestation of International Style architecture, with its seemingly homogeneous collection of white prismatic volumes, more recent scholarship has shown that the exhibitors were not so unified in their approach—even if their interests were similar—and displayed a great range of idiosyncratic solutions to the modern house.[16]

A year later, in late June 1928, at the first meeting of the Congrès Internationaux d'Architecture Moderne (CIAM), at La Sarraz, Switzerland, attendees, many of whom had participated in the Stuttgart exhibition, signed a declaration asserting the essential connection between architecture and everyday life. It begins:

> The undersigned architects representing the national groups of modern architects, affirm their unity of viewpoint regarding the fundamental conceptions of architecture and their professional obligations toward society.
>
> They insist particularly on the fact that "building" is an elementary activity of man intimately linked with evolution and the development of human life. The destiny of architecture is to express the orientation of the age. Works of architecture can spring only from the present time. . . . They affirm today the need for a new conception of architecture that satisfies the spiritual, intellectual and material demands of present-day life.[17]

As early modern designers conceived it, modern architecture aimed, primarily, to satisfy the needs and desires of ordinary people. Their concern was especially applicable in the design of houses.

This seemingly evident correlation has been strangely problematic to the history of modern architecture, which has generally discounted the position of domestic architecture in the sweep of its innovations. Its involvement with fashion, consumerism, national and international politics, and gender and social prejudices has been the subject of recent critical analysis.[18] However, its engagement with contemporary domestic situations, which was extensive, has gained little attention—and that primarily in terms of negation, as for example in the recent anthology titled *Not at Home: The Suppression of Domesticity in Modern Art and Architecture.*[19] In the introduction to this fascinating collection of essays, Christopher Reed hints that it was the humble position of the house that has made it anathema in later accounts of the modernist story. "Perhaps because most architects' careers begin with domestic commissions," he suggests, "modernist architects have insisted even more vehemently than modernist painters on their antipathy to the home."[20]

Although this may have been the case as modern architecture reached its maturity after the Second World War, the founding members of CIAM were not prepared to dismiss the home as inconsistent with their avant-garde intentions. They were, however, antagonistic to habitual modes of composition and decoration that, as they saw it, hampered emerging patterns of everyday living. Another critic of modernist houses, Witold Rybczynski, voices strong antipathy for the modernists' evident insensitivity to domestic comfort in his book *Home: A Short History of an Idea.* He does acknowledge, however, the difficulty of the task they confronted. With regard to the austerity of the Pavillon de l'Esprit Nouveau, he admits that "one cannot help sympathizing with Le Corbusier's efforts to come to grips with the problems of modern living, something that set his plain pavilion apart from the sumptuous interiors of the Art Deco ensembliers. He was trying, however awkwardly, to make the home a more efficient place, and to deal with everyday life, instead of with the esoteric, almost outdated problems of decor."[21]

In this book, I argue that modern architecture placed particular emphasis on the problems of domestic settings and that concern for the issues associated with contemporary dwelling shaped virtually all aspects of modern architecture. It is my intention not to endorse the results of these efforts, which were often inadequate to the physiological and psychological needs of their inhabitants (a point that has been raised all too often), but to demonstrate that the house was central to the development of modernist architecture in Europe, particularly as it came to be in France.

One subtle but tangential demonstration of this point has arisen recently in discussions about the intimate connections modern architecture developed with fashion (until a few years ago, another largely neglected area of study).[22] In his superb study of wall color and fashion in modern architecture, Mark Wigley argues that the modern architects' choice of pure wall colors, especially white, was closely linked with modes of contemporary dress. Modern architects, he suggests, were obsessed with fashion. The point is convincing, but it threatens to obscure another: modern architects were obsessed with *clothing*—and by way of clothing, fashion—because of its functional and spatial contiguity with the house. At the root of their fascination with fashion and clothing lay an obsession with the house. Many of the architects Wigley implicates in a general obses-

sion with fashion equated modern dress specifically with the dwelling, and not necessarily with architecture in general. This makes sense, because, after all, it is really only the house, of all building types, that is intimate and flexible enough to function like one's own dress or suit. This is evident, for example, in Hermann Muthesius's seeming equation of architecture and clothing. Wigley suggests that Muthesius would have argued, "Dress is architecture and architecture is dress." He supports this general point, citing Muthesius's more specific assertions "that 'the dwelling is, however, only the wider dress that surrounds us,' in another he talks of 'our clothing, the narrower dwelling that surrounds us.'"[23] Similarly, Wigley cites a 1924 essay by Walter Gropius, "Wohnhaus-Industry" (Housing-industry), in which Gropius declares, "The majority of citizens of a specific country have similar dwelling and living requirements; it is therefore hard to understand why the dwellings we build should not show a similar unification as, say, our clothes, shoes or automobiles.'"[24] The correlation of dress and architecture in the writings of Le Corbusier and Adolf Loos also is virtually always stated in relation to the house. Thus, as Wigley notes, one might

I.6 Le Corbusier and Pierre Jeanneret, Pavillon de l'Esprit Nouveau, Exposition Internationale des Arts Décoratifs et Industriels Modernes, Paris, 1925, interior of exhibition hall

understand the intensely private characteristics of Loos's houses from his assertion that "a person's life habits, his clothing and physiognomy, all crystalized together in his dwelling."[25] Or that, in the polychrome buildings Le Corbusier developed in the late 1920s, it is the role of the white *house* facade, specifically, to explain the function of color in architecture. White, Wigley explains, "is the means for appreciating the color of the house. It is the standard against which color is to be read. More precisely, it is the standard against which the space produced by those colors can be read."[26] The epochal concerns of fashion and color stood out most vividly against the modern house. And it is probably proper to say that "dress is architecture and architecture is dress" only in direct reference to the connection between modern clothing and modern houses.

Tag Gronberg has shown in another recent study that the house was a fulcrum with which Le Corbusier turned architecture *away* from the issues of fashion toward the problems of living in the contemporary city. The house modeled in the Pavillon de l'Esprit Nouveau, which was situated not far from the luxurious displays of the Parisian department stores (the purveyors of contemporary fashion), rejected the rarefied spaces of the fashionable dwelling and turned instead toward the practical realm of the ordinary dwelling. Assembled by the thousands in blocks and towers, this purified, unfashionable house unit would become the building block of the geometrically pure, luminous new city, a diorama of which was displayed in the pavilion's adjoining exhibition hall (figs. 1.6, 1.7). Gronberg suggests that "the 1925 exposition afforded Le Corbusier an effective rhetorical foil, a context in which he could pit the serious business of architecture and urbanism against the frivolity and waste of luxury consumption."[27] Gronberg suggests that in so doing, Le Corbusier pitted the masculine aspects of the former against the feminine characteristics of the latter. In other words, Le Corbusier's rejection of fashion—often considered to be the province of women—was a subtle expression of male dominion over architecture. But it can be said with equal force, as Alice Friedman declares in *Women and the Making of the Modern House,* that the modern architects' emphasis on the house privileged and strengthened a traditional province of feminine authority, in some cases affecting "a powerful fusion of feminism with the forces of change in architecture."[28] Whatever the underlying motives—gender, power, consumption, fashion, geometry, color—for modernist architects of the 1920s, the modern house was the pivot on which the issues turned. And it seemed that solutions to many of the problems of the age hinged on the solution to the problem of the modern house.

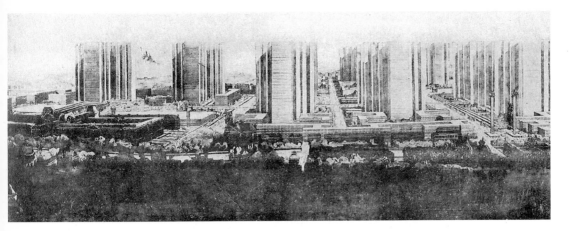

Nevertheless, being perhaps too mundane, too closely tied to crass consumerism, too intimate with the complicated, shifting, often unutterable roles of gender, and too much aligned with the decorative arts, the modern house also became, until recently, too easy to overlook or to suppress.[29] The house did not always fit well with histories of modern architecture that ascribed the logic of new functions, the new application of pure forms, new materials, and new construction methods, as its "predisposing causes," to use the words of Reyner Banham.[30] If it was susceptible to standardization and mass production and the rationality that these predisposing causes implied, the modern house was equally subject to individual expression (by way of decor or wall coloration) and so resisted classification among other modern building types. Likewise, the concerns associated with the house fit poorly with the histories of modern architecture that place its origins further back. The ordinary dwelling lay well outside the interests of "the first moderns," who attempted to formulate universally applicable laws for architectural aesthetics.[31] Thus, even if the modern architecture that took shape in the late 1920s benefited from the academic rationalism of the eighteenth century and the technological developments that followed, it did not share the same concerns. It responded to the heterogeneous conditions of everyday life, and until at least the late 1920s, its primary concern was "the problem of the house."

Although this book focuses on the development of modern architecture in France and the house's role in it, I believe that a similar study of Austria, England, or Germany—indeed, any country in Western Europe—would yield the conclusion reached here: Modern architecture reflected the necessities and possibilities of dwelling as much as, if not more than, the logic of new building techniques and the legacy of immemorial forms. As evidence for this, one need only consider that among the many new and arresting building types that developed with the industrialization and massive urbanization of Western Europe in the nineteenth century, it was the "problem of the house" that became "a problem of the epoch"—not only for Le Corbusier, who made this pronouncement in 1923, but also for a great many of his contemporaries in France. It was also a major preoccupation for the architects who exhibited houses alongside his at the 1927 Deutscher Werkbund exhibition The Dwelling, in Stuttgart, and for the hundreds of product designers who displayed their work in the nearby exhibition halls (fig. 1.8).[32] Many of the major protagonists in the

I.8   The Dwelling,
Werkbund exhibition,
Stuttgart, Germany,
1927, main hall

development of early modern architecture, including the contributors to the Stuttgart exhibition, were deeply involved, if not primarily concerned, with domestic settings. Peter Behrens, Walter Gropius, Le Corbusier, Adolf Loos, Ludwig Mies van der Rohe, Hermann Muthesius, and Otto Wagner—to name only the most recognizable examples—all designed furniture, interiors, and houses during the early decades of the twentieth century. And by the late 1920s, the contemporary house and its furnishing had long been a central theme in the development of modern design in Europe.

It is worth pursuing this point a little further with respect to Germany, since its antagonistic relationship with France often gave impetus to innovations in French design. In 1903, a generation before the Stuttgart exhibition, Hermann Muthesius vigorously prodded his contemporaries with the dire assertion that "the German has no proper house." Having recently returned from an extended stay in England, where the single-family house and a culture of domesticity was very well developed, Muthesius considered this to be symptomatic of a serious cultural malaise. The German's lack of interest in the house, he lamented, "is a deeply rooted cancer of our German art. A change in this situation can only take its start in the German house, which is essentially yet to be created."[33] The need to solve this problem motivated the development of the German regional "crafts workshops" *(Werkstätten)* and the Deutscher Werkbund, which substantially reformed the design and production of German household products and interiors by the beginning of the First World War. But even after nearly a decade of intensive, coordinated effort, Germany had not yet solved the persistent problem of the house. This, at least, was how Muthesius saw it. In an address to the Werkbund in 1911, he was quick to praise progress in German decorative and industrial arts, but he had harsh words for architecture: "If a nation produces good furniture and good light fittings, but daily erects the worst possible buildings, this can only be a sign of heterogeneous, unclarified conditions, conditions whose very inconsistency is proof of the lack of discipline and organization."[34] Despite its failure to devise buildings appropriate to modern conditions, however, success in the design and production of furniture and other household products, which "imparted fruitful inspiration to architecture," anticipated similar results in architecture. Germany had, in any case, established a standard for the design and fitting out of contemporary domestic interiors against which the rest of Europe was compelled to measure itself (see chapter 2).

In 1915, the English architect W. R. Lethaby complained that, while Germany had looked to England for inspiration in the arts at the turn of the century (as evidence, he cited Muthesius's extensive analysis of "the English free architecture"), it had far outpaced England in capitalizing on English innovations.[35] "They saw the essence of our best essays in furniture, glass, textiles, printing, and all the rest, and, laying hold on them, coined them into money." He said much the same for German architecture: "we first seem to have arrived at the thought of an architecture which should develop in its own sphere, and not be forever casting back to disguise itself in the skins which it had long ago sloughed off. . . . [but] German architects have seized on this theory of a 'real architecture'—or they have reached it for themselves."[36] By 1915, this had become a widely accepted view: that what Germans lacked in creativity, they more than made up for in organization and zeal.

Whatever foreign critics might have had to say about German tastes and tactics in the recent development of its capabilities in artistic design—and their views in this regard were almost invariably unfavorable—few could help but admire the systematic planning and effectiveness of the whole German endeavor. The economic benefits of these developments were clear, but the cultural implications were even more significant. Lethaby seems to have been resigned to accepting German success as an inducement to reinvigorate an English culture of design, saying that "the first thing in the arts which we should learn from Germany is how to appreciate English originality."[37]

Even more than the English, French designers were loath to emulate German techniques or sensibilities; they therefore competed directly with Germany, perpetuating traditional French styles or working to develop a uniquely French modernism that could counteract German progress in the arts. In other countries, the response to German developments was often more direct. Arts workshops analogous to those in Germany formed in Austria (e.g., the Wiener Werkstätte, founded in 1904), for example, and the Deutscher Werkbund spawned offspring in Austria and Switzerland.[38] The initiative in Switzerland originated with the recasting of the Ecole d'Art in La Chaux-de-Fonds, Le Corbusier's hometown. The school had trained craftsmen of the local watchmaking trade for decades, but the industry's imminent failure in the early 1910s propelled one influential faculty member, Charles L'Eplattenier, to seek broader outlets for his students' talents. To help justify reform of the school—which involved expanding its decorative arts program and adding interior decoration and architecture to the curriculum—its supervisory board commissioned Charles-Edouard Jeanneret (later known as Le Corbusier) to undertake a comprehensive evaluation of German decorative arts production and education initiatives.[39] After Jeanneret presented his report, the board took the unusual step of publishing 500 copies of the study at its own expense for distribution in Austria, Belgium, France, Germany, and Switzerland, "convinced," as the board declared in 1912, "that the information it contains must be publicized in the interest of developing the Decorative Arts in our country."[40]

French contemporaries, such as Hector Guimard, called the study "quite remarkable."[41] More recently, architectural historians have called it "surprisingly influential."[42] Reading the study today, it seems exceptional not only for its unusually thorough description and analysis of German activities in the decorative arts and architecture but also for its precipitous assessment of the broader situation in the arts, particularly with regard to the simmering conflict between French and German designers. A characteristic passage in the study reads:

> Now here is an aspect of something new and unexpected: France persists in renouncing its painters and sculptors, the Institute condemns and undermines them. But Germany positions itself as a champion of modernism, creating nothing in the domain of the fine arts to prove itself so, but revealing its new tastes through the systematic absorption (purchase) of the works of Parisian painters and sculptors (Courbet, Manet, Cézanne, van Gogh, Matisse, Maillol, etc.) and, on the other hand, revealing itself almost without warning to be colossal in power, in determination, and in achievement in the domain of the applied arts. These facts clearly place the two countries face to face: revolutionized Germany, evolved France.[43]

This passage makes it evident that the competitive tension between French and German designers was palpable even for an outside observer of these developments. It is thus hardly surprising that, as a Swiss Francophone, Jeanneret would have sided with the French. That the board of the Ecole d'Art would have endorsed his position, particularly since the study voices strong distaste for German sensibilities, is somewhat more surprising. Despite its evident admiration for the educational system and decorative arts production in Germany, the *Etude sur le mouvement d'art décoratif en Allemagne* (Study on the decorative arts movement in Germany) expresses disdain for German tastes and the aggressive tactics that brought Germany to the forefront of the movement. The study seems to say that although Germany succeeded in producing good work, the promise of exceptional work lay with the French. Although there is no need now to make such qualitative judgments, a primary purpose of this book is to show how the development of modern domestic architecture in France proceeded in the face of circumstances that included as a prominent and wide-reaching feature the antagonistic relationship between French and German decorative artists.

In France, German successes spurred nationalistic sentiments, which served to highlight both the native capabilities and the prevailing limitations of its designers. By 1912, when Jeanneret published his study, French designers had only begun to respond significantly to the German "threat." Although this was due partly to a lack of comprehensive organization, it also reflected a persistent sense of complacency. Even more than England, France could look back on a well-established tradition of superiority in the decorative arts and domestic furnishings. While French designers assured themselves of French superiority, though, German success in the decorative arts stirred up intensely competitive sentiments. Much of the decorative arts industry in France retrenched in an effort to sustain the vitality of traditional French styles; however, competitive pressures also compelled a number of progressive French designers to develop a uniquely French version of "modern" design centered on the decorative arts and, more particularly, on the domestic interior.

After the war, the theme of artistic unity, centered on the modern house, became an increasingly important motive for architecture throughout Europe. It became, for example, the very core of the program of instruction at the Bauhaus in Dessau, Germany. Although the Bauhaus had been deeply involved with the decorative arts and furnishings from the beginning, its new program of 1926 emphasized the predominance of domestic architecture among its list of concerns. The program pointedly opens with the assertion "The Bauhaus wants to serve in the development of present-day housing, from the simplest household appliances to the finished dwelling."[44] The Deutscher Werkbund, which re-formed itself several years after the war, also focused heavily on these topics. The exhibition it sponsored in Stuttgart in 1927, The Dwelling, commemorated the twentieth anniversary of the group's founding and was designed as a culmination of its efforts to effect sweeping reforms in German design. The house, including its furnishings and equipment, was no less a factor in the development of French modern design after the war, even if its production was more heterogeneous and its "modern movement" ill-defined.

In part because of this lack of definition, France provides an especially interesting case of modern architects' preoccupation with the house.

Because France engendered a strong tradition of academic rationalism in many endeavors, not the least in design and building construction, the emergence of the dwelling as an important if somewhat diffuse theme in modern design seems to strike out against a well-established trajectory. With all of its emotional and perceptual overtones, the modern dwelling in France reveals the depth of the anti-academic and even anti-rational strains of French modern architecture. Chapter 1 explores the origins of this situation. It also discusses how developments in the French decorative arts and domestic interior design, inflected by French painting, led to a substantive reevaluation of the middle-class house.

Chapter 2 focuses on a series of interior ensembles exhibited in the Paris Salons d'Automne of 1910 to 1913, which vividly illustrate how the design and selection of furniture and decorative art objects, and their arrangement according to compositional principles that originated in Cubist painting, suggested new ways of thinking about architecture. These interiors appeared at a time when France found itself compelled to strike a defensive posture in the development of furniture, interiors, and domestic architecture, all fields of traditional strength. The necessity for defensive action—particularly against Germany, a deeply loathed cultural, political, and economic rival—was both shocking and humiliating for French designers. Nationalistic sentiments that followed this realization accelerated design innovation. This rivalry powerfully affected much of the production and critical analysis of both French and German design in the years preceding and during World War I, and its echoes reverberated, although more quietly, after the German defeat in 1919.

Much, but not all, innovation in domestic architecture suffered a hiatus with the onset of war in 1914. For many artists and designers, the four years of war completely curtailed production. The war also greatly exacerbated nationalist and anti-German sentiments while emphasizing the values of everyday existence in France, whether in the trenches or on the home front. For a few progressive, noncombatant designers who were able to continue their work during the war, reconstruction of war-damaged areas became the central concern. Here again, reconsideration of the house played a major role. Chapter 3 explores the consequences of the war and its effects.

After the war, continued development of the modern house in the hands of the *architectes-décorateurs* helped to consolidate principles that characterized a distinct strain of modern architecture in France. Although these designers never formed a distinct, autonomous group, they shared common aims that led them to define their efforts in similar ways. Chapter 4 examines the work of Pierre Chareau, Le Corbusier, Eileen Gray, Francis Jourdain, and Robert Mallet-Stevens in the 1920s. It also discusses the nature of their program for modern architecture, particularly as it appeared in their houses and interiors, as Le Corbusier described it, and as contemporary designers and critics understood it.[45]

An undercurrent that influences all of the analysis in this book is the recognition that France has generally fit uncomfortably into historical accounts of modern architecture in Europe.[46] This is largely because its modernist tendencies developed among independent individuals who did not seek to establish a discernible movement; they also worked outside the traditional reach of architecture—in the decorative arts, interior design, and film and in the design of single-family dwellings. Furthermore, being directly antagonistic to the French academic tradition, these designers consciously placed themselves outside the conservative traditions of French architecture. They generally aligned themselves with French popular culture and the politics that accompanied it—a "new liberalism," to use a term coined by William Logue, which was "the political expression of the middling centrist view of life." From early in the Third Republic, this widespread political movement sought to develop, in all areas of cultural life, "the humanism of moderation, modesty, and morality. It is the expression of a desire to live above the brute existence of the poorest and the idle luxury of the richest."[47] The protagonists in this story were also deeply implicated in the economic trials of France during the Third Republic, in its acrimonious competition with German commercialism before World War I and in its struggles to establish a new postwar economic order. As the French avant-garde tried to shake off entrenched aristocratic and academic traditions in art and architecture, it focused on the circumstances of the middle class, on the preoccupations, habits, spaces, and materials of everyday existence.[48] These were embodied most fully in the modest dwelling.

This book benefits from the work of many scholars who recently have sought to uncover the complex relationships that developed between modern art, design, and architecture and European culture of the late nineteenth and early twentieth centuries. Several books that were particularly helpful in untangling the sometimes antagonistic relationships that developed between the avant-garde and popular culture in France are *The Popular Culture of Modern Art*, by Jeffrey Weiss; *The Transfiguration of the Commonplace: A Philosophy of Art*, by Arthur Danto; *In Defiance of Painting: Cubism, Futurism, and the Invention of Collage*, by Christine Poggi; and *Privacy and Publicity: Modern Architecture as Mass Media*, by Beatriz Colomina.

My book investigates a more centrist movement, which sometimes inter-
sected with the efforts of avant-garde painters but generally addressed the
needs of popular French culture with a view toward genuine, mutual support. In this regard, it is in some ways a companion to *Modernity and Nostalgia,* by Romy Golan, which examines the expression in art of a common
sense of loss that preoccupied France after the First World War. Another
recent book, *Art Nouveau in Fin-de-Siècle France: Politics, Psychology and Style,*
by Debora L. Silverman, also contends that the material culture of France
during the formative years of modern design was clearly reflective of a
collective French psychology, an idea that is implicit in the arguments put
forth here. Another book that has influenced my view of the role of material culture in the development of modern architecture is an excellent study
by Frederic Schwartz, *The Werkbund: Design Theory and Mass Culture before
the First World War.* For its treatment of the French decorative arts, in
particular, *Modernism and the Decorative Arts: Art Nouveau to Le Corbusier,* by
Nancy Troy, has been extraordinarily helpful. Many recent essays con-
necting Cubism and Purism with architecture have also been useful. These
include *Cubism in the Shadow of War,* by David Cottington, and antholo-
gies collected by Nancy Troy and Eve Blau, *Architecture and Cubism,* and
by Carol S. Eliel, *L'Esprit Nouveau: Purism in Paris, 1918–1925.*

Finally, because my account of the development of modern architecture in France seeks to insinuate several underrepresented figures into a
more inclusive and subtle history of modern architecture, it has benefited
greatly from recent scholarship that has uncovered their individual
achievements. To single out just a few of these: *Frantz Jourdain and the
Samaritaine,* by Meredith Clausen; *Jourdain,* by Arlette Barré-Despond
and Suzanne Tise; *Rob Mallet-Stevens, Architecte,* edited by D. Deshoulières
and H. Jeanneau; *Pierre Chareau: Architect and Craftsman, 1883–1950,* by Marc
Vellay and Kenneth Frampton; and *Eileen Gray,* by Caroline Constant. From
among the extensive scholarship on Le Corbusier, works on his early career
by Geoffrey Baker and Alan Brooks, as well as the recent exhibition catalog edited by Stanislaus von Moos and Arthur Rüegg, *Le Corbusier before
Le Corbusier: Applied Arts, Architecture, Painting, Photography, 1907–1922,* have
been especially helpful.

1 RAISING UP THE BOURGEOIS HOME

It is not till we come down to our own times, whose aspect presents so much of confusion in all departments of culture, that we find a schism often manifest, and always inexplicable, between the daily occupations and needs of the people and the character of their habitations. . . .

Let architects of ability, therefore, who have not the ambition to secure a fauteuil *at the Institute, or who have not set their minds on forcing open for themselves the doors of administrative boards which are entirely under the control of a privileged body, set themselves to work and seek for a solution of the problems suggested in the domestic architecture of the day. . . .*

—EUGÈNE-EMMANUEL VIOLLET-LE-DUC

At the end of the 1880s, French building design appeared to be following an auspicious trajectory mapped out for it by science and industry. French engineers were creating a succession of increasingly massive, highly visible public structures intended to confirm that they had mastered space and gravity through the rational application of the harmonic laws of statics.[1] In addition to demonstrating mastery over the natural order of things, these monuments served to exhibit the vigor of industry in France and the progressive attitudes of its liberal, republican populace. Dominating the horizons of Paris, Gustave Eiffel's 300-meter tower (fig. 1.1) and its immense companion across the Champs de Mars, the Gallery of Machines by Ferdinand Dutert (fig. 1.2), were the most vigorous manifestations of these aspirations. Yet less than ten years after France proudly displayed them at the 1889 Exposition Universelle in Paris, such works had lost much of their appeal, and one had to look elsewhere to understand the state of French design.

1.1 Exposition Universelle, Paris, 1889, aerial view showing the 300-meter tower by Gustave Eiffel with the Gallery of Machines, by Ferdinand Dutert, behind it

1.2 Ferdinand Dutert, Gallery of Machines, Exposition Universelle, 1889, interior under construction

The apparently sudden disappearance of French enthusiasm for immense, public works of engineering seems to support an increasingly untenable but still widely held notion that, despite a promising start at the end of the nineteenth century, France ultimately had little to do with the emergence of a modern movement in Western architecture, and only a small remnant of "structural rationalists" were left to represent its concerns. When one considers how actively France was contributing to other modernist movements before World War I, however, it seems unlikely that this could have been the case. French art was at its most fertile: the Impressionist, Nabis, Symbolist, Realist, and Cubist movements permanently altered painting and sculpture. Claude Debussy, Maurice Ravel, and Erik Satie were redefining the place of music in contemporary life. Henri Bergson was positioning modern philosophy in the realm of "common sense" and appealing directly to artists with his theories. And competition in the decorative arts between the great economic powers of Europe—England, Germany, and France—was at its most intense. Progressive strains in each of these disciplines exhibited decidedly anti-rational tendencies, carrying them further and further from the motives that had inspired Enlightenment thinkers and the designers of steel bridges, exhibition halls, and towers of the late nineteenth century. At the same time, modern art in France moved increasingly to align itself with the liberal politics of the middle class, and in doing so, it concentrated almost exclusively on the ordinary events and materials of everyday life. Did architecture in France stand outside of these developments?

By the 1920s, people had long ago begun to care more about how the developments of modern industry could improve their everyday lives than how such innovations embellished the urban skyline. In the liberal environment of republican France, people became more concerned with quality of life than with the eternal preoccupations of reason and truth. They preferred to contend with the complexities of everyday experience rather than the precise laws that ordered the world around them. Thus, for many reasons, the locus of modern architecture in France, and elsewhere in Europe, moved toward the home. And this is why, thirty-four years after a 300-meter tower of steel rose skyward in Paris to announce a new era for architecture, Le Corbusier could proclaim that "architecture has for its first duty, in this period of renewal, that of bringing about a revision of values, a revision of the constituent elements of the house."[2] In France, the groundwork for this task was laid in the decades preceding World War I. However, it was not architects but painters as well as designers of furniture and domestic interiors who constructed the foundations of modern architecture.

THE ORDINARY SUPERSEDES THE EXTRAORDINARY IN THE EXPOSITIONS UNIVERSELLES

That the rather mundane task of developing "a revision of the constituent elements of the house" might be considered the "first duty" of architecture could hardly have been guessed when, in 1892, the great historian and professor of architecture Auguste Choisy predicted that a new architecture would arise out of the logic of building structure. He announced that "a new system of proportion has been created, whose harmonic laws will be none other than those of statics."[3] The Eiffel Tower and the Gallery of Machines, built three years earlier, demonstrated clearly that France had already mastered these laws. Such monuments, whatever their artistic limitations, made French architecture and engineering the envy of the world.[4]

Despite the promise of these remarkable structures, however, within only a few years, critics of design widely contested Choisy's view. In 1896,

Emile Zola, who had spoken with great enthusiasm about technological progress in the 1880s, declared, "I believed absolutely that a new material, iron, would create the basis for a new and modern style. . . . Now it seems that we shall have to wait a long time for such a style."[5] He lamented later that "modern society is racked without end by nervous irritability. We are sick and tired of progress, industry and science."[6] In 1900, Vicomte Melchior de Vogüé, a critic who had also spoken with enthusiasm about the Eiffel Tower and the Gallery of Machines in 1889, declared that they represented a culmination of an old era in architecture rather than the beginning of a new one.[7]

In a study of the political and psychological dimensions of the Art Nouveau movement, Debora Silverman ascribes this drastic shift in attitude to a changing view of people's psychological interiors. The citizens of Paris, in particular, felt increasingly at odds with the external realities of the modern city. They sought to distance themselves from the collective culture, to isolate themselves in comfortable and familiar settings. "If the late nineteenth century produced the possibilities for a dynamic and collective existence," Silverman notes, "it also gave birth to the triumph of psychological man, whose liberty and isolation were heightened by the monumental configuration emerging in the metropolis."[8] In these circumstances, a public *image* of technological progress inevitably yielded to a more personal *application* of technology.[9] And modern architecture could no longer demonstrate its progressive aims in increasingly familiar public monuments of steel and glass nor in some new rational ideal based on the well-understood principles of statics. Instead, it had to accommodate itself to the demands of a new self-awareness of the middle class.

The fading interest in large, explicitly rational buildings was a symptom of the larger cultural movement that refocused artistic activity in France on middle-class domestic life. As these changes took shape at the turn of the century, modern design in France anchored itself in household, rather than public, settings. People may have been "sick and tired of progress, industry and science," as Emile Zola declared in 1896, but they could not do without them.[10] Emphasis on the quality of everyday life and on the consumption of goods associated with it brought the products of technological development directly into people's homes. The ubiquity of these products, which followed the increasing prosperity of the middle class, made the great marvels of engineering seem less impressive than they had been. But even as the products of technology lost their ability to enthrall, they proliferated. People no longer wanted merely to witness the products and possibilities of modern technology; they wanted to benefit materially and directly from them. Mass-produced furniture, tableware, fabrics, electric lighting, and small machines for the home became necessary adjuncts to everyday life. They lost their novelty and were finally pressed into domestic service.[11]

This rapid change in attitude toward the products of technological advancement also reflected collective attitudes and shifting demographics, which France shared with most of Europe. By the end of the nineteenth century, Paris had swallowed up a large portion of the French population. A culture that had been mostly rural and stratified only a generation before was contracting into a homogeneous urban mass. Many working people found themselves forced into industrial servitude and into living environments bereft of even basic comforts. Constant exposure to these environments discredited the optimistic dream of social progress represented by public structures like the Eiffel Tower and the Gallery of Machines but made the promise of industrialized production of inexpensive furniture and domestic equipment increasingly appealing. Consequently, by the beginning of the twentieth century, technological advances continued to increase in scope, while their most visible products were substantially

1.3 Ferdinand Dutert, Gallery of Machines, Exposition Universelle, 1889, interior

1.4 Charles Garnier, Histoire de l'Habitation Humaine, Exposition Universelle, Paris, 1889, view of Japanese house (left) and Chinese house (right)

reduced in scale. Indications of this were nowhere more evident than on the floors of the great exhibition halls (fig. 1.3).

France held large international expositions in 1855, 1867, 1878, 1889, and 1900.[12] These became vastly popular events, with attendance at each nearly doubling that of the preceding. Organizers strove to make the exhibitions above all *popular* events, events accessible to anyone. That France held these expositions in the center of Paris, despite great logistic difficulties, attests to their populist appeal. Indeed, Eugène-Emmanuel Viollet-le-Duc argued against hosting the 1878 Exposition Universelle outside of Paris largely on the grounds "that our artisans, our laborers must be able to visit them frequently and at length without wasting time on long trips and without being obliged to spend much."[13] The Exposition Universelle of 1889 attracted 28 million visitors in six months. Its colossal exhibition buildings must have been immensely impressive to just about any visitor, but their effect was rivaled, if not dwarfed, by the massive scale of the whole undertaking. The event boasted more than 61,000 exhibits spread over 250 acres in the center of Paris.[14] Like the Crystal Palace of the Great Exhibition in London nearly half a century before, its monumental buildings were designed to be the characteristic architectural manifestations of the age. They certainly asserted French capabilities in engineering and architecture.

At the close of the 1889 exposition, Charles Garnier, who was the official "architectural adviser" *(architecte-conseil),* summed up his impressions of the event, declaring, "Let us salute the Exposition Universelle in all its brilliance and in all its scope; it is the glorification of art, of science, of industry and of the labor of the whole world. It is above all proof of the power of architecture."[15] Although the Eiffel Tower and the exhibition halls contributed significantly to this assessment, Garnier's own offering at the exposition gave more subtle evidence for the vigor of architecture.[16]

In the shadow of the tower, Garnier had assembled an ambitious exhibition describing the history of human habitation (fig. 1.4). It consisted of nearly forty full-scale house ensembles representing dwellings from all parts of the world and from time periods spanning prehistory to the Renaissance. Each fully furnished house occupied a garden with vegetation indigenous to its original setting. These exhibits generally concentrated on humble dwellings and attendant vernacular styles. Visitors to the exposition could therefore witness not only the monumental constructions of contemporary France but also the immense variety and possibility evident even in the most humble works of architecture.[17] This diverse image of architecture was complemented, of course, by the many, varied pavilions contributed by guest nations.

The Exposition Universelle of 1900 brought together a similarly diverse, contradictory, and scintillating array of pavilions, displays, and entertainments—more than 70,000 in all. Without the dominant unifying message of the Gallery of Machines and the 300-meter tower, however (although they were reused for the exposition), the architecture seemed to succumb to its own exuberant quest for novelty (fig. 1.5). Few of the buildings contributed by France or its guests could rival the clarity of the great monumental buildings from 1889. The public's enthusiasm for the event, which was undiminished, therefore found other outlets, and visitors expecting to be overwhelmed by its sheer scale were not disappointed. They were dazzled, in particular, by vast nocturnal displays of electric lights, a novelty that promised to insinuate itself into every corner of the city and affect every facet of life (fig. 1.6).[18]

For their part, design critics unleashed their scorn on the immense and frenetic exhibition halls, but they found much to admire in the boudoirs and bathrooms in the decorative arts pavilions (fig. 1.7). One contemporary critic, André Hallays, complained:

1.5   Le Chateau
d'Eau, Exposition
Universelle, Paris,
1900

1.6   Exposition
Universelle, Paris,
1900, night scene
showing electric
lighting display

The "palaces" that have been erected on the Esplanade des Invalides are masterpieces of ugliness. Viewed as a whole, as one leaves the Pont Alexandre III, they inspire terror. If one examines the crazy decoration on each façade, they leave one dumbfounded. Architects, sculptors, ornamentalists and painters seem to have been trying to outdo one another in incoherence.[19]

In his recent analysis of the exhibition, Philippe Julian explains, however, that

Behind these palaces stood pavilions where a more imaginative, less official style was permitted. Here, rather than in the official sections, flowered the Art Nouveau movement which for the past ten years had been striving to change traditional decorative styles, and even the whole aesthetic creed. . . . This new enthusiasm was accompanied by the idea that the art of the future world would be an art for all, not only replacing the clutter of furniture in the apartments of the bourgeoisie, but bringing gaiety into the homes of the workers. And so the pavilions on the Esplanade des Invalides which proclaimed the supremacy of art were visited and discussed much more than the industrial pavilions on the Champs de Mars, where machinery belonged essentially to the nineteenth century.[20]

As with earlier events of this scope in France, organizers of the 1900 Exposition Universelle sought to address the interests of the working class. In this case, it was not just the scheduling and location of the exhibits that made the event accessible for working-class visitors. Working-class themes also dominated the exposition and were evident everywhere in murals, sculptures, and ornaments on public buildings. Julian asserts that "most of the artists who received commissions for the decoration of the exhibition had to glorify the workers, for the movement initiated by Napoleon III [for the 1855 exposition] had become an act of faith: the workers were to take part in the Great Festival of Progress which their energies had made possible."[21] Concern for the working class was also evident, although less explicitly, in the interiors of the pavilions on the Esplanade, where domestic life in contemporary France had become an important theme. Although many of these interiors displayed a sense of opulence consistent with traditional French tastes, their frequent references to regional folklore, crafts, and vegetation resonated with visitors from a wide range of social situations. The possibility of Art Nouveau's broad applica-

1.7 Eugène Gaillard,
bedroom, L'Art
Nouveau Bing
Pavilion, Exposition
Universelle, Paris,
1900

tion to contemporary life, not merely its novelty, conveyed the sense that it represented a genuine and appropriate modern movement.

Art Nouveau also gained prominence as well as notoriety at the exposition because it gave evidence of a pan-European artistic movement. To an optimistic few, this hinted at a convergence of values among nations often divided for political and military reasons. More commonly, however, critics of Art Nouveau argued that the infusion of foreign influence into French design threatened national integrity by diluting uniquely French tastes, of which the French were inordinately proud. Hallays, for example, asserted rather caustically that "the most original feature of this decorative parody is its universality. The Modern Style is European. . . . Obviously at the origin of this Belgian movement one finds the influence of English art. But today, in everything called Modern Style, in France, in Germany, or elsewhere, one finds only a slavish imitation of Belgian art."[22] This suspicion of foreign influence was one reason for the movement's rapid fall from popularity after 1900, despite its broad appeal.

STRUCTURAL RATIONALISM AND THE NEW FRENCH HOUSE

Although the international expositions established highly unusual conditions for displaying the products of contemporary design, they did tend to exemplify more general circumstances. Many of the exhibits brought together work that had been developed for Salon displays, salesrooms, and private houses.[23] The aim was to capture the imagination of potential consumers while appealing to their practical requirements. Design in these settings naturally manifested a fascination with everyday life. In fin de siècle France, this preoccupation appeared most vividly in the production of Art Nouveau designers and of the painters who seceded from the strictures of academic art.

This preoccupation also affected a more unlikely group of designers: the proponents of what was later called "structural rationalism." Just as the visual prominence of the Eiffel Tower and the Gallery of Machines belied important trends in contemporary design, the apparent rationalism of designers such as Eugène-Emmanuel Viollet-le-Duc gives only limited insight into their work, which was oriented by a host of practical concerns, with structural clarity being only one. The seemingly incongruous combination of structural monumentality and the intimacy of domestic space that was evident in the exhibitions corresponded with the work and theoretical writing of Viollet-le-Duc. One of his principal aims was to develop a uniquely French style of contemporary, popular architecture. Accordingly, he reasoned (as did Auguste Choisy and Charles Garnier) that domestic architecture of the past—not just its monumental constructions—should inspire contemporary French designers:

> If we inquire into the history of the past, we shall find that however debased any period may have been, there was not a private house that did not answer to the requirements of the civilisation under whose auspices it was built. In the Ancient World, both in Asia and in the West during the Mediaeval period, the dwellings were the veritable garb, so to speak, of the manners, customs and modes of living of those who occupied them. It is not till we come down to our own times, whose aspect presents so much of confusion in all departments of culture, that we find a schism often manifest, and always inexplicable, between the daily occupations and needs of the people and the character of their habitations.[24]

Viollet-le-Duc contended that one of the main reasons for this schism was the stifling effect of the architectural section of the Academy of Fine Arts, whose original mandate had been to formulate and uphold a normative theory of architecture. (Auguste Choisy's assertion that a new system of architectural proportions would arise on the basis of statics was the latest manifestation of this idea.) Viollet-le-Duc argued, however, that the academy's doctrinal presumptions had so weakened the creative capacities of its members and aspirants that they were incapable of effecting any practical advancement in architecture, much less fulfilling its original mandate. Even worse, the academy's reactionary stance in the face of cultural and economic change precluded even good-faith efforts to advance its doctrine. "All its efforts," he declared, "tend, not to the propagation of doctrines, whether true or false, but to the maintenance of its position and the exclusion from it of those who are not Academicians, or do not aspire to be so, or who are unwilling to acknowledge its supremacy."[25] In this environment, it was clear that progress in architecture would neither proceed from the Academy of Fine Arts nor show in the public buildings it sponsored. Despite the academy's oppressive effect on French architecture, however, Viollet-le-Duc saw in these disheartening circumstances some hope for change:

> There have been times when public architecture, having lost all character of its own, followed in the wake of enfeebled art; but during those very periods domestic architecture, not subjected to the narrow ideas of a Government or of an Academy, was still able to imprint its own seal upon its designs.
>
> It has been reserved for our own age to allow this last vestige of originality to be lost. Let architects of ability, therefore, who have not the ambition to secure a *fauteuil* at the Institute, or who have not set their minds on forcing open for themselves the doors of administrative boards which are entirely under the control of a privileged body, set themselves to work and seek for a solution of the problems suggested in the domestic architecture of the day. . . . A vast field of study and labour is presented here, and we may even assert that the clear and practical solution of these problems would be the best means of preventing the shameless perversion of principles exhibited in the construction of our public buildings.

Designers seeking to develop an architecture appropriate to contemporary life therefore could find their best opportunities in houses and the objects used to furnish them. Practical, rather than ideological or doctrinal, considerations would hold sway. As Viollet-le-Duc argued:

> It is therefore to the resources supplied by our own common sense and reason that we must apply for the solution of the problem, proceeding as our predecessors had the wisdom to proceed: that is, by adopting new arrangements without troubling ourselves about the forms

applied to old ones whose conditions were different from those we have to deal with.[26]

Even in an assessment as optimistic as this, however, it was clear that these designers could effect change only if their middle- and working-class clients supported it. Substantive change required, therefore, the enlightened endorsement of private clients and consumers. Viollet-le-Duc reasoned that this necessitated a vast cultural effort, because "the general level of a nation is raised only by the instruction and education of the lower strata."[27] Public education was, as William Logue has argued, "the key issue of the early Third Republic."[28] Its largely successful development of a liberal system of education contributed significantly to the shifting orientation of French art and architecture in the late 1800s.[29] By the end of the century, the working and middle classes had become far more capable of articulating their demands and cultivating their own tastes than ever before.[30] Consequently, the middle-class house as a matter of artistic consideration became a primary concern. In her analysis of the French interior at the turn of the twentieth century, Lisa Tiersten proclaims that "the bourgeois home had become the epicenter of a new aesthetic democracy in early twentieth-century France."[31] Despite this, or perhaps because of it, the continued dominance of conservative academic training in architecture limited the penetration of these tendencies into the work of officially sanctioned architects.

As many architectural historians have noted, the architectural establishment in France produced few influential innovators, perhaps only two: Tony Garnier and Auguste Perret.[32] Although both did exercise their creativity in the suitably academic effort of promoting the rational development and refinement of reinforced concrete, and even though both were students in the "academic succession" of Auguste Choisy and Julien Gaudet, their work can hardly be said to have been based primarily on the principles of statics.[33] They often dedicated their work to far more quotidian concerns.

Garnier's most important undertaking was Une Cité Industrielle (1901–17), an immense project for an industrial town of 35,000 inhabitants in southeastern France (fig. 1.8), with "a design that completely satisfies the material and moral needs of the individual."[34] It proposed factories, hospitals, parks, communal gardens, housing, and modern infrastructure for power and transportation—all carefully zoned to maintain efficiency, environmental quality, and hygiene. Quality of life was its fundamental concern.

Garnier also designed the project to accommodate the regional culture

of southeastern France within a modern, industrial town. Accordingly, he proposed that the building materials used be indigenous to the region.[35] This entailed the use, primarily, of concrete and ferro-concrete for major structures in the city (fig. 1.9), with allowances for "different," presumably indigenous, "construction methods and materials."[36] In all cases, his proposed uses, especially of the two types of concrete (unreinforced and reinforced), were based less on the apparent rationality of the materials than on pragmatic, aesthetic, and emotional considerations.[37] "These two materials," he explained in the introduction to *Une cité industrielle*,

are highly plastic, and require specially prepared formwork; the simpler this formwork, the easier the installation and the lower the costs. This simplicity of means logically leads to a simplicity of structural expression. It is also worth noting that if the construction remains simple, without ornamentation or moldings and with sheer surfaces, the decorative arts can be effectively employed in all their forms, and each

1.8 Tony Garnier, *Une Cité Industrielle*, 1917, overview of public area

artistic object will maintain a cleaner and fresher expressiveness, thanks to its independence from the structure itself. Moreover, the use of concrete and cement enables us to obtain large horizontal and vertical surfaces, endowing the building with a sense of calm and balance in harmony with the natural contours of the landscape.[38]

These considerations were especially important for the residential quarters of the town, which are the subject of well over half of the more than 300 illustrations in the folio published in 1917 (fig. 1.10). Perspective drawings in *Une cité industrielle* show a range of modest houses that are strongly but simply modeled in concrete (they are, however, significantly overstructured). Their surfaces are raked by Mediterranean sunlight and softened by the dappled shadows of trees and the foliage of hanging plants.

A villa that Garnier built for himself in 1910–12 at Saint-Rambert, France, exemplified this use of concrete, particularly in the congruity of the wall surfaces with the interior decoration (figs. 1.11, 1.12). Garnier published photographs of the house in the 1917 and 1932 editions of *Une cité indus-*

1.9   Tony Garnier, Une Cité Industrielle, 1917, transit station

trielle. They show that the walls, floors, and ceilings are smooth and joined without moldings. Most of the walls are painted simply, although those of at least one room bear trompe l'oeil frescoes. Throughout the house, concrete window seats, benches, and beds, softened by ornamental cushions, emerge from the walls and floors. A heavy concrete mantel in one bedroom supports several vases and a marble bust. The house is full of such objects—fragments from antiquity, potted plants, ornamental rugs, ceramics, glass, sculptures, paintings. Their delicacy balances the austere concrete surfaces and the freestanding furniture, which is ponderous in its simplicity. Despite the austerity of the building—its street facade is uncompromisingly plain—and the hardness of its materials, the interiors of the house give an impression of coolness and habitability, of generous light, secure corners, and accommodating surfaces. The use of reinforced concrete in such circumstances, although very effective, is hardly rational.

Ricardo Mariani has argued recently that to consider Tony Garnier a precursor of rational modernism is not only to misunderstand the depth of his influence on modern urban planning, which was minimal (the 1917 publication of *Une cité industrielle* passed virtually without mention in the art critical press until much later), but also to misinterpret his ideological

1.10 Tony Garnier, Une Cité Industrielle, 1917, residential area

1.11 Tony Garnier, architect's villa, Saint-Rambert, France, 1910–12, exterior view of garden facade

1.12 Tony Garnier, architect's villa, Saint-Rambert, France, 1910–12, bedroom

commitments.[39] Garnier's industrial city demonstrates a subtle concern for the political, social, and economic exigencies of everyday life for working-class people in the newly industrialized regions of southeastern France. Its concerns are local, specific, and mundane, even if it suggests a general model for dealing with such conditions. As a model for "rational" modern architecture, Une Cité Industrielle is problematic also because it emphasizes that architectural planning can go only so far toward satisfying the "moral and material needs of the individual." The domestic interiors of the residential quarter, which comfortably accommodate a great range of decorative appurtenances, emphasize the importance of flexibility and openness to individual interpretation. If Garnier's work in Une Cité Industrielle is revolutionary for its use of concrete, it is not because of the way concrete contends with the laws of statics. Une Cité Industrielle is revolutionary because of the subtlety with which the material insinuates itself into the environments and lives of ordinary people.

Auguste Perret also pioneered the use of reinforced concrete in architecture, a matter that has long been central to scholarly reflection on his work.[40] In a recent study of Perret, however, Karla Britton stresses that this emphasis on concrete, and its significance for building structure in particular, has obscured other important aspects of his work and its influence among the architects and artists of his generation.[41] She suggests that Perret chose to work in concrete for its plasticity, its ability to promote simultaneously a stable, historical tradition and a more fluid, changeable sense of modernity. Perret himself frequently emphasized that architecture always responds to a great range of "permanent and . . . transitory conditions." The former include "laws of stability, the nature of materials used, atmospheric variables," and the latter, "purpose, function, use, rules and regulations and fashion."[42] Although it has come to be identified strongly, sometimes almost exclusively, with the reinforced concrete structural frame, Perret's work captured the attention of his contemporaries for other forceful qualities: its perpetuation of historical forms, its alliance with a tradition of building craft and the sensual qualities of material, and its ability to accommodate the practical necessities of contemporary life.[43] Many of these qualities counterbalanced the apparent rationality of his buildings and showed their wide divergence from the ideological and dogmatic pretensions of his academically trained contemporaries. Although he was trained by Auguste Choisy and Julien Gaudet, Perret claimed to have been most profoundly influenced by the writings of Eugène-Emmanuel Viollet-le-Duc.[44]

One of Perret's earliest and best-known buildings, the 1903 apartment at 25 *bis* rue Franklin in Paris (fig. 1.13), attests to the breadth of his interests. Architectural historians often cite the ten-story apartment block as an important "proto-modernist" building, primarily for its use and clear indication of a reinforced concrete frame (fig. 1.14). However, Perret's treatment of the material in this early building demonstrates some uncertainty, since the entire building facade is wrapped with decorative tiles. Plain rectangular tiles cover the main structural members, and these frame concrete infill panels (designed by the sculptor Alexandre Bigot) that are vigorously ornamented with patterns of ceramic laurel leaves. Although the square tiles obscure the concrete frame, they specifically emphasize its effect on the shaping of the building. This frame-infill relationship is typical of Perret's later work, but in most subsequent projects, he left the concrete frame exposed. The ornamental motifs are unusual among Perret's buildings, though, being reminiscent of contemporary Art Nouveau decoration.

Kenneth Frampton proposes that Perret used the ornamentation on the rue Franklin apartment to recall tectonic rather than stylistic precedents, noting that the tile patterns allude to traditional wood construction.[45] Britton argues that Perret used the tiles for a more practical reason: to protect the concrete, a material as yet untested in these circumstances, from environmental damage.[46] It also seems plausible to suggest that Perret added the tiles to help to soften the impact of the building in its residential context. Sigfried Giedion hints at this accommodating aspect of the building, noting that, instead of exhibiting the purity of the concrete frame—as was the case of contemporary buildings in Chicago—"the familiar European restlessness is still present to a considerable degree" in Perret's apartment building.[47]

This apparent restlessness resulted primarily from the building's response to specific, transitory conditions. Aside from its calculated display of the concrete frame, some of the most innovative aspects of the building relate to limitations imposed by its residential program and site. Tight spatial constraints and interior lighting problems of the mid-block building made for difficult interior planning; however, the concrete frame, which obviated interior structural walls, allowed for unusually flexible and open room configurations (fig. 1.15). The main floor of each apartment consists primarily of three large, interconnected central bays surrounded on all sides by passages or auxiliary rooms into which they project. The walls separating the three central rooms (dining room, salon, and bedroom on floors one through seven) fall along the column lines; to the front and back of the apartment, however, the rooms open much

1.13 Auguste Perret,
25 *bis* rue Franklin
apartment, Paris,
1903, exterior view

1.14 Auguste Perret, 25 *bis* rue Franklin apartment, Paris, 1903, exterior detail

more freely into the adjacent spaces. For example, the narrower structural bay behind these rooms contains the entry foyer with a built-in bench, a vestibule with four closets, and a dessert room annex to the kitchen where it wraps around the side of the dining room. The dining room projects into this dessert room annex to make space for a buffet. On the opposite side, the main bedroom projects into the vestibule to make an alcove for the bed. The vestibule wraps the bedroom, becoming a hall that gives access to a smaller bedroom on the street front. The three main rooms also project forward toward the street. On the first floor, they meet together on a broad street-facing terrace. There are similar terraces on the top three floors. The main rooms on intermediate floors let balconies onto the street-front court. The traditional rear courtyard serves mainly as a narrow light shaft for the main stair, whose exterior wall, thanks to the concrete structural frame, consists almost entirely of glass blocks. Perret's creative interpretation of building setback regulations and the flexible definition of the courtyard also help to bring about the sense of spaciousness and brilliance that distinguishes the building interiors.[48] The structure also maximizes interior living space within the building envelope suggested by building codes by minimizing floor depth (made possible through the use of concrete), and including a habitable attic story with a roof garden, which Perret used as his own flat. Despite these innovations, the house also blends with the adjacent buildings, picking up cornice lines and rooflines and matching the warm gray tone of their stone facings.

Perret's flexibility with regard to such conditions, and to stylistic interpretation, helps to explain why his other buildings varied so much in

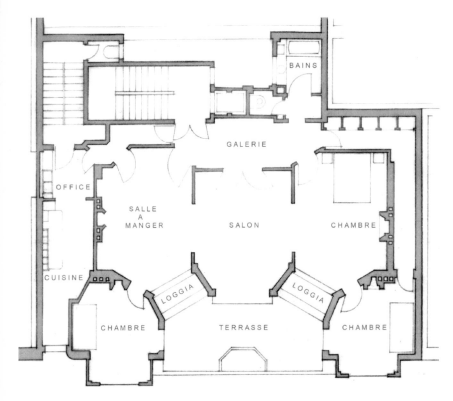

appearance despite their almost exclusive use of concrete. Flexibility and
practicality—as well as rationality—characterize many of his early buildings in concrete. The Ponthieu Garage (1905), the Champs-Elysées theater
(1910–13), and the church of Notre Dame du Raincy (1922–24), for example, all differ as markedly in the way they accommodate their programs
as in their stylistic treatment.

In a series of twenty or so house-studios Perret built in the 1920s and
after, a sense of accommodation became the most remarkable, though subtle, design characteristic.[49] The painter Jean Dubuffet, who lived for a time
in the Mela Muter studio of 1927–28 (figs. 1.16, 1.17), summed up this impression in a letter to Perret, saying, "At first, one doesn't see anything unusual
in this building, it seems rather ordinary, but in use, over time one marvels."[50] This small, two-story house consists essentially of four structural
bays containing modest living quarters, a garage, an atelier, and a generous patio. The irregularly shaped garage bay faces the quiet allée Main-
tenon and sits back several feet from the main bay. The bay contains the
unadorned entry, introduced by a low stoop and leading into a large, bright
exhibition space, through which one passes to reach the patio, kitchen,
dining/living room, and stair to the bedroom and painting studio on the
upper floor. Large windows on the alley and patio sides of the gallery wash

the room with light. The studio above, which includes the entire front half of the house, draws in even more light with lofty windows that span the bay on both the alley and patio fronts. Aside from its abundance of natural light, everything about the house seems modest: its diminutive scale, unobtrusive front door, compact living quarters, and the neat but rather rough concrete and brickwork. Dubuffet described the house as "comfortable, refreshing," and wrote about the pleasure he took in opening and closing doors in the house (the house must have felt quite solid), in passing from room to room, and particularly in using the stair. Because of its location at the juncture of the four bays, the stair connects every room in the house except the bathroom on the second floor. Perhaps Dubuffet's pleasure derived from the sense that to use the stair was to traverse and summarize the house and the program of living and working that engendered it.

Structural rationality certainly underlies much of Perret's work, but

1.16 Auguste Perret, Mela Muter studio, Paris, 1927–28, exterior view

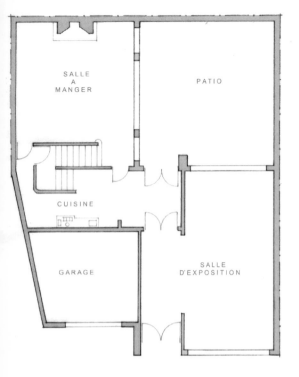
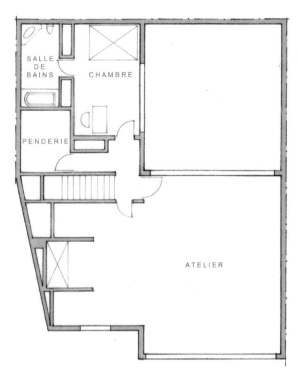

1.17 Auguste Perret,
Mela Muter studio,
Paris, 1927–28, plans

to focus too closely on this aspect of it is to miss a more general and vital program he envisioned for architecture. This was to develop modern buildings that are eminently but subtly usable and that blend with the circumstances surrounding them. Perret articulated this view most succinctly in the concluding remarks of a lecture on architecture, which he delivered to the Institut d'Art et d'Archéologie in 1933, saying, "the architect who, without betraying the constraints of a modern building programme, nor the use of modern materials, creates a work that will always seem to have existed, that is, in a word, banal, is entitled to feel content."[51] This program was especially suited to domestic architecture, which was an important if seldom discussed part of his oeuvre.

A discussion of Perret's architectural work should not pass without some mention of the friendships and intellectual associations he cultivated during the 1910s and after. Perret was closely involved with the Cercle des Artistes de Passy from the time of its founding in 1912 and acted as vice president of the group that succeeded it during the war, Art et Liberté; he also participated frequently in the informal meetings of Cubist artists sponsored by the Villon-Duchamp brothers in Puteaux.[52] Perret employed Le Corbusier for sixteen months from late June 1908 to fall 1909 and was for many years a frequent correspondent, adviser, and mentor. Perret often brought together poets, composers, sculptors, painters, decorative artists, architects, fashion designers, and critics whose interests in modernism were no less profound than their commitment to the continuity of French cultural tradition.[53] Around 1910, a number of these artists had begun to collaborate in Salon exhibitions. Like Perret, they proposed to develop an architectural framework that could suitably accommodate the many products of contemporary life: the banal and the unusual, the cheap and the valuable, the artless and the artistic. The culmination of this collaboration, Un Salon Bourgeois (also known as the Maison Cubiste) of 1912, is the subject of more extensive discussion in chapter 2. Although Perret did not participate in the project, he collaborated with many artists over the next decade in the design of studio-houses, such as the Muter studio, which he developed with the Polish painter Marie Mela Muter. During the 1920s, he built several houses in and near Paris with similarly voluminous work spaces and modest living accommodations for the sculptors Chana Orloff (1926–29) (fig. 1.18) and Dora Gordine (1928–29), the glass painter and frequent collaborator on Perret's church projects Marguerite Huré

1.18 Auguste Perret, Chana Orloff studio, 1926–29, Paris, interior view

(1929–31), and the painter Georges Braque (1927–30). He also designed an unexecuted project for Marc Chagall in 1927.

The breadth of interests Perret cultivated belies his limited classification as an architect of reinforced concrete.[54] It suggests that to label him as part of the "academic succession" of structural rationalists is seriously to underestimate his compass. Indeed, it is not surprising that both Perret and Tony Garnier developed turbulent relationships with the Academy of Fine Arts, despite both having excelled in their studies at the Ecole des Beaux-Arts. Garnier, a Rome Prize winner and thus one of the school's most promising students, designed his industrial city "against great opposition" while he was a pensioner at the French Academy in Rome.[55] As a Rome Prize winner, Garnier would normally have been expected to return to Paris to design important public buildings; he worked instead in Lyon for most of his career. Perret left the school after only three years, despite notable success, to work for his father's contracting business. Moreover, Garnier's concern for "the material and moral needs of the individual" and Perret's contentment with the "banal" in architecture were decidedly against the grain of academic thinking. These were interests shared very actively, however, by progressive artists and the designers of domestic interiors and mass-produced houses in France. And it was they, rather than academically trained architects, who sought most energetically to accommodate contemporary domestic life in France during the last decades of the nineteenth century and the first decades of the twentieth. And so it is in the work of these artists, and not of architects, that one must look for the first definitive stirrings of modern architecture in France.

THE LIBERALIZATION OF THE BOURGEOIS FRENCH INTERIOR

To examine these developments in the design of French domestic interiors, one must return to the middle of the nineteenth century. At that time, France had dominated the decorative tastes of Europe for nearly three centuries and had virtually no rivals in the production of fine art, luxury furniture, and work in glass, porcelain, and precious metals. However, the Great Exhibition of the Works of Industry of All Nations hosted by the British crown in 1851 presented a potentially different situation. England's competitive if sometimes aesthetically bereft showing at the Great Exhibition demonstrated vividly that France had failed to keep pace with industry's incursions into the provinces of design. There were execrable chairs in molded gutta-percha, tasteless, machine-carved buffets, and flimsy, pressed-tin candelabra, but the exhibition portended the emergence of a huge middle-class market for interior furnishings. This market appeared to be developing almost independent of French influence, which was, for many conservative French designers and critics, a source of smug satisfaction.

The situation became more dire throughout the next decade as the English government actively sought to raise the quality of industrially produced ornament and to improve the marketability of its manufactured furniture and decorative objects. This was the particular responsibility of the Department of Practical Art, which was founded by Prince Albert and Henry Cole soon after the Great Exhibition. The establishment of a state-sponsored department for this task exemplified the seriousness of the issue in England, for it was a matter that had impact not only on artistic tradition but also on emerging industries, international markets, and national prestige. Responding to an increasingly alarming threat of English competition, France quickly organized its own Exposition Universelle, which took place in Paris four years later. However, the wide popular appeal of British genre painting at the 1855 Exposition Universelle, along with England's continued dominance in the industrialized production of consumer goods, merely exacerbated French concerns.[56] The 1862 International Exhibition in London proved to be as menacing as the Great Exhibition of 1851.

In an effort to combat the threat of international competition in a more systematic and vigorous way, a group of French designers, design critics, and manufacturers formed the Central Union of Fine Arts Applied to Industry (Union Centrale des Beaux-Arts Appliqués à l'Industrie) in 1864. Its original aim was to coordinate the industrialized production of furniture and decorative art objects and to market them to middle-class consumers in France and throughout Europe. Members of the group were careful to ensure, however, that French tastes did not suffer from their efforts. They professed "to honor, encourage, and stimulate in industrial works everything that contains art . . . to propagate in France . . . the realization of beauty in utility; to aid men in the elite in their efforts to raise the standards of work . . . to encourage the emulation of those artists whose works, while popularizing the sense of beauty, also maintain the just pre-eminence attributed to our industrial arts by the world."[57] The group struggled with this mission from the outset, partly because it lacked a state-imposed mandate, but mostly because its members, who were drawn largely from the conservative academic, social, and political elite, distanced the organization almost immediately from industry and from the burgeoning middle-class culture.[58] Despite their rhetoric and the almost certain economic disadvantage that would follow, they undermined the goal of "popularizing the sense of beauty." They chose instead to emphasize France's preeminence in the luxury crafts. By 1882, when the group changed its name to the Central Union of the Decorative Arts (Union Centrale des Arts Décoratifs), its goals had changed as well. The group now sought, as Debora Silverman notes, to "purify the sentiment of beauty and aristocratize the crafts."[59] This shift reflected the widely held and persistent belief among conservative designers that industrial production and the historically luxurious tastes of France were fundamentally incompatible.

Department stores and foreign producers, rather than French crafts workshops, therefore took control of the market for low-priced furnishings and commandeered a vast segment of the crafts trade in France. Pandering to the tastes of French consumers, department stores continued to produce an eclectic array of highly ornamented, low-cost domestic furnishings and bibelots for middle-class buyers. At the same time, decorative handbooks and women's journals encouraged consumers to assume control over the furnishing of their own houses (fig. 1.19). Lisa Tiersten notes that these journals promoted the increasingly widespread view "that it was not only psychologically unhealthy to live in an environment designed by a total stranger, but that the moral sanctity of the home was compromised by the intrusion of outsiders."[60] The notion that bourgeois homeowners, or even common laborers, might become the arbiters of French taste, at least in domestic settings, became an important theme among progressive designers over the next several decades. Designers would have to capture the sentiments of these consumers and accommodate their desires. A contemporary art critic, Gustave Geffroy, conveyed the sense of this powerful groundswell in 1895, saying:

> Today the human masses can live a personal life . . . they are already emerging from the shadows, are advancing . . . to occupy the scene of history. . . .
>
> The necessary assimilation of the masses to the life of the spirit was begun and will be achieved by art.[61]

This idea emerged forcefully among the painters of Geffroy's generation, who began to concentrate their attention on everyday themes. It was also taken up by influential artist-designers such as Le Corbusier, Francis Jourdain, André Mare, and others, who designed interiors and houses on the presumption that their compositions were meant merely to represent configurations that middle- and working-class inhabitants might bring about themselves.

Seeking to accommodate the tastes and budgets of a new class of consumers, manufacturers of the late nineteenth century reduced the cost
of these supposed art objects by using cheap materials, sweatshop labor,
and serialized industrial processes. Department stores marketed their products heavily to the middle class. Proponents of an emerging bourgeois style
of interior decoration (who were often allied with department stores)
encouraged women in particular to express their individuality and that
of their families in the composition and furnishing of their homes. Tiersten suggests that in the typical middle-class domestic settings, "the quality of the objects themselves did not matter so much as their disposition
and arrangement, the aesthetic composition of which revealed the orig-

1.19 M. Cottin, *Les
petits riens*, in Henri
de Noussane, *Le goût
dans l'ameublement*
(Paris, 1896)

inality and artistic vision of the lady of the house."[62] Not surprisingly, many proponents of traditional French tastes sneered at these bourgeois pretensions and sought to protect French luxury goods from this form of popularization.[63] Inspired by Edmund de Goncourt, who criticized "the ugliness and bad taste of contemporary industrial society," the group sponsored a small cadre of decorative artists committed to hand labor and the perpetuation of French patrimony in the arts.[64]

Nevertheless, middle-class taste exerted an increasingly strong influence on French design.[65] Siegfried Bing was an important agent in the broad incorporation of middle-class tastes in a new kind of French domestic interior and a proponent of at least some modernization of production methods. He was an extraordinarily successful art dealer and important contributor to the efforts of the Central Union of the Decorative Arts during the 1880s and 1890s.[66] Bing made a name and a fortune for himself in the 1880s as a collector of Japanese and American art. In 1895, he applied his considerable energy to the establishment of higher standards for middle-class French tastes. This effort centered on the foundation of a new gallery in Paris—indeed, a new kind of gallery—which would, in his words, "fight to eliminate ugliness and the pretentious luxury of every object, to effect the penetration of taste and the charm of simple beauty even into the least objects of utility."[67] He called it L'Art Nouveau. For a decade, the movement that bore its name affected nearly every aspect of design in France.

An important part of Bing's plan for the gallery was to accept any work, even if it was not French, as long as it expressed new sentiments and was of the highest quality. So from the beginning, Bing chose to display objects designed by American, Belgian, English, and Japanese artists alongside the products of their French contemporaries.[68] The collection included a great range of artistic productions intended primarily for use in domestic interiors, including sculpture, easel painting, furniture, cabinetry, ceramics, stained glass, jewelry, wallpapers, tapestries, rugs, and embroidery. Bing commissioned many of the pieces specifically for the venture and exercised strict control over the choice of the other objects. Many of his French collaborators were Nabis and Symbolist painters, such as Albert Besnard, Pierre Bonnard, Maurice Denis, Henri de Toulouse-Lautrec, and Edouard Vuillard; others, such as Emile Gallé and René Lalique, were decorative artists. He also secured the services of English painters, especially Frank Brangwyn and Charles Conder, Belgian architect Henri van de Velde, and American glassmaker Louis Comfort Tiffany. Bing later admitted, with a bit of hyperbole, that his first exhibit consisted of "the thousand ill-assorted things that I had collected in a haphazard way."[69] But there was a consistency in the work; every piece expressed a uniform "hatred of stagnation."[70]

Even more remarkable than the collection's great range was the method of display. Unlike traditional galleries, which tended to separate the products of various disciplines, L'Art Nouveau brought most of the objects together as complete ensembles. Each room encompassed a range of artistic productions coordinated to give a single impression (figs. 1.20, 1.21). Assembled together in a converted Parisian mansion, these rooms presented a new conception of the bourgeois house. L'Art Nouveau was the first Parisian gallery to arrange primary exhibits as complete room ensembles emulating a furnished house rather than by genre, although it was certainly inspired by La Maison d'Art, a gallery that had opened in Brussels the year before.[71]

Like the gallery's interiors, L'Art Nouveau's exterior represented the work of a diverse range of artists (fig. 1.22). Primarily the work of French architect Louis Bonnier and English painter Frank Brangwyn, with input from the Belgian Victor Horta, it presented a range of nontraditional ornaments—broad, painted friezes, stenciled ornamental motifs loosely arrayed on the plastered surfaces of the ground floor, an elaborate glass-and-metal cupola surmounting the corner turret, and, framing the main entrance, two columns expanding upward to form elaborately sculpted sunflower plants (fig. 1.23). The overall impression was of a typically French, Parisian house, but one that had been substantially modified and updated.

Many critics complained nevertheless that L'Art Nouveau's infusion of foreign work into Paris demeaned French tastes and instilled an unhealthy sense of competition in an already beleaguered segment of French patrimony.[72] Bing argued, however, that introducing French artists and consumers to the finest work from other regions of the world would stir up the most fertile parts of the French imagination. Foreign competition had always been good for French art. During its greatest periods, Bing contended, French design had been receptive to external influences. Just as the monarchy of the eighteenth century had drawn inspiration from East Asia for its grand and unified styles of interior ornamentation, he argued, France might once again look beyond its borders for inspiration.[73] For the furniture and decorative objects produced in his own workshops, which he established adjacent to the gallery, he set forth "the following program, to the exclusion of all other considerations. Thoroughly impregnate oneself anew with the old French tradition . . . enrich the old patrimony with the spirit of modernness, bearing in mind

the eternal law which ordains that everything which fails to keep progressing is doomed to perish."[74] Displaying these and other objects designed and built in the same spirit, L'Art Nouveau would manifest a genuinely modern movement that could "subordinate the general character of our environment to all the conditions of modern life."[75]

Cultivating a taste for "modern life," the gallery gave a unique impression not just of newness but also of livability—a sense that art and everyday life could coexist even in the relatively modest circumstances of the bourgeois French home. This was an important source of the explosive popularity of the Art Nouveau movement. A perceptive British contemporary, Gabriel Mourey, reflected that "it must not be forgotten that this exhibition was not destined only for the *dilettante* knowing all the aesthetic ideas, and whose education in artistic things by study or taste had already prepared him to be able to express a personal opinion. No, in this matter, we must keep in mind what we call the mass, who do not make revolutions, but consecrate them, if they are skillfully prepared."[76] Even if most of its products were quite expensive, Bing's gallery responded masterfully to an increasingly widespread interest in bourgeois home decor. The rise of the Art Nouveau movement paralleled the sudden popularity of decorating handbooks and the frequent appearance of articles on the subject of home interiors in popular journals, many of which encouraged bourgeois housewives to cultivate eclectic tastes, to choose furnishings carefully and arrange them creatively.[77] One of the great strengths of Art Nouveau as it developed in France was that people did identify with its products. People liked them and wanted to buy them. By the turn of the century, Bing enjoyed the dubious compliment of excessive imitation. By 1902, he could complain of a "daily mounting flood" of horribly conceived objects exhibited and sold as products in the "art nouveau style."[78] He lamented that an American company had even claimed to have invented "a machine for the making of *Art Nouveau*."[79] Not surprisingly, many of the so-called Art Nouveau products marketed by department stores and other large-scale producers were ill-conceived and poorly executed. Their popularity, along with that of the Art Nouveau movement, waned quickly. Soon after the turn of the century, "the realization of beauty in utility" and "the necessary assimilation of the masses to the life of the spirit"— eventualities that French design reformers had long anticipated—still seemed a long way off.[80]

These goals were taken up nevertheless and promoted with extraordinary vigor by Frantz Jourdain (father of Francis Jourdain), an important Art Nouveau designer and one of the key proponents of modernization

1.20 Henri van de Velde, L'Art Nouveau gallery, Paris, 1895, smoking room

1.21 Henri van de Velde, L'Art Nouveau gallery, Paris, 1895, dining room

and liberalization in French art and design during the first decades of the twentieth century. Although trained as an architect at the Ecole des Beaux-Arts—which he disliked and left without completing qualifications for a diploma—Jourdain became an active critic of the Ecole and an outspoken reformer of art. He argued forcefully for the rejuvenation of contemporary art and the independence of artists from state intervention. He was also an extraordinarily effective organizer of diverse artistic tendencies. As an influential member of many progressive groups of artists, designers, and critics, and a vocal proponent of liberal political causes, he persistently championed efforts to reform French artistic culture. He lobbied arts organizations to open themselves up to the contributions of architects and decorative artists. And he exhorted architects to address a broader range of issues, particularly in relation to everyday life in the city, rather than focusing almost

1.22 Louis Bonnier, L'Art Nouveau gallery, Paris, 1895, exterior view

1.23 Louis Bonnier, L'Art Nouveau gallery, Paris, 1895, exterior detail

exclusively on the design of costly monuments and public buildings.[81]

Jourdain was the only architect to participate in the formation of the Société Nationale des Beaux-Arts, a group of artists that seceded from the conservative Société des Artistes Français in 1889. Through his tireless insistence, he eventually managed to secure entry of architects and decorative artists into its Salons. He presided over the Société du Nouveau Paris for many years, from its inception in 1902; an important goal of the society was to encourage architects to expand their activities into the everyday matters of civic infrastructure and housing. Low-cost housing was also the main concern of another group he helped to establish in 1902, the Société Française des Logements Hygiéniques à Bon Marché, which was instrumental in securing artistic services and public support for the construction of working-class housing in Paris. Its first project was a mixed-use building designed in 1903 by Henri Sauvage and Charles Sarazin, one of the first buildings in Paris to make use of a reinforced concrete frame. This and other buildings sponsored by the group provided an important demonstration of how the liberal principle of *solidarisme*, which had recently gained currency under the premiership of Léon Bourgeois, could allow artists, with the backing of the state, to promote the cultural diffusion of artistic tendencies while assuring their independence from state intervention.[82]

Frantz Jourdain's most important contribution to the reform of art in France and its diffusion to the public was the Salon d'Automne. This organization, which he founded in 1903 with the critic Ivanhoë Rambosson, gathered progressive designers, artists, and patrons seeking to reassemble the various arts—painting, sculpture, decorative arts, and architecture—into a unified force. It was motivated by a conviction that the ancient hierarchy of the arts, which placed painting and sculpture above the so-called lesser, or decorative, arts, was no longer tenable. In a retrospective analysis of the organization's founding principles, Jourdain explained that a primary goal of the group was to establish that "there is no such thing as a major or minor art, but only talented artists and worthless artists, whatever their medium. Convinced of the necessity of respecting the unity of art, we consider it timely to establish the absolute equality of painting, sculpture, the decorative arts, engraving, and architecture, while eliminating useless classifications and iniquitous hierarchies."[83] This conviction underlay the selection and organization of work for the group's annual exhibition, which it held in the Grand Palais during the fall—in opposition to the official spring Salon of the Academy of Art. Just as Bing had proposed that his gallery L'Art Nouveau would use every kind of art to "subordinate the general character of our environment to all the conditions of modern life," the founders of the Salon d'Automne sought to demonstrate "the chaotic order of life" through the catholic selection and display of artworks.[84]

In 1905, the committee of the Salon d'Automne began to encourage the development of integrated art ensembles that would envisage everyday living environments. Its members foresaw ensembles in which contemporary music, furniture, decorative arts, and painting would complement the progressive attitudes of the rooms' inhabitants.[85] These displays, while differing radically from art exhibitions at the official Salons, were similar in conception to carefully unified interiors displayed in L'Art Nouveau a decade earlier. But their development over the succeeding decade challenged even the most progressive interpretations of contemporary domestic environments.

Many of these developments proceeded directly from the methods of display promoted by the Salon d'Automne. From the beginning, new associations formed as the work of painters and designers commingled in its galleries each fall. Later, as painters, sculptors, decorative artists, and interior designers collaborated on interior ensembles for the Salon, these associations extended outward to affect new conceptions not only of art but of the artistic arrangement of living environments. Paintings took on decorative characteristics; interior designs followed compositional strategies of paintings. A number of these collaborative environments are examined in chapter 2.

DOMESTIC THEMES IN THE FINE ARTS

Just as L'Art Nouveau encouraged collaboration of Symbolist and Nabis painters in the development of Art Nouveau architecture and decor, the Salon d'Automne facilitated the engagement of Cubists with modern domestic architecture. These conjunctions were consistent with the long-standing goals of art reformers in France, who as early as the 1860s had sought to break down distinctions among the arts and to reunite art with French popular culture. In disciplines that had been dominated for so long by the theoretical aims of the Academy of Art, however, collaboration was easier to bring about than popularization. Any attempt to show that the lives of ordinary people could be the legitimate subject of artistic attention represented a substantial and controversial departure from accepted norms. It was this shift in attention, perhaps more than the weighty questions of artistic technique or the increasing clamor for access to exhibition space, that led to the acrimonious secessions of the Salon des Refusés in 1863, the Salon des Indépendants in 1884, and the Salon d'Automne in 1903. It also established an important trajectory for modern art in France.

Although their approaches varied, virtually all progressive art movements of the late nineteenth and early twentieth centuries in France contended with the circumstances, perceptions, and objects associated with everyday life.[86] These tendencies were abetted in part by a decline in state influence and consequent increase in private funding for art. Much of this funding came from a growing number of bourgeois buyers who gained access to fine art through galleries and entrepreneurial art dealers. At the same time, the liberalization of French politics during the Second Empire and the Third Republic fostered the burgeoning involvement of artists in political and social affairs, which often helped to bring their work to the attention of the public. Finally, the increasingly accessible (and often rather undisciplined) display of art, particularly at the Expositions Universelles, meant that people gravitated to and purchased the art that appealed to them, regardless of official sanction and often in spite of sharply negative critical reaction. Genre painting, in particular, became immensely popular because of these exhibitions.[87]

In subsequent decades, painters who "examined the commonplaces of everyday life" in France, to use the words of Gabriel Weisberg, achieved unprecedented prominence.[88] For example, the historical-genre painter Jean-Louis-Ernest Meissonier, who was acclaimed as "the greatest painter in the world" in 1867 and was eventually given the Grand-Croix of the Legion of Honor, frequently painted *petite-genre* scenes (fig. 1.24).[89] The canvases of his younger contemporaries, Realist painters such as Gustave Courbet and Jean-François Millet, were more challenging but equally popular. They frequently depicted contemporary scenes from life in rural France, leaving both subject matter and technique dangerously unrefined (fig. 1.25). Realist painters later depicted urban working-class settings in similar terms (fig. 1.26). These paintings not only challenged traditional academic themes and techniques but also raised questions about how artists should respond to contemporary experience.[90] Reacting against the picturesque, narrative tendencies of the Realists, the Naturalists sought merely to capture ordinary moments in life without reinterpreting them. Their goal, as Geneviève Lacambre explains, was "to convey a life-like impression, to record all aspects of modernity wherever it could be detected."[91]

During these same years, Claude Monet, Paul Cézanne, and other Impressionists extended this understanding beyond the choice of subject matter into the questions of how people perceive the world and, thus, how artists should represent it. They subscribed to a notion of common sense vigorously advocated by Henri Bergson.[92] Bergson argued that, contrary to the esoteric assertions of contemporary philosophy, common sense leads one to believe rightly "that matter exists just as it is perceived."[93] The Impressionists shared this view because it seemed clear to them, as George Heard Hamilton suggests, that "intuitive experience was the only source for the knowledge of reality, and that art was a direct revelation of such experience."[94] This suggested that a work of art, if properly constructed, should be as accessible to someone with little experience of art as it is to a supposed expert, and that its significance should no longer rest on hidden sources of meaning, such as allegory, history, and theology.

Dissatisfied with the implied limitations, the Symbolist and Nabis painters of the late 1880s and 1890s focused attention on emotional rather than perceptual experience. Artists such as Paul Gauguin and Maurice Denis concentrated on "those forces hidden beneath the surface of the com-

1.24 Jean-Louis-Ernest Meissonier, *The Laundresses in Antibes*, oil on wood, 1869

monplace," to use the words of Robert Goldwater.[95] Rather than merely depicting the reality of everyday life, they sought to convey its emotional undercurrents.[96] To do this, a painting had to be more than an image of reality, and it had to appeal to more than the sense of vision. These painters demonstrated that a depicted scene, being always insufficient to represent its emotional content, gained strength from its colors and composition. In 1890, Denis emphasized this point with the bland assertion that "a picture—before being a war-horse, a nude woman, or some sort of anecdote—is essentially a surface covered with colors arranged in a certain order."[97] Denis and his contemporaries therefore used color and the composition of shapes on the canvas to affect the subconscious workings of the mind (fig. 1.27). This emphasis on surface naturally led them to associate painting with decoration, which was, in their view, its original purpose.[98] Albert Aurier, a contemporary of Denis, argued that "painting can only have been created to decorate the banal walls of human edifices with

thoughts, dreams and ideas."[99] For these painters, and for many French artists of succeeding decades, the seemingly mundane appeal of *décoration* became the primary means with which to express emotion in art. The domestic interior naturally provided the most suitable circumstances for this kind of work, and so it was that the fortuitous collaboration of Siegfried Bing and Albert Besnard, Maurice Denis, Henri de Toulouse-Lautrec, Edouard Vuillard, and others on the decoration of L'Art Nouveau helped to revolutionize the relationship between painting and domestic space in France, bringing them together in the increasingly vital context of the bourgeois house.

Decoration was also a central concern of the Fauves, who came to prominence at the Salons d'Automne of 1905 and 1906. The Fauves, of whom Henri Matisse was the most prominent, attempted to achieve emotional effects primarily through compositional relationships on the canvas. Matisse described this sort of composition as "the art of arranging in a decorative manner the various elements at the painter's disposal for the expression of his *feelings.*"[100] These elements included colors, contours, and the shapes of objects one might encounter in day-to-day experience, such as furniture, fruit, and plants (fig. 1.28).[101] Matisse imagined that his decorative paintings might provide an escape from the nagging concerns of everyday life. "What I dream of," he said, "is an art of balance, of purity and serenity, devoid of troubling or depressing subject matter, an art which could be for every mental worker, for the businessman as well as the man of letters, for example, a soothing, calming influence on the mind, something which provides relaxation from fatigues and toil."[102] Being decorative and thus popular rather than esoteric, this kind of art could insinuate itself comfortably into the domestic situations of ordinary people.

Although its appeal was hardly popular and its effect anything but soothing, Analytic Cubism also emphasized the arrangement of mundane elements on the canvas. Georges Braque and Pablo Picasso produced a great number of paintings after 1907 in which bottles, tables, letters, guitars, cups—"objects of the most predictable familiarity," in the words of Leo Steinberg—became primary subject matter.[103] But these objects took shape as if subdivided, reduced to facets and contours, and blended with adjacent objects and intervening spaces so that they could no longer be understood as discrete objects independent of their contexts (fig. 1.29). In this way, Cubist compositions implied that the ubiquitous and banal products of contemporary society are so thoroughly integrated into people's habits that objects and circumstances become virtually indistinguishable. The power of Cubist paintings derives, therefore, from a delicate balance

1.25 Jean-François Millet, *The Gleaners*, oil on canvas, 1857

1.26 François Bonhommé, *Interior of a Forge*, the Power Hammer in 1862, drawing, 1862

between banal objective content and complex spatial composition. Colin Rowe and Robert Slutzky explain that the paintings "transpose insignificant singularities into meaningful complexities."[104] The early collages of Braque and Picasso clarified this method further by devaluing the media used to depict their banal subject material (fig. 1.30). In an extended analysis of these collages, Christine Poggi explains that what remains significant after this diminution of both content and technique is composition: "In place of the unique indexical markings of the artist's hand, still of primary significance in Symbolist and Fauvist works, we find only fragments of previously established codes of representation: newspaper clippings, bits of wallpaper, musical scores. . . . In these early collages originality derives from the imaginative manipulation of conventional signs."[105]

Despite their use of ordinary materials and subject matter, Braque and Picasso were not interested in whether middle-class French people liked or understood their work. Jeffrey Weiss notes that their collages were "composed of popular source material and rarefied aesthetic meaning." Their aim was, at least in part, to emphasize "the tension between popular culture and incomprehension in modern art."[106] These intentions remained virtually incomprehensible to any but a few sympathetic artists and the most perceptive of critics and connoisseurs, and the evident cheapness (in the worst sense of the word) of these works of art offended bourgeois sensibilities.[107] Nevertheless, their collages did affect middle-class environments by way of other artists who used Cubist techniques to help resolve tensions between bourgeois tastes and the contemporary avant-garde.

Not long after Braque and Picasso assembled their first collages, a group of artists and designers sympathetic to their work—many of them members of the Puteaux Cubists—began developing domestic interiors. These were targeted directly at the middle class, not simply as a challenge to popular tastes but as a potentially viable line of development in the modernization of ordinary households. They were collagelike assemblages that brought together familiar or familiar-seeming objects in order to make extraordinary compositions. Although these interiors bore little outward resemblance to Cubist paintings or collages, they shared a fundamental principle: like Cubist paintings, they gained significance because of the relationships established among elements rather than from anything especially notable in the elements themselves. They also commented on and benefited from strategies that bourgeois families used to furnish their homes, where the calculated disposition of objects, often quite varied in origin and quality, was meant to convey a unified impression of well-being

1.27 Maurice Denis, *April*, oil on canvas, 1892

1.28 Henri Matisse, *Harmony in Red*, oil on canvas, 1908

1.29 Georges Braque, *Violin and Palette*, oil on canvas, 1909–10

1.30 Pablo Picasso, *Guitar and Wineglass*, collage, 1912

and prosperity.[108] So the work of these artists was both a challenge to and an accommodation of contemporary middle-class approaches to the assembly of settings for domestic life. It subtly but significantly affected the design of modern domestic architecture as it developed in France over the next two decades. This and the continued competitive pressure, especially from Germany, in the design and production of interiors, furniture, and utilitarian and decorative objects for middle-class households propelled notable changes in French conceptions of modern architecture. The next chapter examines these developments—dominated first by German competition and later by the work of the Cubists—as they appeared in the Salons d'Automne of 1910 to 1913.

2 DESIGN AND DOMESTIC SETTINGS

THE SALONS D'AUTOMNE OF 1910 TO 1913

*If a fastidiously drawn scale drawing, of a temple overloaded with useless
columns can be mounted on a chassis and served up to the public classified
as "architecture," then a living room or kitchen, displayed as they really are,
complete with furniture and utensils, which they can move around in, can
also be classified as architecture, and as living, animated architecture, which
will captivate and interest the visitor in another way.*

—ROBERT MALLET-STEVENS, "LE SALON D'AUTOMNE"

Supported by a now vital reform movement and increasingly creative interaction with modern painters, French decorative arts and domestic architecture were beginning to enjoy a lively, if sometimes tumultuous,
resurgence during the 1910s. Even so, French design continued to face well-
organized competition from abroad. Germany, in particular, posed a new
and largely unanticipated threat to French tastes.

In the previous decade—under the auspices of various state-supported
crafts workshops, or *Werkstätten*, and the Deutscher Werkbund—the German state, industry, and artists had fully reorganized the design, production, and marketing of furniture and utilitarian and decorative objects in
Germany. Initially, German production methods followed those of the
English Arts and Crafts movement, sharing its heavy emphasis on simple
composition and exquisite care in the crafting of objects for domestic interiors.[1] The German crafts workshops refined British methods of hand production for a vast range of products and quickly found effective ways to

EINRICHTUNG
Nr. I
Wohn- und Eßstube: Fichte, rot lackiert, Messingbeschlag

GESAMTBILD

(96) 8 Sofa, 190 cm lang, 70 cm tief, 95 cm ganze Höhe
(96) 6 Tisch zum Ausziehen, 100×80 cm, 75 cm hoch
(96) 4 Wäscheschrank, 90 cm breit, 50 cm tief, 150 cm hoch
(79) 5 3 Stühle
(96) 3 Kleiderschrank, 110 cm breit, 200 cm hoch, 56 cm tief

**2.1 Richard
Riemerschmid,
machine-produced
furniture, 1905**

mechanize their production processes. In 1905, for example, Richard
Riemerschmid developed a line of machine-made domestic furnishings
for the workshops in Dresden (fig. 2.1). These *Maschinenmöbel* (machine-
furniture) used standardized parts in painted pine, which could be assembled in various configurations to make a range of pieces—chairs, couches,
cabinets, tables. Exposed connectors demonstrated the simple, straightforward joinery of the parts. Bruno Paul introduced a similar line of furniture, which he called *Typenmöbel* (type-furniture), for the Vereinigte
Werkstätten in Munich three years later. In 1910, Charles-Edouard Jeanneret (later known as Le Corbusier) visited the workshops that manufactured these and other products and found the modern facilities partially
mechanized, beautifully organized, and incredibly clean.[2]

By this time, large-scale industry was also beginning to participate in
the movement to reform objects for household use. The immense indus-

trial conglomerate Allgemeine Elektricitäts-Gesellschaft (AEG) in Berlin was the most important contributor to this effort. In his study, Jeanneret (who not only visited the firm in 1910 but also worked for its artistic director, Peter Behrens, for five months that same year) explained that "the board of directors [of the firm] has found a way of exploiting the reform movement asserting itself in architecture, by imprinting its consumer goods with a character of perfect convenience ruled by the laws of taste."[3] Under Behrens's artistic leadership, AEG developed lines of inexpensive domestic products—lamps, electric teakettles, clocks—that adhered closely to the principles of the movement (fig. 2.2). Through mass production of high-quality domestic furnishings—something decorative arts movements elsewhere had long resisted—Germany quickly gained access to lucrative international markets for its consumer products. In France, this fact gained consequence as imports of German furniture and other domestic goods increased steadily into the 1910s.[4]

2.2 Peter Behrens, electric teakettle produced by the Allgemeine Elektricitäts-Gesellschaft, 1910

Meanwhile, German work also gained critical acclaim throughout Europe, even inside France. This was particularly painful for France, which had for centuries enjoyed a widely acknowledged superiority over Germany in matters of art and taste.[5] French designers and critics still maintained, as Jeanneret did in 1912, that German aesthetic success was either accidental or derivative (often clumsily so) of English or French achievements, but they could hardly do so with confidence for much longer.[6]

One aspect of design that Germany had perfected—but to which French designers could wistfully lay some claim—was the interior ensemble. Almost immediately after taking on the genre, the German workshops displayed brilliantly executed interior ensembles in local, national, and international exhibitions. Demonstrating organization on a larger scale than any of their competitors, their rooms represented the production of many collaborating designers rather than the comprehensive work of an individual, as was usually the case in France. The German designers also developed harmonious sequences of rooms, showing the effectiveness of their principles at the scale of an entire house. In their most important collaborations, each room not only demonstrated its own coherence but also fit neatly into a larger whole. The Vereinigte Werkstätten, a prominent annual design exhibition held in Munich during the summer of 1908 under the leadership of Bruno Paul, displayed a series of interiors that brilliantly demonstrated this collaboration (figs. 2.3, 2.4). From one room to the next, carefully coordinated materials, color, and stylistic treatments attested to the rigor and clarity of the designers' intentions. A delegation from the city of Paris observed with alarm the organization and superb

2.3 Bruno Paul,
small dining room,
Die Austellung
München, Munich,
1908

2.4 Richard
Riemerschmid,
corner of a woman's
room, Die Austellung
München, Munich,
1908

craftsmanship evident in German decorative arts production.[7] In response to their experience in Munich, the delegates voiced a dire warning for France:

> The commercial defeat which has threatened us for many years is no longer to be feared, indeed, it has already occurred. . . . We cannot compensate for the advance which Munich has been able to accomplish to our detriment in the industrial domain. Only in five or six years from now will we see and experience the complete results, when this army of students begins to produce industrially. . . . The only thing we can try to do with any hope of success is to begin to prepare the future generation to enter into competition with these countries.[8]

The exhibition in Munich was not only evidence of a commercial conquest, however. It presaged a cultural setback comparable, in the view of some critics, to the ruinous military defeat of 1870.[9] This weighty apprehension was much different from the nagging concern for national prestige and prosperity that had preoccupied French designers for more than fifty years in their mostly friendly rivalry with English counterparts. It took on far greater urgency when Germany entered the fray. Virulent political competition between France and Germany, based on historical enmities and widely divergent political philosophies, strongly affected French attitudes toward anything German, especially German art.

1910—THE GERMAN CHALLENGE

To spur a response to this challenge, and "to begin to prepare the future generation to enter into competition," Frantz Jourdain, on behalf of the Salon d'Automne, invited the designers from Munich to mount a display at the Salon of 1910. Jourdain asserted that the exhibition of German work alongside French work would provide the French public an opportunity to "study each entry impartially."[10] He contended that exposing the work to direct critical assessment would encourage French designers to understand their own weaknesses.

As it turned out, French designers were particularly vulnerable. The year 1910 was not, by most accounts, a good year for design in France. In the decorative arts, productive collaboration between artists and industry remained unrealized. At the Salon of the Société des Artistes Décorateurs, which took place earlier in the year, Charles Saunier noted some promising developments but held out little hope for them. "A style appears to be underway but there is insufficient cooperation between artists and industry and not enough interest on the part of the public." This indifference made the upcoming exhibit of the Munich designers at the Salon d'Automne particularly ominous, and Saunier anticipated that the event would be very difficult for France: "The production of Germany which will be demonstrated in the [1910] Salon d'Automne is considerable, menacing—a 'grave moment' for the decorative arts in France. Their furniture may not be to French tastes, but this will not be the case for other objects." The German exhibit was threatening not only because it virtually guaranteed an embarrassment for the French; it also was sure to emphasize the already bleak commercial prospects for French designers. Saunier lamented, "Foreigners are passing us by and inundating Paris with their products."[11] The 1910 Salon d'Automne promised to make this situation vividly and painfully evident.

For French domestic architecture, circumstances seemed even less encouraging. In an assessment of architectural work presented in the Salons of 1910, M. P. Verneuil made the melancholy pronouncement that "architecture has given us few interesting works this year." And he asked, "How can one not regret, in our Salons, the absence of projects for simple but comfortable houses, country houses or city houses, conceived according to a clear and logical plan and with facades impressed with the same simplicity, which would finally release us from the bad taste that reigns as an absolute master over our small-scale architecture?"[12] Under these circumstances, the German contributions to the Salon d'Automne, which were sure to recall the ensembles that "were so successful in Munich in 1908," could hardly fail to make an impression.

The official guide to the 1910 Salon noted that the method of display the Germans brought to the event would naturally orient it toward architecture. "For this reason," it declared, "an architectural character rules over the exhibition of decorative arts."[13] At the moment of the 1910 Salon d'Automne, neither French decorative artists nor architects could hope to deliver much by way of a competitive response. Jourdain maintained high hopes for the exhibit precisely because of this: the Salon was a provocation, and France was almost ready to face it.

The results were as distressing as feared—and as far-reaching as hoped.[14] The contingent from Munich succeeded in presenting an exhibition that fulfilled all expectations. As in the 1908 exhibition, its members chose to create complementary, unified interiors, carefully coordinating every detail and each exquisitely crafted piece (figs. 2.5, 2.6).[15] Its eighteen room ensembles included all of the more public rooms in a typical

2.5 Theodor Veil,
reception room,
Salon d'Automne,
Paris, 1910

2.6 Richard Berndl,
large salon, Salon
d'Automne, Paris,
1910

bourgeois house—reception hall, library, music room, dining room, salon. It also included two bedrooms, a boudoir, and a bathroom as well as more mundane spaces such as a corridor and an entry vestibule. French critics of the exhibition expressed amazement at the effectiveness and originality of the German display, even if, as they often claimed, the ensembles were not to French tastes because of the weighty proportions of the furniture and bold use of color.[16]

They could not help but note, by contrast, the disorganized appearance of the French contribution to the exhibit. Despite having the advantage of exhibiting in their home city, some French designers did not even complete their interiors for the opening of the Salon. And critics admitted that the finished ensembles were less coherent than those of their German competitors. Verneuil, for instance, complained that "the *munichois* show us the benefits of a common effort, as opposed to the individual effort that prevails among us, where veritable anarchy reigns."[17] An interior by André Groult, for example, presented a variety of furniture in different colors and materials, assembled against a strongly patterned wallpaper and complemented by an eclectic selection of paintings—still lifes and portraits—hung almost haphazardly on the wall (fig. 2.7). He noted in a more conciliatory tone, however, that "the *munichois* spent a long time preparing their important exhibition: *they work according to a common idea*, enjoying the collaboration with industry or valu-

able subsidies. Our artists on the contrary, display only their *personal* and current works, *which were not made with an exposition in mind*, and without help of any sort."[18]

While Verneuil could find some consolation in the independence of French artists, other critics were not as sanguine. François Monod wrote later, reflecting on the competitive situation between the two countries, that the problems exhibited by French designers were indicative of broad failures in education and production. If "one now compares France with Germany, and with the other countries of Central Europe," he lamented, "one is obliged to concede our evident inferiority from either the standpoint of our organization of decorative arts education, or—the one is the function of the other—the standpoint of our modern decorative art *production*. . . . The schools [in Germany] are animated by the same will as German industry, 'the will to stamp even the most modest manufactured object, the article of everyday use, with the cachet of art.'"[19]

Although French critics reacted favorably and reflectively to the organization and quality of the German offering in the 1910 Salon d'Automne, their response to its aesthetic merits tended to be defensive and nationalistic. Verneuil, for example, protested that German tastes could never suit the French. "Could such an exhibition have any influence on French decorative arts? I do not hesitate to say no, and no absolutely. The Bavarian is certainly closer to us than the Prussian, but he remains German nonetheless. And our Latin taste will never receive any direction from German taste."[20] Despite this kind of reaction, the failure of French designers in 1910 also raised important questions about the state of French tastes. Charles Saunier asked, "Where is the style, the French modern style? One cannot fail to note that the English style exists, that the German style has also affirmed its vitality at the last Salon d'Automne."[21] Even if German design was not to French tastes, as Saunier had declared a year earlier, the French still had little to match it. But this realization, too, could be turned to positive ends. And, by the Salon of the following year, it was already possible to perceive clearly distinguishable schools of thought that were emerging in the design of French domestic interiors.

Despite the evident failure of French designers, the 1910 Salon d'Automne presented a crucial moment, a turning point for the decorative arts in France. It provided French designers with a clearer sense of mission than they had felt for decades: an intense desire to dominate Germany in the decorative arts. Saunier summed this up, reflecting on the exhibition, in January 1911: "It was not without inquietude that I anticipated the participation of Germany in the decorative art section of the most recent Salon d'Automne. . . . Following the exposition of the Salon d'Automne, the crushing blow that menaced was avoided, but the alarm was real. The Germans have shown what one can gain by following suit."[22] In other words, the embarrassment of the 1910 Salon d'Automne was not the humiliating defeat it could have been; rather, it encouraged a vigorous response, as Frantz Jourdain had hoped.

The 1910 exhibition clearly showed the limitations that French designers had to overcome. Funding and organization were the matters of deepest concern. Nevertheless, critics and designers generally agreed that it was the continued *independence* of French artists and designers, not their formal organization, that would help France to strengthen its position in the decorative arts. So even if the success of the designers from Munich was directly attributable to generous state subsidies, or to the kaiser's educational program, French designers were hesitant to demand the same from their own government. Direct intervention by the state had been anathema in France for a long time, and French artists and critics were not inclined to accept any policies that might force them to relinquish artistic control. They were, in addition, vigorously resistant to any suggestions that they emulate "German" methods of production. Even if a lack of state or institutional backing appeared for the moment to be a distinct disadvantage, designers in France worked to remain unencumbered by the requirements and inertia of large organizational structures.

The Salon d'Automne, under the continued leadership of Frantz Jourdain, was particularly effective in turning this desire for independence to positive ends. Despite his admiration for German efforts, Jourdain asserted, "in art more than in any other intellectual manifestation, centralization is detrimental. Existing, by its very essence, only within a context of liberty and individuality, Art begins to wilt and decay under any sort of tyrannical tutelage."[23] After 1910, the Salon's liberal selection of works by painters, sculptors, and decorative artists, and its continued encouragement of artistic collaboration, resulted in eloquent French versions of the domestic interior ensemble. It became clear in the 1911 and 1912 Salons particularly that French designers had benefited, after all, from their failure to match *munichois* designers in 1910.

1911—*CONSTRUCTEUR/COLORISTE*

Spurred to action after the 1908 and 1910 exhibitions in Munich and Paris, a number of French designers began to make more assertive attempts to exhibit their work in unified and sometimes collaborative ensembles. Pre-

2.8 Maurice Dufrène,
cabinet and armchair,
Salon d'Automne,
Paris, 1911

dictably, the most nationalistic critics were quick to dismiss these efforts
as another unfortunate sign of French weakness and the spreading
influence of German imperialism. Even so, French designers dealt with
interior ensembles very differently than did their German counterparts,
rarely conforming entirely to the requirements of a group. M. P. Verneuil
repeated his criticism of this tendency in 1913, declaring:

> One can regret that among the attempts to realize modern interiors
> there has been lacking until now the homogeneity that would accen-
> tuate their character and presence. This is due to the general spirit of
> individualism that reigns today, in which individualism is, from the out-
> set, the absolute rule. In an ensemble to whose creation a number of
> artists contribute, the dominant thought of each is not to create homo-
> geneity, to harmonize perfectly the part which he contributes to the
> those of his collaborators, but solely to affirm his personality in an
> absolute and vivid manner.[24]

Despite the artists' evident lack of discipline, however, distinct tendencies began to emerge in 1911. As Verneuil explained it, there were two kinds of designers producing ensembles in France during the early 1910s: "1. artists we have followed for years in the salons: Dufrène, Jallot, Gaillard, Gallerey, Majorelle, Selmersheim . . . whose work exhibited mastery, consistency, and perhaps excessive conservatism, and 2. artists 'discovered' by the Salon d'Automne: Jaulmes, Süe, Mare, Groult, Huillard . . . whose work exhibited greater vitality, newer ideas, less care, less homogeneity."[25]

The designers of the first group, whom the critics labeled the *constructeurs*, worked on their own and presented luxurious, subtle, homogeneous interiors reminiscent of earlier court styles or of Art Nouveau.[26] They opposed German successes by attempting to reinforce traditional French tastes, using fine materials and muted colors, and emphasized impeccable construction in their furniture (fig. 2.8). The ensembles they presented in the Salons of 1911 and later manifested a mature, luxurious, and very "French" style.

The artists in the second group, the *coloristes*, many of whom were painters rather than decorative artists, often exhibited collaborative work. Their interiors presented jarring colors and strong stylistic juxtapositions. The materials and craftsmanship varied but gave a general impression of indifference to quality. Many contemporary observers saw in the intense colors of these ensembles an attempt to emulate the similarly bold interiors presented in 1910 by the designers from Munich. But the intentions of these French designers were very different from those of their German counterparts. Unlike the work of Bruno Paul and his collaborators, which emphasized unity and harmony among interior surfaces and furnishings, the rooms of the *coloristes* were meant to express the fortuitous effect of relationships among disparate objects. These designers, not being skilled furniture makers, were often compelled to select rather than construct many of the pieces that constituted their ensembles. Consequently, their furnishings tended to be eclectic, gathering together elements drawn from a great range of sources including French neoclassical furniture (Directoire, Restoration, Louis-Philippe), provincial crafts, contemporary sculpture and painting (particularly Cubism), and so on. Whatever the origins of these pieces, however, the *coloristes* were not particularly concerned with the significance of individual objects in an interior. Léandre Vaillat, a contemporary critic writing about the *coloriste* contribution to the 1911 Salon d'Automne, declared that "they are more concerned with the general impression than with the search for the right shape; they create what might be called an atmos-

2.9 André Mare,
study, Salon
d'Automne,
Paris, 1911

phere in the home."[27] They were more interested in the interactions among objects and the overall effect produced by assembling them together.

An interior of a study exhibited by André Mare at the Salon d'Automne provides a vivid example of the *coloristes'* approach (figs. 2.9, 2.10). The heavy furniture, inspired by the provincial crafts of Normandy and built to Mare's designs, contrasts strongly in color and styling with the large white mantelpiece carved by the Puteaux Cubist sculptor Roger de La Fresnaye. These larger pieces and the plain walls surrounding them set a ponderous tone, which is quickened, however, by many smaller pieces: brilliantly hued embroidered pillows on the settee and armchairs, a large bright rug with floral borders, an austerely geometrical pendant lamp, a number of framed and unframed Cubist prints and paintings hung in no apparent order, books roughly stacked in their cases, folios and rumpled piles of loose papers on the shelves and desk, a simple glass vase with flowers,

2.10 André Mare, study, with mantelpiece by Roger de La Fresnaye, Salon d'Automne, Paris, 1911

turned silver candlesticks, and a neoclassical urn on the mantel. The room gives, above all, an impression of having been lived in, worked in. In photographs of the exhibit, the furniture seems to have crept slightly out of position (no piece of furniture has more than two legs on the rug), the cushions and pillows on the settee have been tousled, the books and papers look used, the prints and paintings appear to have been hung by an inexpert hand. There is certainly no clear unity of style, but a unity of composition is almost palpable in the photograph. The *idea* of a study is pervasive and active. This theme is supported by no single piece alone; it derives from the heaviness of the principal elements contrasted with the casual clutter of the less consequential things in the room.[28]

There can be little doubt that the *coloristes* wanted their interiors to accord well with contemporary bourgeois sensibilities, but they also sought to present effects similar to those of Cubist paintings. Like a Cubist painting, a *coloriste* interior emphasized compositional effect rather than individual objects. Its lines were often disjointed and awkward, its compositional elements unremarkable or banal, its colors unpredictable.[29]

As the work of the *coloristes* developed, the eclectic nature of their choices and a general bias in favor of things suitable to middle-class tastes further distinguished their work from that of the *constructeurs*. This was especially evident in their Salon d'Automne offering of the following year, a large-scale collaborative effort titled Un Salon Bourgeois but generally known as the Maison Cubiste, which is described below. These tendencies also provided the *coloriste* ensembles with a potential commercial advantage: because any number of appropriate elements could constitute an adequate solution to a given theme, clients with limited resources did not need to purchase complete ensembles in order to adopt the modern tastes of *coloriste* designers for their homes.[30] The ensemble could bear alterations in the choice and arrangement of individual elements without affecting the overall impression significantly. This had always been something of a problem for the strongly unified interiors of the Art Nouveau movement and, later, of the *constructeurs* and had been a major impediment to their commercial success.

Mare and his collaborators stood to benefit from an issue that was emerging with increasing force among critics of the decorative artists in France: the question of affordability. It was not only pressure from Germany that threatened traditional French decorative arts but the structure of contemporary French society as well. In August 1911, the French critic Louis Hourticq commented on this situation. He noted that "a modern style is rendered difficult by a vast, disparate society; whereas formerly a royal court always controlled style." Modernization of French design depended on acceptance by a broad segment of the population, and for that it seemed almost inevitable that new modes of production had to take their place alongside new ways of designing: "If the new style never adopts mechanical production methods, it will hardly be of any use in our society," Hourticq asserted.[31]

The promise of success in 1911, however limited, lifted some of the gloom that had followed the Salon d'Automne in 1910. Just before its opening, organizers of the Salon d'Automne and representatives from the other major decorative arts groups in France convened to plan for an international exhibition of modern decorative arts, to be held in 1915. Its principal aim would be to demonstrate unequivocally the continued preeminence of French tastes. Promoters of the idea declared, "It is not at all a question of demonstrating once more the superiority of our historical styles, but of provoking the realization and the diffusion of modern French styles."[32] Although some questioned whether the date for the exhibition was a bit premature, a vibrant, modern decorative art in France seemed to be gaining momentum.[33]

1912—UN SALON BOURGEOIS

Unfortunately, the events of 1912, with a few notable exceptions, failed to live up to this promise. The theme of usefulness and of an appeal to French society in general continued to occupy an important place in discussions about the decorative arts and domestic architecture. For the first time, working-class themes appeared in the pages of *Art et décoration*, the most influential French journal on the decorative arts. In an article titled "Logis d'ouvriers" (Workers' housing), for example, Maurice Guillemot declared, "The people have a right to beauty. This phrase which, for many, seems essentially paradoxical, has become essentially trivial, has become trivial for having been repeated; one can modify and complete it by saying that the people also have a right to hygiene, to comfort, to everything that makes life better."[34] But even as the attitudes of art critics in France were changing, designers generally failed to respond.

In an assessment of the Salon of the Société des Artistes Décorateurs in the spring of that year, Gabriel Mourey complained that while the Germans continued to move forward, complacent French designers produced virtually nothing of use:

> German industries, better informed about the exigencies of the public than ours, and giving good account of the fact that in the twentieth century, in a democratic country, it is not for the aristocracy that the diffusion of a style should operate but for the bourgeois masses and the popular masses. . . . Here, just like always, it is useless objects, luxurious objects, art objects that are the most numerous and also, it must be said, the most successful. So much for our incontestable superiority.[35]

The problem persisted in other art exhibits throughout the year. Looking back on 1912, M. P. Verneuil, who was often ready to see the merits in French work, could find little to praise. In an assessment of the Salons of that year, he declared with disgust: "1912 certainly will not distinguish itself from others for the appeal of its decorative arts sections at the salons. We have never been presented with less that is unanticipated, less that is novel. . . . It would seem that our decorators are incapable of bringing about a truly virile and truly vital movement." Verneuil complained also that, while the decorative arts languished, architecture was making no progress at all. "What is absolutely lacking, unfortunately, is an architectural movement, for which we have so long awaited in vain. . . . It is as if we do not seem to understand here what they understand perfectly elsewhere. Look at Austria, and look at Germany. The movement there is

3.
UN SALON BOURGEOIS.

Plan

above all architectural; and logically the ornamental arts have followed thereby forming a complete and homogeneous movement."[36] Although Verneuil was, as always, quick to point out that the foreign innovations were not necessarily to French tastes, he lamented that French superiority in the arts had all but evaporated. This assessment was surprisingly harsh and voiced deepening frustration with France's inability to compete, even as a complacent faith in French superiority became less and less tenable.

2.11 Un Salon Bourgeois (Maison Cubiste), Salon d'Automne, Paris, 1912, catalog

2.12 Un Salon Bourgeois (Maison Cubiste), Salon d'Automne, Paris, 1912, plan showing bedroom (4), hall (2), and salon (3)

No doubt the most innovative essay in decorative art and architecture to take place during 1912 was Un Salon Bourgeois, a massive collaborative effort exhibited by the *coloristes* at the Salon d'Automne (fig. 2.11).[37] The project was bizarre in appearance and quickly dismissed as "evidence of Cubist madness," to use the words of one contemporary critic.[38] It was significant nevertheless for demonstrating the refinement of the compositional techniques that André Mare and his collaborators had introduced the year before. Mare again directed the collaboration, and he composed two of its three rooms—a bedroom and a salon (fig. 2.12). He was also responsible for the design of the furniture in the exhibit. The collaborators made it clear from the outset that the project was meant to appeal specifically to a middle-class audience, as its official title suggests.

As they had with the interiors of the previous year, the *coloriste* artists relied on the assembly of disparate objects and strong color contrasts to achieve balance in the project (fig. 2.13). Several months before the exhibition, Mare articulated the compositional rules of the project in a letter to his collaborators:

> First of all, make something very *French*, stay within the tradition. Let us allow ourselves to be guided by our instinct which forces us to react against the errors of 1900, and this reaction should be constituted in the following way: 1st—Return to simple, pure, logical and even slightly harsh lines . . . 2nd—Return to very bold, very pure, very daring colors. . . . Be vigorous and naive in drawing; render the awkward detail without allowing it to impose itself; be awkward rather than skillful. For the decoration, take up once again the motif[s] which did not

2.13 Un Salon Bourgeois (Maison Cubiste), Salon d'Automne, Paris, 1912, view of salon

change from the Renaissance until Louis Philippe. . . . in sum, make things that are a little severe in outline, the harshness of which will be mitigated by a pleasant decor, boldly colored, and the whole in a tradition that is very French.[39]

The entry portal designed by Raymond Duchamp-Villon introduced these themes to contemporary visitors, highlighting in its own details the vigorous, bold, awkward characteristics of the ensemble as well as its references to historical French styles (figs. 2.14, 2.15). The pilasters flanking the doorway conjure the image of a traditional domestic threshold, but the heavy, crystalline ornamentation heaved out over the stoop hints at a fundamental transformation of this image. Had the whole facade been built, this ambiguous reading would have expanded to include the entire housefront. The plaster maquette that Duchamp-Villon prepared for the exhibit shows the typical division of ground floor and *piano nobile* of a Parisian mansion, accentuated by a broad, unarticulated cornice terminating on either side of the portal to make room for the ornamental mass over the doorway. Five segments of heavy balustrade rest on this cornice. These reinforce the horizontal division of the facade while easing the transition from the seven bays on the ground floor to the three bays on the upper. Another strong cornice, broken by the upward thrust of three dormers, and a mansard roof terminate the building. A vaguely heraldic emblem occupies the top of the central bay. Two oval windows flank it. Smaller details on the portal, particularly the wrought iron window guards with their sinuous lines and floral motifs and the potted plants by the front doorstep, soften the harsh angularity of the building. The effect is both familiar and jarring, nostalgic and overtly contemporary.

While the facade is certainly reminiscent of seventeenth- and eighteenth-century prototypes, as many architectural historians and critics have pointed out, it cannot be dismissed as merely another slightly "modernized" revival, nor should it be seen as a failed attempt to break old habits with the design of something new and "Cubist" in style. Reyner Banham's critique of Un Salon Bourgeois is indicative of this view:

> The one surviving record of the Cubist architecture of Raymond Duchamp-Villon suggests that it is a long way from the progressive trends of the time of its conception, 1912. It is little more than the routine structure of a symmetrical villa in the Mansardic tradition tricked out with fans of prismatic mouldings instead of Rococo (or even Art Nouveau) details. The fact that this no more than superficially Mod-

2.14 Raymond Duchamp-Villon, model of the facade, Un Salon Bourgeois (Maison Cubiste), Salon d'Automne, Paris, 1912

2.15 Raymond Duchamp-Villon, entry portal, Un Salon Bourgeois (Maison Cubiste), Salon d'Automne, Paris, 1912

ern design was deemed worthy of illustration in Apollinaire's *Les Pein-
tres Cubistes* suggests that the Movement as a whole was thoroughly
out of touch with forward ideas in architecture—a point that is worth
making in view of what has been so often said or implied about connections between Cubism and the International Style.[40]

As a discrete work of architecture, Duchamp-Villon's facade for Un Salon
Bourgeois is certainly susceptible to this kind of critique. It *is* both derivative and strange, and as a supposedly Cubist house, its facets and contours seem overly constrained and thus ineffectual. However, seen in its
larger context—as part of a didactic exhibit on one hand and as the entry
and frontage to a series of interrelated interiors on the other—the facade
is more than a shallow application of "Cubist" forms to an otherwise standard bourgeois housefront. The awkward conjunction of elements in the
facade, for example, is consistent with the rules of composition proposed
by André Mare. It also corresponds to the visual analysis of Cubist painters
who observed and similarly interpreted the confusing aggregation of
objects, movement, and energy of modern life in their paintings and collages. Duchamp-Villon explained that his aim was to design "a new architectural setting" that would resonate with this energy. As he asserted in
a letter to Walter Pach, it is "not that we should try to adapt the forms
and lines of even the characteristic objects of our time, which would only
be a transposition of these lines and forms to other materials and therefore an error—but rather we should tirelessly fill our minds with the relationships of these objects among themselves in order to interpret them
in synthetic lines, planes and volumes which shall, in their turn, equili-
brate in rhythms analogous to those which surround us."[41] For Un Salon
Bourgeois, this could move both outward, to the urban context, and
inward, to the rooms of the house.

Although the Salon Bourgeois exhibit gave no information about how
the facade would relate to the street or adjacent buildings, one could
imagine that, set in the living context of the city, its unusual compositional relationships would be absorbed by the intense visual cadence of
the modern street. In this context, its adjustment of historical precedent
would seem subtler and yet more evident than in the context of the exhibition. As the entry portal to a series of *coloriste* interiors in the ensemble,
the facade played a different role. It established a frame of reference for
the project and inaugurated a series of energetic relationships among the
objects assembled in it.

Raymond Duchamp-Villon's facade was only one of many elements constituting the artistic and architectural whole that Mare envisioned for the project. In the ensemble, interior and exterior walls, furniture, ornament, and artwork all contributed to remake the modern architectural situation, to create an appropriate frame for contemporary domestic life, not merely a new architectural style. Seen in this light, Duchamp-Villon's statement regarding the facade—that "we should tirelessly fill our minds with the relationships of these objects [the characteristic objects of our time] among themselves"—reveals a sophisticated understanding of the project that is not readily evident when one examines the facade itself. He implied that architecture would derive not from the style of extant objects but from a critical assessment of the relationships established among them—in the context of contemporary life.

The three interiors of Un Salon Bourgeois set out to demonstrate how these relationships would play out in contemporary middle-class interiors. The rooms were even more assertive than the facade in their seemingly uninhibited compositional effects. Flanking either side of the vividly patterned entry vestibule, a bedroom and salon confronted visitors with a bewildering assembly of objects, patterns, shapes, and brilliant colors.

No longer evoking the sobriety of Mare's study from the year before, these rooms announce themselves with aggressively patterned walls contrasted by strong, boldly colored furniture and a great range of small decorative objects. The bedroom walls carry a rhythmic pattern of flowers and swags. In the wall coverings of the salon, arabesques of intertwined foliage wrap flowers in swirls of color. In each of the rooms, a heavy fireplace sculpted by Roger de La Fresnaye stands in stark contrast to these frenetic patterns. Like Duchamp-Villon's facade, these pieces invoke but significantly alter neoclassical motifs—engaged columns, scrolls, cornices—to create a sense of familiarity touched nevertheless by an awkward impression of newness. The furniture in the rooms is also stolid, but brightly painted and accented with busily patterned upholstery or embroidered pillows. The floral rugs are bold and colorful. Smaller objects further complicate the scene. Poised on the mantel in each room, on the tables, and on the desk are a variety of decorative and more or less useful objects: ornate mantel clocks, vases, crystal perfume bottles, enameled urns, a vividly ornamented tea set by Jacques Villon. The walls support Cubist paintings by Marcel Duchamp, Albert Gleizes, Robert de La Fresnaye, Fernand Léger, and Jean Metzinger. The visual force of these three "bourgeois" rooms is intense, but it is also reminiscent of the typical bourgeois home. Compare, for example, the effect of Un Salon Bourgeois to the statements of two contemporary experts on domestic interiors cited by Lisa Tiersten in her analysis of turn-of-the-century home decorating in France:

> According to the decorating expert Henri de Noussane, modern decoration was an exercise in pastiche: "The salon of the bourgeois home and apartment should be furnished in a modern style. Understand well what we mean by modern: it signifies a mélange of styles." The etiquette expert Emmeline Raymond offered the same advice as a dictum: "the more modern the salon, the more that decoration which is truly modern must be kept out of it. It should contain furnishings of every possible style."[42]

This way of composing domestic interiors, which encouraged home owners to choose whatever suited their tastes regardless of its adherence to any calculated program, was clearly not what the critics of the decorative arts and architecture were looking for in modern design. These critics excoriated Un Salon Bourgeois, largely because it seemed to embody, in a particularly vivid way, Verneuil's complaint about "the general spirit that reigns today, in which extreme individualism is the absolute rule."[43] Clearly, each piece in the ensemble retained its identity as the work of an individual. And, brought together, they established anything but a familiar sense of homogeneity. However, each piece contributed to a coherent plan, a plan that responded not to the privileged sense of repose that characterized later Art Nouveau and *constructeur* interiors but to the complex, vital circumstances of the urban middle class in modern France.

What seemed to be missing from the project, however, was a sense of habitability. One critic commented that, while the ensemble achieved a sense of "gaiety," it was neither simple nor hygienic (as evidence, he cited placement of the bed in an alcove).[44] If the principles of habitability, simplicity, and hygiene were the primary motivations for modern design in France—as they were almost certainly in Austria, England, and Germany—Un Salon Bourgeois could be easily dismissed as a failure. However, these adjectives hardly applied in France, where patrimony, taste, and individuality were all much stronger motivators for conservative and progressive designers alike. They were also important for the public served by these designers, especially the increasingly influential middle class.

French patrimony, especially, was very much in the public debate at the moment. So, as Mare had indicated to his collaborators before the exhibition, the development of a peculiarly "French" sensibility was essential to the project. Although this reflected contemporary sentiment, it was also, at least partly, a defensive tactic aimed to calm critics protesting that the *coloriste* use of vivid colors and ponderous forms was derivative of recent German interiors. Despite André Mare's efforts to "make something very French," however, Un Salon Bourgeois created an uproar for the Salon d'Automne precisely because of the supposed foreign origins of Cubism and the biases of the Salon. Critics of the ensemble complained bitterly that the jury for the Salon in 1912, which included eighteen "foreigners" and only four Frenchmen, had succumbed to external influences. Most damning for Un Salon Bourgeois was not its similarity to German ensembles, however. It was the insidious influence of Cubism—disavowed by the French, for the moment, as the invention of a Spaniard—that rankled critics. Because of strident reaction against the exhibit, the Salon d'Automne nearly lost its authorization to use the Grand Palais for its exhibitions. In order to save the Salon, Frantz Jourdain was forced to apologize for having allowed too much foreign influence into the jury of the Salon and to set restrictions on the kinds of work that could be included in future exhibits.[45]

Despite the furor the exhibit caused, foreign influence on Un Salon Bourgeois appears to have been minimal. So it is useful to examine some of the other points in Mare's directives. For example, his call for "simple, pure, logical and even slightly harsh lines" was less important for its advocacy of anything uniquely French than for establishing that the experience of contour and color was a primary motivation in the work. Mare's eclectic choice of styles, whether French or otherwise, presumed that seemingly unrelated objects could contribute to the broad effect of the ensemble. When Mare encouraged his collaborators to "be awkward rather than skillful," he seems to have disavowed the insistence on quality craftsmanship typical of the English and German decorative arts. However, this was almost certainly motivated by practical rather than political ends. The awkward detail was forgiving of unskilled craftsmanship. Unlike other groups of progressive decorative artists in France and elsewhere, the *coloristes* were essentially indifferent to the methods of production associated with the items in their ensembles. They exhibited hand-produced objects as well as pieces manufactured by commercial enterprises. (A similar attitude espoused later by Le Corbusier allowed machine- and hand-produced objects to coexist comfortably in domestic situations.) The compositional rules of Un Salon Bourgeois allowed it to be effectively independent of production methods, which makes the ensemble all the more striking in its larger European context. At a time when designers elsewhere in Europe were heavily involved with new production methods for the decorative arts, the *coloristes* were envisioning a domestic framework that could interpret and accommodate the profusion of things already available in modern France.

If Un Salon Bourgeois gave full expression to the painterly intentions that Mare had introduced in his Salon d'Automne interiors of 1911, it also showed that these intentions could include architecture as well as the decorative arts. This continuity among painting, interiors, and architecture was unusual even in the liberal context of the Salon d'Automne. In fact, Un Salon Bourgeois was the first specifically architectural work to be displayed in the Salon. In this regard, the ensemble, particularly the facade by Raymond Duchamp-Villon, anticipated an important development for the public exhibition of design in France. When the Salon d'Automne first included architecture (or rather, *art urbain,* as it was called) as a category in 1922, its exhibition catalog declared: "The street in modern life, so often necessarily exterior, is becoming like an extension of the dwelling."[46] Duchamp-Villon's contribution to Un Salon Bourgeois emphasized the essential connection between the modern French domestic interior—as it was taking shape in 1912—and its public countenance.

Un Salon Bourgeois was not merely a strange Cubist fantasy or a dead-end attempt to discover a new style of modern architecture. It was an intelligent and subtle essay on the possibilities for modern design in France. It would be difficult to argue that Un Salon Bourgeois spawned the new architectural movement Verneuil and other critics were looking for; however, it articulated the unique relationship between the decorative arts and architecture that was developing in France.[47] Viewed in retrospect, it could be said that Un Salon Bourgeois presaged a moment, more than a decade later, when architecture and the decorative arts converged in France, and when designers and critics could declare, as did Henri Verne and René Chavance, that "there is no longer a difference between architecture and decor."[48]

1913—THE GOOD AND WELL-MADE THING

If the 1912 Salon Bourgeois hinted at new compositional relationships between bourgeois domestic furnishings and domestic architecture, exhibits at the 1913 Salon d'Automne demonstrated more clearly what role furniture, and the production of furniture, might play in shaping domestic architecture for the French middle class. By 1913, technological innovations in the manufacture of consumer products had begun to alter significantly the balance of western European trade in furniture and household equipment. Under the leadership of crafts and trade organizations like the Vereinigte Werkstätten in Munich and the Deutscher Werkbund, Germany had pursued this course most aggressively over the previous decade. The competitive pressures these organizations exerted were felt keenly throughout Europe. Groups in Austria and Switzerland responded by establishing their own versions of the Werkbund. In England, proponents of the Arts and Crafts movement acknowledged that Germany had outpaced England in crafts production, despite England's earlier advantage, but found themselves unable to regain the advantage.[49] In France, where resistance to German competition was most intense, the increasing ubiquity of quality mass-produced items for household use—whatever their origins—exerted pressure from within. In these circumstances, usefulness, practicality, and economy began to emerge as primary virtues, even in objects ruled by traditional French tastes. At the same time, the traditional French emphasis on luxury in household decor came increasingly into question. As the middle class continued to gain economic and political ascendancy in France, circumstances dictated a change in how people valued design and how they interpreted its effect on their everyday lives.

This became increasingly evident in the decorative arts Salons, particularly the Salon d'Automne, where the lines between art and practicality had long since been blurred. As interior decor and domestic architecture exercised stronger mutual influence, they opened themselves to new interpretations. The architectural ensemble suggested not only that the interior and its furnishings should play a crucial role in the development of a new architecture but also that the middle-class consumer and occupant must help to drive changes in the French conception of architecture. Robert Mallet-Stevens, an architect and interior designer associated with the *coloristes*, hinted at this idea in 1911:

> If a fastidiously drawn scale drawing, of a temple overloaded with useless columns can be mounted on a chassis and served up to the public classified as "architecture," then a living room or kitchen, displayed as they really are, complete with furniture and utensils, which they can move around in, can also be classified as architecture, and as living, animated architecture, which will captivate and interest the visitor in another way.[50]

Several of the interior ensembles exhibited at the decorative arts Salons in 1911 and 1912 developed the point further. Un Salon Bourgeois, for example, showed that exterior architecture could be complicit in this method

2.16   Louis Suë and Jacques Palyart, boudoir, Salon d'Automne, Paris, 1913

of display. It suggested that modern interiors must be capable not only of absorbing a great range of contemporary objects but also of extending outward to participate in the modern city street. Un Salon Bourgeois, as well as André Mare's study of 1911, also implied that a "living, animated architecture" might include standardized elements and mass-produced objects just as readily as it included finely crafted furniture and works of art. The selective inclusion of objects in these interiors and their casual arrangement suggested further that inhabitants had an important role to play in shaping contemporary domestic architecture.

In 1913, the most assertive and progressive proponent of these changes was not, however, associated with the *coloristes*. Although the *coloristes* had been instrumental in proposing a new conception of the middle-class interior, virulent reaction against the Cubist associations of Un Salon Bourgeois (and the infiltration of supposedly foreign influence into the Salon that it seemed to represent) prevented similar collaboration in the Salon d'Automne of 1913.[51] As a result, much of the avant-garde character that had marked exhibits of former years failed to materialize. Arlette Barré-Despond notes that "the Salon d'Automne of 1913 was of a remarkable—and well-remarked—discretion. Care had been taken to scatter the few cubist, futurist, Fauve, and Orphist pieces among the rest of the exhibited works. As one critic lamented, 'Nothing is left, or rather, all that remains is decent and well-behaved. . . . '"[52] Many of the *coloristes* continued to work in a loosely affiliated group, but their individual ensembles exhibited hardly any of the audacity of the year before. Gustave-Louis Jaulmes exhibited a dining room, which M. P. Verneuil praised as "gay and distinguished, delicate and very French."[53] Verneuil found Mare's boudoir to be somewhat disconcerting but "rather interesting." It presented "a mélange of things, some worse, some better than others," that nevertheless seemed gradually to bring themselves to coherence.[54] Louis Sué, in collaboration with Jacques Palyart, produced a boudoir whose vivid combination of patterns and colors made it the most audacious offering

2.17   Robert
Mallet-Stevens, hall,
Salon d'Automne,
Paris, 1913

in the Salon, even if it did not represent a radical departure from what had been done before (fig. 2.16). Robert Mallet-Stevens contributed a hall, starkly patterned in vermilion, black, and white, and a somewhat more restrained music room in intense shades of green, yellow, blue, and white, both of which were destined for a sumptuous villa in Deauville (figs. 2.17, 2.18). In 1913, the *coloristes* tended to emphasize, above all, the uniquely French character of their work. Its more progressive aspects, particularly any attempt to interpret the contemporary lifestyle of the middle class and to compose the objects associated with it, were more subdued than in previous Salons. These themes appeared forcefully, however, in the work of another exhibitor in the Salon who was destined to inspire the modernization of French design: Francis Jourdain, the son of Frantz Jourdain.

The interiors that Francis Jourdain displayed in the 1913 Salon d'Automne—a bedroom (fig. 2.19) and a salon/dining room (fig. 2.20)— could hardly have been more different in appearance from those of Un Salon Bourgeois. This point was illustrated in the comments of Verneuil, who criticized Jourdain's rooms for excessive simplicity.[55] However, they were similarly bold in intention.

A photograph of the bedroom shows furniture that is particularly aus-

2.18 Robert Mallet-Stevens, music room, Salon d'Automne, Paris, 1913

2.19 Francis Jourdain, bedroom, Salon d'Automne, Paris, 1913

2.20 Francis Jourdain, salon/ dining room, Salon d'Automne, Paris, 1913

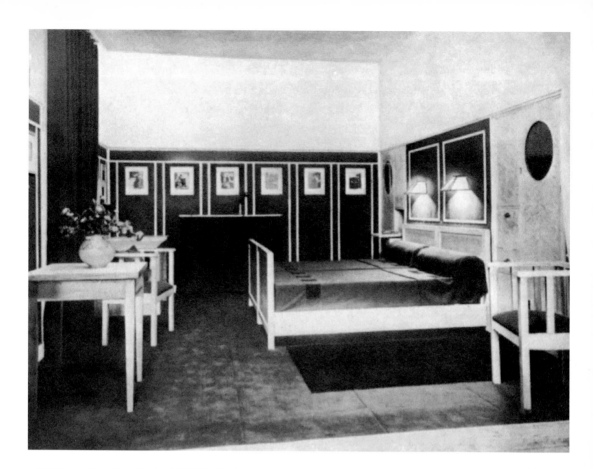

tere, white, rectangular. Orange wall panels and a black rug set off the pieces. To the contemporary eye, the ensemble was harsh. "Not a single ornament intervenes to break the implacable rigidity of its lines," protested Verneuil.[56]

The furniture in the salon/dining room is heavier, warmer, but still devoid of ornamentation. It integrates rhythmically with the walls, drawing the architecture of the room into the composition: the recession of alcoves, nooks, and drawers playing against the thrust of shelves and cabinets. A few simple objects (a book, ceramic bowls, a large metal pot with a spray of flowering branches) rest on the ledges shaped by this interplay of wall and furniture. In the center of the room, a dining table bears a basket of fruit. The table and the chairs surrounding it stand resolutely upright on stout rectangular legs. They are so straightforward as to seem awkward. (Many years later, Jourdain explained that "a table [is] essentially a plank on four legs."[57] The table in the salon/dining room is little more than this.) Refusing to obscure their fundamentally purposeful nature with ornamentation, Jourdain designed furniture and walls that would impart a sense of clarity and habitability to his interiors. The materials also contribute to this. The polished wood of the room is satisfying but not lavish. The buffed metal drawer pulls and cabinet door handles accommodate the hand comfortably, and their smooth shapes are simple enough to facilitate high-quality mass production. The objects on the shelves and table harmonize with but are not dictated by the room. Although essential to the decor, they also seem to be adaptable. They can be replaced or supplemented without compromising the effect of the ensemble, and one can easily imagine the idiosyncratic personal belongings and heirlooms of a family taking their places comfortably in the room.

Jourdain wanted to show that, above all, a modern interior is meant to be habitable, comfortable, and affordable. The economics of a middle-class interior required not luxury but practicality, not forced gaiety but ease. Every piece in the Salon d'Automne ensembles—the freestanding and built-in furniture as well as the hardware and decorative objects—contributed to fulfilling these requirements. The rooms demonstrated an antithesis to a still prevalent conception of the sumptuous French interior, which was elegant and visually arresting but virtually uninhabitable. Advertisements for Jourdain's commercial enterprise, Les Ateliers Modernes, emphasized, therefore, that his interiors contrasted as much with the elegantly coordinated work of the *constructeurs* as with the brazen efforts of the *coloristes*. "For the Frenchman," one ad declares, "a modern interior is still 'one in which a person cannot live.' This is evident, on one hand, in examples which purport to resolve the problem of a style—the 'modern style' of Belgium, of Nancy, of Faubourg Saint-Antoine, the 'modern style' of stylized flowers—and, on the other hand, in exceptional interiors, interiors for exhibition—specimens of old styles made over, badly composed, in the various colors demanded by the season."[58] Jourdain sought, above all, to develop modern rooms that were flexible and habitable, not merely remarkable.

In this regard, one of the more significant innovations Jourdain introduced in the 1913 Salon d'Automne was the designation of one ensemble as both salon *and* dining room. Eliminating superfluous detail and blending functions, it proposed a very modern, refined solution to a widespread concern—the furnishing of a cramped urban flat. This simple move suggested a middle-class clientele for whom space and budgetary limitations recommended the confluence of domestic activities. It also presaged an important development in progressive domestic architecture that took place in France after the war: the creation of "living rooms" that would perform the functions of many rooms at once.[59] In 1925, for example, Henri Sauvage described this phenomenon, declaring, "In the dwelling of the past . . . to create the dining room, the salon, the office was to organize life according to a new plan. To abolish these distributions today, in order to reestablish the multipurpose room, is to institute a practice of private life. . . . The salon becomes the *living-room*."[60] He explained that "the dwelling of tomorrow . . . will be flexible. Intended for tenants whose occupations, mores, and habits vary from one to the other, the apartment will consist of nothing more than an anonymous frame in which the inhabitant, without being compelled by preexisting ornamentation, will arrange the decor according to personal taste."[61] This kind of thinking was evident, too, in the work of Pierre Chareau, whose ensemble in the 1925 Exposition Internationale des Arts Décoratifs et Industriels Modernes in Paris prompted one critic to assert that "it is in the setting of an ordinary apartment that . . . a completely new program, founded on the abolition of specialized and limited rooms, elaborates itself. Already the dining room, the *salon*, the office combine themselves into a unique room, the *living room*. The apartment simplifies itself, as if the difficulties of domestic life control it from within."[62] In 1913, Francis Jourdain suggested that rooms of this sort would accommodate the "practice of private life" without dominating it. "Our rooms," he said, "are no longer ceremonial. Our rooms harmonize with simple, bright furniture of beautiful materials and human proportions, ingenious enough to satisfy, in a limited space, all of our daily needs of well-being, convenience and practical elegance."[63] This new, compact program for French domestic architecture, which brought together the functions of the domestic salon and the dining room in a single, economical ensemble, preoccupied many French modern designers after World War I.

Although some critics responded favorably to this kind of innovation in the interior ensembles of 1913, they lamented that it emphasized, more than ever, the stagnation of contemporary French architecture. In an assessment of the Salon d'Automne of that year, M. P. Verneuil complained, as he had done repeatedly in the preceding years, that contemporary architecture had virtually nothing to show for itself. "One must regret," he protested, "that alongside the decorators, the architects have not at least made an equivalent effort . . . and we demand immediately . . . from architecture, properly speaking, from truly modern, new architecture, houses appropriate to our desires and to our tastes today."[64] Similarly, Gabriel Mourey complained that, while the decorative artists were making some progress, there were "very few" architects who seemed capable of addressing "the new problems imposed on architecture by the conditions of real life, by recently developed materials, by the pressing needs made greater every day by social progress."[65] Francis Jourdain, more than any other French designer at the time, was addressing these issues seriously. He had, in the words of one critic, "the blood of architecture in his veins."[66]

If Jourdain's new, architectural approach to the domestic interior was unusual for its spatial and programmatic arrangements, it was also daring for its overt acceptance of foreign influence. Advertisements for Les Ateliers Modernes appearing at the time of the exhibition declared, "Francis Jourdain is today the closest to the great Viennese, Adolf Loos."[67] Jourdain saw himself as a direct counterpart of the Viennese designer and critic in a number of ways. Jourdain designed ensembles that, aside from exhibiting a superficial resemblance to those of Loos, explicitly articulated virtues Loos promoted in his writings about design: simplicity and lack of embellishment, careful articulation of surface materials, and openness to the personal effects of occupants (fig. 2.21). Both designers asserted that especially in domestic situations, careful construction and efficient use of space, rather than purely aesthetic considerations, reflected the sophisticated sensibilities of their clientele. Accordingly, their work did not pander to stylistic expectations. Like Loos, Jourdain insisted that each of his designs relied for its success on a unified feeling that was virtually impossible to encapsulate in formulaic descriptions or carefully framed illustrations. Jourdain presented his work with the declaration that "neither a drawing nor

2.21 Adolf Loos, Loos apartment, Vienna, 1903

a photograph can give an image of it, any more than of a living being. Our senses must experience it directly."[68] He sought to produce comfortable, harmonious, modern interiors that developed their character not from historical French styles but in the quality of their design and construction and in their relevance to contemporary domestic life.[69] Livability, rather than style, was the crucial issue. One critic declared at the time that "Francis Jourdain consults life, studies our needs, examines our morals, and scrutinizes our tastes."[70] The result was something that seemed familiar and accommodating while it deviated from entrenched traditions.

Aside from emulating the work of Loos, Jourdain was instrumental in introducing Loos's writings to French designers. Jourdain and Georges Besson commissioned the first French translation of "Ornament et crime" and published it in *Cahiers d'aujourd'hui*, of which they were the editors, in 1912.[71] (A decade later, Loos published a compilation of his early essays for the first time in Paris "since no German publishing house dared to take it on in 1920."[72] He moved to Paris permanently in 1922.) Suzanne Tise asserts that Francis Jourdain's efforts to introduce the work of the Viennese designer to France was comparable at least to his father's efforts in bringing the *munichois* designers to Paris several years before:

> Just as Frantz Jourdain must be credited for introducing the work of German designers to the Parisian public for the first time when he invited the Vereinigte Werkstätte in Munich to participate in the Salon d'Automne of 1910, Francis Jourdain and Georges Besson (and not Le Corbusier and Ozenfant as is commonly believed) were the first to introduce the theories of Loos to the French artistic community. Publishing his text ["Ornament et crime"] was a courageous move at a time when French attitudes toward Germany were far from friendly, and when conservative critics in Paris were characterizing modern art as a dangerous influence from Germany that would destroy the French tradition.[73]

Despite the dangers of associating oneself with foreign designers, especially those of German extraction, admiration for Loos became an important virtue of progressive designers in the 1910s and 1920s—a point frequently reinforced by Le Corbusier in the years after the war.[74]

Although Le Corbusier may have been aware of Loos's writing through the *Cahiers d'aujourd'hui* publication of 1912, it was Jourdain's radical but subtle innovations that caught his attention before the war. Late in the fall of 1913, Le Corbusier (who went by his given name, Charles-Edouard Jeanneret, until 1920) visited Paris to acquire ideas and materials for several projects he was developing in La Chaux-de-Fonds. In previous visits to Paris, he had discovered the work of the *coloristes* at the Salon d'Automne, and he arrived in Paris intending to study their most recent Salon entries. Although he took extensive notes on their work (including six detailed pages on the rooms exhibited by Robert Mallet-Stevens), he later declared Jourdain's interiors the most provocative in the exhibition, asserting that, against the revivalist tendencies of the *coloristes*, Jourdain's work was refreshingly clear and forward-looking.[75] It succeeded, he said in a flattering letter to Jourdain, in "furnishing *principles*" for design "at this time when the fury of 'decorative art,' the folly of the *Beautiful* overwhelms and stupefies the simple, instinctive, necessary and only true sentiment of the *Good*—the Good or *Well Made Thing* being Beautiful in and of itself."[76] These were principles Jeanneret strove to develop in his work; while he remained skeptical about the very notion of "decorative art"—a skepticism that became more intense over the following decade—he took up Jourdain's notions of simplicity, instinct, and necessity in his work on domestic interiors and housing during the war.

2.22 Charles-
Edouard Jeanneret
(Le Corbusier),
Jeanneret-Perret
residence, La
Chaux-de-Fonds,
Switzerland,
1913–14, salon

Jeanneret, who was twenty-five years old in 1913, had spent most of his adult life amid the tumult of French-German competition in the arts: he had worked with the most progressive French and German architects (Auguste Perret and Peter Behrens) and had recently authored what was being recognized as the most thorough analysis of the decorative arts movement in Germany. He was therefore especially attuned to the recent influence of furniture and product design on the production of architecture in both Germany and France. Furthermore, his status as a French-speaking Swiss national gave him a propitious vantage point from which to view the cultural implications of these developments. As the sole instructor of architecture at the newly reconfigured Ecole d'Art in his hometown of La Chaux-de-Fonds (a post he assumed in 1912), Jeanneret had been charged with making these connections explicit. During his two-year tenure at the school, he taught courses on "geometrical elements, their character and their relative value in decorative and monumental applications" and on "architectural applications" in the design of furniture and decorative objects. He also coordinated construction projects designed to give students practical building experience in architecture, interior dec-

oration, and the production of decorative objects. In addition to his teaching, he maintained an active architecture and interior design practice. The letterhead for his practice referred to him as "consulting architect for all questions of interior decoration, remodels, furnishing, garden layouts, etc."[77] Although the interiors he designed in 1914 and 1915 for his parents' house and the Ditisheim and Schwob apartments reflected some *coloriste* sensibilities, his understanding of the vital relationship between interior decoration and architectural form and production were moving in the directions Jourdain proposed.

Photographs of the living room of the Jeanneret-Perret house show an eclectic arrangement of custom-made and "found" furniture and decorative objects (fig. 2.22). The complex mixing of these elements, along with the floral wallpaper patterns and the almost haphazard placement of pictures on the wall, echoes the interiors of Un Salon Bourgeois. The interiors Jeanneret designed for the apartments of Hermann and Ernst-Albert Ditisheim, however, reveal a shift in sensibility. The smoking room of 1915, for example, is more reserved, its casual arrangement of furnish-

2.23 Charles-Edouard Jeanneret (Le Corbusier), smoking room, Hermann Ditisheim apartment, La Chaux-de-Fonds, Switzerland, 1915

ings and pictures and the heavy formality of the marble mantelpiece (fig. 2.23) recalling André Mare's Salon interiors of 1911 and 1912. The large pieces of furniture in other rooms align more closely with Jourdain's work, their austere massing and use of painted wood and Eternit asbestos panels emphasizing solidity and economy over chromatic vibrancy and historical quotation (fig. 2.24).

Jourdain's principles, so closely tied to the production of furniture and interiors, affected Jeanneret even more profoundly in his business ventures and speculative design projects after 1914. With his forced resignation from the Ecole d'Art in La Chaux-de-Fonds in April 1914, following a tumultuous battle between proponents of the Old and New sections of the school, Jeanneret concentrated on private commissions (mostly interior designs) and on publications whose aim was to promote the changes he and his colleagues in the New Section had set out to achieve.

When Jeanneret's former teacher and longtime mentor Charles L'Eplattenier had formed the New Section in 1911, he proposed to shift the focus of the school away from its emphasis on the regional watchmaking industry to the broader movement that was modernizing design and artistic production throughout Europe. To bolster his position, L'Eplattenier had convinced the school's advisory board to commission a systematic study of German design and production methods. Jeanneret was already seeking employment in Germany when the advisory board asked him to undertake the study. The success of German endeavors in design production was already well known. Jeanneret's *Etude sur le mouvement d'art décoratif en Allemagne* reinforced the point, arguing that the threat of German dominance in European artistic taste was a grave and imminent possibility (a point

2.24 Charles-Edouard Jeanneret (Le Corbusier), cabinet, Ernst-Albert Ditisheim apartment, La Chaux-de-Fonds, Switzerland, 1915

that resonated far more powerfully in Paris than in La Chaux-de-Fonds). In reaction to this threat, and as a complement to the New Section of the school, L'Eplattenier organized a movement to establish an arts and trade organization modeled after the Deutscher Werkbund, which was called L'Oeuvre: Association Suisse-Romande de l'Art et l'Industrie. The group began publication in 1913 of a journal titled *L'oeuvre*.

After leaving the Ecole d'Art, Jeanneret turned his attention with increasing zeal to the architectural manifestations of this new movement. In essays for *L'oeuvre*, he speculated in particular on the development of low-cost housing, a subject that he studied intensively during the next decade. Francis Jourdain's principles of simplicity, instinct, and necessity were very much on his mind as he undertook these projects. More than any other factor, however, the war in France shaped his resolve and gave the task of redefining the contemporary house its epochal significance.

3 THE WAR, HOUSE RECONSTRUCTION, AND FURNITURE PRODUCTION

The soldier, in order to escape from death which filled the air, has dug deeper and deeper into the soil, deeper than the roots of the trees, through the layers of the ground. . . . He has forced himself to lead the life of a caveman or a miner. What we imagined to be the habitat of prehistoric men in their caves is recurring, brought back, as in a cycle of iron, by the conditions created by the most recent progress of science.

—ROBERT DE LA SIZERANNE, *L'ART PENDANT LA GUERRE, 1914–1918*

The war brought the question of housing into vivid focus. If, as Robert de la Sizeranne mused after the war, "recent progress" had reduced soldiers to the barbarism of cave dwellers, the agents of reconstruction strove to turn technological progress to better account.[1] Between 1914 and 1925, Charles-Edouard Jeanneret developed no less than eighteen different mass-production housing schemes.[2] Perhaps the most important of these, for him at least, was a speculative project he began soon after the German army swept toward the Marne River in August 1914. In October, he joined forces with Max Du Bois, an engineer and an old friend from La Chaux-de-Fonds, Switzerland, then residing in Paris, who was an expert in designing with reinforced concrete. Together, they devised a mass-production housing scheme famously called the Maison Dom-ino (fig. 3.1). Its primary aim was to facilitate the rapid reconstruction of housing in areas of France devastated by the war.[3] Over the next several years, Jeanneret developed the proposal further, devising the construction system of

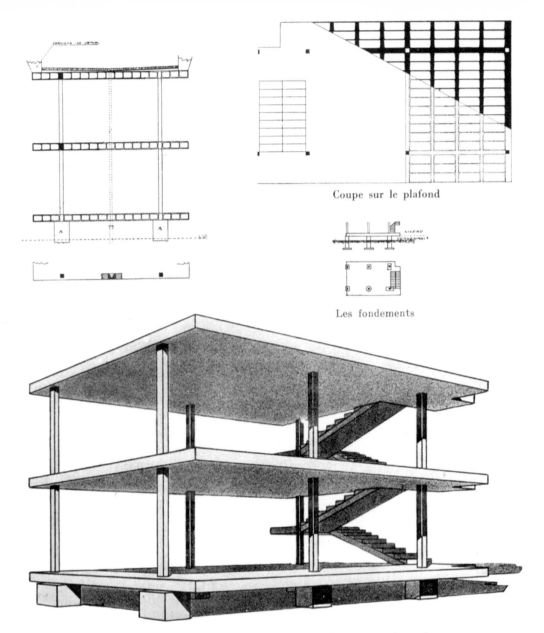

Coupe sur le plafond

Les fondements

L'ossature standard « Dom-ino », pour exécution en grande série

the building frame, unit plans, unit clusters, enclosure and window arrangements, etc. He moved to Paris early in 1917, partly to implement the scheme commercially with Du Bois. (Jeanneret was exempt from military duty in Switzerland because of poor eyesight and, as a Swiss citizen, could travel freely in France.) This amounted to only a short-lived venture into the manufacture of concrete blocks; the undertaking lasted until 1921, and it nearly bankrupted Jeanneret.

3.1 Charles-Edouard Jeanneret (Le Corbusier), Maison Dom-ino framework, 1914–15, diagrams of the framing system

Nevertheless, the Maison Dom-ino propelled Jeanneret into an extraordinarily creative (if not very lucrative) phase in his career. The urban clusters and building construction strategies of the Maison Dom-ino presaged other important urban projects of the 1920s. But the scope of his intentions during the war was already vast, encompassing the design and production of everything from whole towns to interior furnishings. Although his urban schemes have attracted the most attention, his intentions regarding the interior fittings of these large-scale housing projects, which he began to articulate in the 1914 scheme, set the stage for some of his most revolutionary thinking over the following decade. Jeanneret later referred to his work on the interiors and furnishings of mass-produced housing, which were nascent in the Maison Dom-ino, as "a milestone in the evolution of architecture." He went so far as to declare that, as a result of his efforts, "A new term has replaced the old word *furniture [mobilier]*, which stood for fossilizing traditions and limited utilization. That new term is *equipment [équipement]*, which implies a logical classification of the various elements necessary to run a house that results from their practical analysis."[4] Aside from his speculative work as a designer of housing schemes, Jeanneret spent much of his time during the war designing domestic interiors for clients in La Chaux-de-Fonds. So it is hardly surprising that, even in large-scale housing projects like the Maison Dom-ino, he would focus attention on their interior equipment.

Although Jeanneret later claimed credit for revolutionizing the notion of interior equipment, the beginnings of this kind of thinking in France should be attributed at least partly to Francis Jourdain, who had been developing practical, low-cost, "interchangeable" furniture since 1904 (fig. 3.2). And since 1912, Jourdain had been proclaiming that his furniture was not derived from historical French styles; instead, it responded directly to the needs of contemporary people. Octave Mirbeau proclaimed that "the furnishings of Francis Jourdain are essentially objects that testify to our way of life and that merge respectfully with it."[5] Jeanneret had acknowledged the importance of what Jourdain was attempting and was no doubt influenced by it, but it is fair to say that by 1914 he already was prepared to take the issues much further.

Jeanneret envisioned systems of interchangeable parts and their manufacture not only for the Maison Dom-ino frame and wall partitions but also for the integral and freestanding furnishings of the resulting houses. He was also careful to show that these systems were flexible enough to accommodate regional styles and personal tastes and to satisfy all the demands of modern living. He explained, first of all, that the Dom-ino

system "is fabricated with mutually compatible, standard elements, which allow a great diversity of house groupings." After constructing the building skeletons, he continued,

> all that remains is to install a home inside this framework. The arrangement of the "Dom-ino" framework, particularly the position of the posts, permits innumerable combinations of interior arrangements. We have conceived the notion of a Firm, sister to the [one that produced the framework], that would sell all the equipment for the house, that is to say, everything that could be mass produced in factories, following standard measurements and responding to the multiple demands of rational equipment: windows, doors, standard casework serving as cupboards, armoires, or furniture and forming some of the interior partitions.[6]

Despite the overarching reliance on standardization and mass production, Jeanneret also emphasized the flexibility of the Dom-ino house. Both its interior arrangement and its efficacy for reconstruction efforts were testament to this. He explained, for example, that the nonstructural exterior and partition walls could be built with virtually any material, "even stones incinerated in the conflagrations, or from blocks *(agglomérés)* made with wastes from the ruins of the war, etc. etc."[7] Jeanneret even proposed that, owing to the simplicity of the system, people could order the parts and build their own houses. Finally, he asserted that the system would accord well with the traditional houses in the war-ravaged regions of northeastern France for which it was initially designed. In this area of the country, he explained, it was evident "that the window was dominant everywhere, that the historical houses of Flanders were, in reality, houses of glass . . . and that the Flanders Renaissance was so resilient that it could serve admirably as a model for a new architecture in reinforced concrete."[8] This attention to and appreciation of the local vernacular were consistent with much of Jeanneret's thinking at the time. During his sojourns in Germany from 1908 to 1911 and his subsequent travels through southeastern and southern Europe, Jeanneret had made a habit of studying provincial vernacular housing, often recording detailed observations of room arrangements and the routines of their inhabitants.[9]

It is easy to view the Maison Dom-ino project, in retrospect, as rather cold and inhospitable, even imperious in its attempts to subject patterns of living to a rigid structural and rational order. But it seems clear that in the years he developed the Maison Dom-ino, Jeanneret was pursuing other intentions. His work before 1914 lends credence to this presumption. He was keenly interested in making housing that would be inexpensive but hospitable and adaptable, new but not without a sense for history and locality. Considering that Jeanneret declared his admiration for the work of Francis Jourdain only months before he began developing the Maison Dom-ino, it is not surprising that the principles of cost-effectiveness, simplicity, flexibility, and the generous accommodation of everyday life—which were so evident in Jourdain's contributions to the 1913 Salon d'Automne and his advertisements for Les Ateliers Modernes—would be among Jeanneret's primary aims for the Maison Dom-ino project.

These were the principles, too, that drew Jeanneret to the work of Tony Garnier, with whom he maintained an active correspondence during the war. Jeanneret's perspective drawings of the Maison Dom-ino, especially exteriors of housing clusters based on the Dom-ino framework, illustrate a distinct affinity with the residential districts of Garnier's Cité Industrielle. This affinity runs deep in the projects, including not only their appearance but also their material choices, regional affiliation, and attitude toward the habits of their putative occupants. As already noted, Garnier presented the Cité Industrielle as "a design that completely satisfies the material and moral needs of the individual." He strove to illustrate this point in numerous drawings dedicated to the residential sections of the city. He also built three residences at Saint-Rambert: one for himself, another for his wife, Catherine Garnier, and a third for Melle Bachelot. They elaborated the proposed single-family houses in the Cité Industrielle. These houses show that for Garnier, habitability was of utmost concern.

3.3 Charles-Edouard Jeanneret (Le Corbusier), mass-produced houses based on the Maison Dom-ino frame, 1914–15, project perspective

Uniformity and structural clarity contributed to economies of scale; they also provided coherence to the residential areas, but Garnier's drawings illustrate that they did so without compromising a sense of calm and domesticity. Jeanneret pursued a similar objective. He sketched many iterations of the Maison Dom-ino, as single units or combined to make apartment blocks, during the war. Exterior perspectives show the buildings surrounded by lawns, garden courtyards, and tree-lined walkways. People water potted plants on sunny terraces or rest their arms on balcony railings (fig. 3.3). They drape laundry on the windowsills. Interior views, invariably dominated by large windows with divided lights, appear fully equipped with comfortable furniture, flower arrangements, and framed pictures (fig. 3.4).

Although concrete was a notable area of coincidence between the Maison Dom-ino and the Cité Industrielle, it was used in the service of habitability. Garnier proposed that use of a concrete framework would contribute toward making the enterprise simple and practical, but he explicitly advocated using indigenous materials and local expertise for the same reasons. Furthermore, he proposed that the relative neutrality of the concrete building structure would serve to enhance the effect of the interior decor.

If many of these ideas appear to have come to rest in the Maison Dom-ino, it is because Jeanneret was directly inspired by them. Jeanneret saw

parts of the as yet unpublished *Une cité industrielle* in July 1914, just before
the outbreak of the war, at the Exposition International Urbaine: La Cité
Moderne in Lyon, France. Upon returning to La Chaux-de-Fonds, he
immediately wrote to Garnier requesting drawings and photographs of
works in reinforced concrete, evidently for an article he was planning to
write on the subject. This was to follow a piece he had already written
for *L'oeuvre*, which discussed the subject of new materials in architecture.
Owing to the war, Garnier did not respond to the request until more than
a year later, in December 1915, but his letter to Jeanneret was compli-
mentary and cordial.[10] In the meantime, Jeanneret had begun work on
the Maison Dom-ino with Max Du Bois just three months after returning from Lyon.[11]

Many aspects of the Maison Dom-ino scheme for war reconstruction
show that Jeanneret was very aware of the situation in France during the
war and his place in it. Because of his expertise on the decorative arts in
Germany and knowledge of recent developments in France, he was mind-
ful of where the work of contemporary architects and interior designers—
both in France and in Germany—might lead in the production of houses.
He was also acutely aware of how important it was that his project be
viewed as a French solution to the problem of reconstruction. Advocating the use of local materials and expertise was one part of his strategy;
asserting that the Maison Dom-ino scheme accorded well with the
regional houses of Flanders was another. He also had to ensure that his
credentials and affiliations were beyond question.

Any progressive artist in wartime France had to be sensitive to the
nearly insurmountable difficulties he faced in keeping prewar innovations alive. As a foreigner in Paris, Jeanneret was especially subject to
scrutiny. The climate of regionalism and nationalism that developed from

3.4 Charles-
Edouard Jeanneret
(Le Corbusier), interior
of a Maison Dom-ino,
1914–15, perspective
sketch

the outset of the war forced artists in all disciplines to sanitize their work of its connections, real or perceived, to German antecedents. As Kenneth Silver has shown, the pervasive conservatism that surfaced along with the Union Sacré—a solemn pact to dispense with all political differences in the interests of defeating the enemy—also militated against the very notion of progressivism in art.[12] Being relatively unknown as an artist before moving to Paris in February 1917, Jeanneret was not likely to elicit much criticism for his previous work, but he made every effort to strengthen his image as a pro-French expert and critic in the long-simmering conflict between French and German designers. In the spring of 1914, he had already succeeded in having the bulk of his *Etude sur le mouvement d'art décoratif en Allemagne* republished in France (in two installments of *L'art de France*), and by the end of 1915, he was in Paris working on a new book to be called *France or Germany . . .* Evidently this project, which he hoped to complete by the beginning of 1917, would illustrate the countries' rivalry in the decorative arts from the 1870s to the outbreak of the war. Jeanneret was unable to find a publisher for the project and never finished it. Nevertheless, his active interest in the French war effort on the home front, and in postwar reconstruction especially, helped to insinuate him into the cultural scene in Paris when he moved there during the war. His years studying and working in Germany could easily have exposed him to the kind of criticism frequently leveled against members of the prewar avant-garde (especially former *coloristes*); however, he seems to have avoided this.

While Jeanneret was settling into Paris, most of his French-born counterparts were more actively engaged in the war and thus did little design work until after the armistice. Many avant-garde artists were serving on the front lines, and most of those who were not fighting retrenched in the face of the pervasive conservatism of the Union Sacré. Notable exceptions, among architects and designers, were Francis Jourdain and Tony Garnier, who were excused from service on the grounds of health and age, respectively. Both contributed to the 1916 Exposition de la Cité Reconstituée, a rare wartime art exhibit held at the Jeu de Paume in Paris and sponsored by the Association Général des Hygiénistes et Techniciens Municipaux. Jourdain's contribution emphasized an increasingly serious need for solid, inexpensive furniture, while Garnier dealt with the larger problems of remaking ruined towns and cities in the industrialized north.

Jourdain was a professed pacifist, but he served willingly when he was called up in May 1915. He worked as a battlefield nurse at Verdun until 1916, when he was discharged because of weak health. Upon returning to

Paris, he recommenced his work in interior design almost immediately, concentrating on the reconstruction effort. His contributions to the Exposition de la Cité Reconstituée—a dining room and a bedroom furniture ensemble—deviated very little from what he had already been advocating, although the wartime sense of urgency made them especially relevant.[13] He continued to advance the economy and flexibility of his work, particularly in the years immediately after the armistice. One especially notable project was a new series of *meubles interchangeables* fabricated by the Société Anonyme de Pièces Détachées pour Avions, an aviation spare parts firm recalibrated to transfer wartime technology to peaceful purposes. With this furniture, which could be bought as individual pieces (there were six different ones) or as matched ensembles configured for various domestic situations, Jourdain demonstrated that interior household environments could turn the industrial machinery of war to more accommodating ends.[14]

Just as Jourdain's conscientious recasting of the modern domestic interior during the war suggested ways to redirect the aims of industrialization in France, Garnier's *Une cité industrielle,* which he published during the war, proposed the appropriation of technological advances to accommodate and reflect modern dwelling habits. Garnier had developed much of the urban plan and designed its major structures, such as the hydroelectric dam and concrete bridges, by 1904. Over the next ten years, he developed many of its industrial, medical, and institutional buildings, refining them as he designed a number of large-scale commissions to be built in southern France. He exhibited some of these in the fall of 1914 at the international exposition La Cité Moderne, in Lyon, and two years later at the Exposition de la Cité Reconstituée, in Paris, where he showed designs for a hospital, train station, and slaughterhouses, all of which were eventually built in Lyon. In the years immediately preceding publication of *Une cité industrielle* in 1917, however, he lavished much of his attention on designs for the residential quarters of the city. His own house, built at Saint-Rambert in 1911, acted as a test for the middle-class residences in the city, as did a second house he built nearby for his wife in 1913. In his descriptions of the residential quarters of the industrial town, Garnier suggested that the technical difficulties of building houses in concrete contributed to the simplicity of their forms while helping to emphasize elements of the interior decor—furniture, decorative objects, artwork. Thus, the technological advances that made the mass-produced housing scheme possible faded into the background; Garnier appropriated them in the service of domestic satisfaction, stating:

if the construction remains simple, without ornamentation or moldings and with sheer surfaces, the decorative arts can be effectively
employed in all their forms, and each artistic object will maintain a
cleaner and fresher expressiveness, thanks to its independence from
the structure itself. Moreover, the use of concrete and cement enables
us to obtain large horizontal and vertical surfaces, endowing the building with a sense of calm and balance in harmony with the natural
contours of the landscape.[15]

This suggests that in the housing of Une Cité Industrielle, the subtle application of new building technology would serve to cultivate domestic repose
and to facilitate the expression of personal tastes, even in working-class
dwellings. Jeanneret, too, advocated this approach as he proposed various manifestations of the Maison Dom-ino project. The problem of the
house as it developed during the war in France was affected by technological progress, but it took shape in response to the demands of inhabi-
tation. This suggests that matters of interior configuration and external
connection to the land were at least as important as the emergent form
of the modern house.

In 1917, Garnier's message of domestic repose and harmony with the
landscape assumed a gravity it could not have acquired before the war.
Not only was there an urgent need for sensible housing, there was a widespread and burgeoning desire among French artists, indeed among most

3.5 W. E. Troutman,
Inc., trenches in
northeastern France,
"This grim reminder
wends its way north-
ward, from Chateau
Thierry to Soissons,"
1924

of the French, for "a return to the traditional landscape—to the soil, so to speak," in the words of Romy Golan.[16] There was a sense that, whatever political circumstances had precipitated the war, the land was what every French soldier was fighting for: for the reintegration of Alsace and Lorraine, and for the rehabilitation of territory horrendously mutilated in northeastern France.

The extent of this devastation was almost inconceivable, even to those who witnessed it. By the end of the war, nearly 200,000 hectares of agricultural land were utterly devastated, and a similar amount of forest was reduced to wasteland. More than 300 million cubic meters of trench needed to be filled and graded (fig. 3.5). Nearly 300,000 buildings, mostly houses, were completely destroyed and another 500,000 damaged during the four years of intensive shelling. These figures include, in addition to houses, thousands of churches, schools, government buildings, and factories. Throughout the war zone, more than a third of all factories were reduced to rubble. At least four towns (Bailleul, Chauny, Lens, and Liévin) ceased to exist; even building foundations and streets were erased (fig. 3.6). The much larger cities of Armentières, Reims, and Soissons suffered nearly equal damage, with 80 percent or more of their buildings destroyed.[17] Far worse was the devastation of human life: 1.4 million French soldiers died in combat, and nearly three times that many suffered wounds during the war.[18] The war also necessitated widespread evacuation of northeastern France, displacing almost 3 million people. For soldiers fighting in the war, mired for interminable months in fetid trenches, the scenes of utter ruination, of buildings and trees and corpses reduced to mud, strained credulity.

A great number of artists and designers were direct witnesses to this destruction, although few found the time or the will to record it.[19] Guillaume Apollinaire, André Derain, Auguste Herbin, Roger de La Fresnaye, Fernand Léger, Jean Metzinger, and Maurice de Vlaminck all were stationed at the front. André Mare served in the army as a *camoufleur* (a useful position for soldiers with artistic talent). He also maintained contact with his prewar compatriots, the *coloristes* Gustave-Louis Jaulmes, Maurice Marinot, and Louis Suë, who were at the front, too. Mare and Suë hatched a plan in 1917 to form a design collective as soon as the war ended.[20] They founded the Compagnie des Arts Français in 1919, a firm that became enormously influential, if not particularly revolutionary, for its production of traditional French luxury furnishings in the 1920s.

Pierre Chareau also served in the army throughout the war. Before 1914, he had spent six unremarkable years in the Paris office of an English design firm, Waring and Gillow. He did not begin his independent career

as an *artiste décorateur* until after the war, although he sketched out his first major commission—the redecoration of an apartment for Anna and Jean Dalsace (clients, later, of the Maison de Verre)—while on leave just after the armistice in 1918. He exhibited two of the rooms at the first post-war Salon d'Automne the next year under the title A Young Doctor's Consulting-Room and Bedroom (fig. 3.7). This first wartime commission set the tone for a host of residential furniture, lighting, interior, and house designs Chareau developed over the next decade.

Robert Mallet-Stevens was a volunteer in the French air force for the duration of the war, and his interior design and architectural work all but ceased for four years. However, he continued to develop speculative building designs for his *Une Cité Moderne,* a book he had begun as early as 1911 with a series of residential projects. These included two designs for workers' housing, which he produced just before the war, in 1914 (fig. 3.8). He finally published the book, with an introduction by Frantz Jourdain, in 1922.

Certainly the ending of the war revived and even stimulated artistic production in France, as the careers of Chareau, Mallet-Stevens, Mare, and so many others attest. Art and architecture proved to be important palliatives to the devastation wrought by the war. But even during wartime, as the extreme conservatism of the Union Sacré abated, it became more widely accepted that art had its place in war, and that artists—"each according to his own métier," as Charles Morice phrased it—should feel confident in their contributions to the war effort.[21] Thus, even noncombatants like Tony Garnier, Charles-Edouard Jeanneret, and Francis Jourdain had an essential role to play. The principles sustained by designers through the war—simplicity, cost-effectiveness, sensitivity to current patterns of living—perpetuated the prewar efforts of progressive designers and helped to drive the development of modern architecture in France after the war.

3.6 Schutz Group Photographers, "All that is left of the town of Malancourt, in the Argonne Sector," c. 1918

3.7 Pierre Chareau,
A Young Doctor's
Consulting-Room and
Bedroom, Salon
d'Automne, Paris,
1919

3.8 Robert Mallet-
Stevens, worker's
house, *Projet de
maison ouvrier pour
Saint-Cloud*, drawing,
1914

4 THE END OF DECORATIVE ART, THE HOUR OF ARCHITECTURE

And without doubt furniture can lead us toward architecture,
and in place of decoration we shall see the rise of architecture.

—LE CORBUSIER, *THE DECORATIVE ART OF TODAY*

The depredations of the war, and the seemingly irrevocable change
it had wrought on everyday life in the early 1920s, made contemporary
interest in the decorative arts and interior design seem trivial and impru-
dent. This, at least, was how Le Corbusier described the situation in *The
Decorative Art of Today*, which he published in 1925. The war, he declared,
was "the event that upset everything. . . ."

> The old world was shattered, trampled on, rejected, buried. It was over
> and done with. While the event took its course, technology could dare
> everything.
>   Technology.
>   The decorative arts were anti-technology. Their efforts were directed
> to opposite ends from the common effort of the age. They aimed to
> restore manufacture by hand. The physical products of decorative art
> have no place within the context of the age.[1]

The production methods and the modest output of the prewar decorative arts workshops in France—even those that made modest attempts to mechanize—could not hope to rival the productivity of postwar industry. The decorative arts, it seemed, were bound to change.

Le Corbusier's assertion that the decorative arts had no place in modern society challenged, however, a pervasive sense in France of their value as balm for the lingering pain of the war. Despite his vocal enthusiasm for technology, the war had shown it to be hostile, or at best indifferent, to human concerns. The lacerated countryside and the many thousands of homes and lives destroyed in the war provided vivid reminders and instilled a profound distrust of technological advancement. Romy Golan argues that French disillusionment with the effects of technology ushered in a widespread sense of nostalgia in the 1920s, a powerful if sometimes illusory desire to nurse France back to its rustic prewar vigor.[2] In the decorative arts, this contributed to an energetic revival of extravagant bourgeois

4.1   Maurice Dufrène, woman's bedroom, Pavillon des Galeries Lafayette, Exposition Internationale des Arts Décoratifs et Industriels Modernes, Paris, 1925

4.2 Jacques-Emile
Ruhlmann, Pavillon
du Collectionneur,
salon, Exposition
Internationale des
Arts Décoratifs et
Industriels Modernes,
Paris, 1925

tastes, exemplified in the mid 1920s by the exquisitely hand-crafted Art
Deco interiors of acclaimed designers such as those by Maurice Dufrène
(fig. 4.1) and Jacques-Emile Ruhlman (fig. 4.2) or the overtly revivalist
work of André Mare and Louis Suë.

Le Corbusier turned this sense of nostalgia to progressive ends. In a
pictorial history of the decorative arts, titled "Milestones" (Témoins), in
The Decorative Art of Today (fig. 4.3), he reexamined the decorative arts
from 1900 to 1925, not to revive past successes but to show their trajectory.
Forty images of jewelry, posters, clothing, furniture, room ensembles, mass-
produced housing, exhibition structures, and ocean liners demonstrate
that "the spiritual convulsion has led—painfully, slowly, with all its
regrets and backward glances—to clarification."[3] In 1913, Le Corbusier had

attributed "simplicity, instinct, necessity, goodness" to the work of Francis Jourdain, hinting that these would serve as guides to steer the arts away from aestheticism and fashion, from "the folly of the *Beautiful*." In the postwar era, he contended that the best aspects of technology would reinforce these principles and accelerate a purifying trend in design. In much of his own design work of the 1920s, and in that of sympathetic French contemporaries, these same principles also helped architecture to steer clear of the dangerous bravado of technology.

4.3 Le Corbusier, "Milestones" (Témoins), page from *The Decorative Art of Today*, 1925

Photo Stavba.

TÉMOINS

1914 : l'événement bouleversant.
Alors tout y a été à coups de mitraille. Dans les esprits aussi.
Tout fut dit et fait. Le monde ancien fut brisé, foulé, refoulé,

Sensitive to the collective ethos but also aware of the potential benefits of modernization, a small group of progressive designers in France, particularly Pierre Chareau, Eileen Gray, Le Corbusier, Francis Jourdain, Robert Mallet-Stevens, and Henri Sauvage, worked to sustain the progressive development of design that had begun before the war. They sought also to extend its salutary influence to the architectural reconstruction of postwar France. These designers demonstrated that technology inevitably would play a larger role than it had before the war, but that it could improve life only if it was rooted in firm, modest principles. So evident in the "simple, instinctive, necessary" interiors of Francis Jourdain before the war, these principles continued to shape the work of the progressive *architectes-décorateurs* in France as the long-anticipated modern movement in architecture gradually took shape.

In 1925, when Le Corbusier confidently announced the advent of modern architecture in France, he asserted that it had arisen out of the decorative arts: "The spirit which is awakening, springing up full of wonder, fighting against suffocation, winning its place and, as the days dawn, affirming itself . . . this spirit was first enlisted under the banner of decorative art."[4] While architecture foundered for more than half a century, decorative artists had inaugurated a fundamental change in design and brought with it a new conception of architecture:

> The *ensembliers* were right. Some of the questions of architecture were being dealt with in their work. . . .
>
> Now all these efforts, and the crusade mounted by the Ruskins, Grassets and Gallés, had by this time made a profound impression, and the hour of architecture was about to strike—the conclusion of a century of work with machines—a great shift in public opinion had been achieved: attention was focused on architecture.[5]

The architecture that expressed this spirit was modern, unquestionably, but it was not overtly "technological." It was not the ascendant, rational architecture presaged by the Eiffel Tower and the Gallery of Machines a generation before, nor was it the heroic, bellicose spawn of war. It was modest, efficient, and domesticated. Modern architecture, as it developed among these designers, resisted the impulse to glorify technological progress while also avoiding the nostalgic and parochial biases of the war-weary populace: it responded directly to the existing circumstances in France.

Henri Sauvage envisioned the modern architecture of 1925 in modest,

4.4 Le Corbusier and Pierre Jeanneret, Pavillon de l'Esprit Nouveau, Exposition Internationale des Arts Décoratifs et Industriels Modernes, Paris, 1925, exterior view

4.5 Le Corbusier and Pierre Jeanneret, Pavillon de l'Esprit Nouveau, Exposition Internationale des Arts Décoratifs et Industriels Modernes, Paris, 1925, interior view showing furniture by Michael Thonet and paintings by Juan Gris and Le Corbusier

4.6   Le Corbusier and Pierre Jeanneret, Une Ville Contemporaine, displayed in the Pavillon de l'Esprit Nouveau exhibition hall, Exposition Internationale des Arts Décoratifs et Industriels Modernes, Paris, 1925

4.7   Le Corbusier, *immuebles-villas*, 1922, interior perspectives of a living room (above) and a dining room (below)

domestic terms as "an anonymous frame in which the inhabitant, without being bothered with preexisting ornament, will arrange the décor according to his own taste."[6] Le Corbusier and Pierre Jeanneret constructed one such dwelling at the 1925 Exposition Internationale des Arts Décoratifs et Industriels Modernes in Paris (figs. 4.4, 4.5; see also figs. 1.1, 1.2). The Pavillon de l'Esprit Nouveau proposed a neutral setting, one of thousands—hundreds of thousands—that could be constructed to alleviate a shortage of housing in France (fig. 4.6; see also figs. 1.3, 1.7).[7] Le Corbusier envisioned tenants living out their lives in these practical dwellings among their own things—objects selected and arranged to ease their labors, fulfill their aspirations, and make them content (fig. 4.7).

Even if traditional decorative art, handicraft, and ornamentation had little role to play in these circumstances, the principles underlying them did. In his choice and composition of objects for this model middle-class dwelling, Le Corbusier followed aims similar to those that progressive French designers had pursued for a long time: faith that art would bring about the "assimilation of the masses to the life of the spirit" and an interest in "the chaotic order of life," as well as an avowed "hatred of stagnation." He also emulated tastes that had begun to develop in the decorative art ensembles a decade earlier, tastes based on "simple, pure, logical and even slightly harsh lines," and followed a tacit presumption that French middle-class people had enough taste to furnish their own homes artistically.[8] Le Corbusier looked for simplicity, instinct, and necessity in the objects he chose to furnish and equip the modern dwelling unit, and he composed them to bring out fortuitous relationships.[9]

He saw his own work as a continuation of reform in the decorative arts but also as part of a profound cultural shift. "It is a remarkable fact," he said, "that we are in the presence of a *basic* movement, a social movement. I am convinced that in fact what is happening is an architectural movement, a general architectural movement, that is emerging at its due time, when its hour has come—an historic architectural movement."[10] The need for simple, comfortable, tasteful dwellings after the war was acute. Severe postwar inflation, declining value of wages, and a series of monetary crises in 1919, 1924, and 1925 made it more so. For a great number of people, particularly those who had enjoyed a fairly high standard of living, even minimal standards were difficult to attain. In their analysis of the latter part of the Third Republic, Philippe Bernard and Henri Dubief remark that "the middle classes, who in France had been richer and more numerous than in other countries, had been most affected by the general impoverishment of the country. At the end of the war *ren-*

tiers, members of the liberal professions, landlords and civil servants often felt they were ruined."[11] And for many who in the past could afford luxurious dwellings, simple comforts had to suffice.

Given the almost uniformly bleak circumstances that confronted French people after the war, very few decorative artists or architects could choose to ignore the problem of affordable, tasteful housing. Even organizations not formerly known to concern themselves much with middle-class or working-class preferences attempted to reorient their focus. Thus, when the Salon des Artistes Décorateurs reconvened in the spring of 1919, Louis Hourticq could note with pleasure that "one of the innovations of this exposition was evident in the program which invited our decorators to present practical and inexpensive furniture intended for our devastated country. The problem must have pleased them, since they have justly combated applied luxury, fashionable richness, in the name of logic and integrity. Many have responded with joy to this utilitarian program."[12] He declared that "the war has influenced our decorators by obliging them to work also for the new poor."[13] That same year, the architect H. M. Magne voiced a widely held sentiment among designers: "our role is precisely to improve life."[14]

TOWARD A UNION OF MODERN DESIGNERS

Francis Jourdain had endeavored to improve life since before the war. In the 1920s, he continued to develop ways of furnishing the tightly constrained spaces in which most people in France were compelled to arrange their lives. For a brief period, he also worked for the American luggage manufacturer Innovation, producing extraordinarily compact "furniture": efficient armoires and trunks for long-distance travel. With financial backing from the Innovation company, he opened a shop in Paris, Chez Francis Jourdain, whose primary goal was to provide furniture to clients of modest financial means. In addition to producing interiors for private clients (often of the *rentier* class), the shop marketed a line of inexpensive "interchangeable" furniture, similar to what he produced before the war; its six pieces could be combined in many different ways to suit the budgets and space limitations of working-class buyers.

For a few years immediately after the war, these sorts of economical endeavors seemed to take hold in the Salons. Many prominent decorative artists and art critics in France endorsed efforts to make furniture and interior finishes less expensive; they also allowed that, for reasons of cost, the strict coherence and "completeness" of an ensemble was no longer absolutely necessary. Some variety in the furnishings created or chosen for an ensemble allowed consumers to assemble furnishings gradually if they could not afford to purchase entire room arrangements.[15] Designers whose work did not allow this flexibility found themselves the subject of serious criticism, not only for failing to account for the straitened economic circumstances of the time, but also because they showed insensitivity to contemporaneous styles of living. In 1919, Jean-Louis Vaudoyer criticized the *ensembliers* because they "too often confuse decor, *mise-en-scène* . . . with the comfort of private life." He suggested that any visitor to the Salon d'Automne could easily perceive this problem:

> Before the exhibits of the *ensembliers* play the following game: place there, in your imagination, one of the objects that make up your personal effects, your cherished legacy, and try to choose a place in one of these ideal rooms, where everything has been anticipated for the pleasure of your eyes and the comfort of your limbs. Suddenly the ensemble will become false, injured, made ridiculous, and your prized *souvenir* will look like a clumsy Huron entering the *salon* of the beautiful St. Yves.[16]

This sort of criticism represented at least tacit affirmation of *coloriste* principles of composition, even if many of the *coloriste* designers, such as Louis Süe and André Mare, showed only minimal interest in marketing to middle- or working-class buyers after the war.[17]

Although the need to accommodate domestic life comfortably may have become a virtual prerequisite for interiors after the war, too much emphasis on economy did not necessarily receive correspondingly favorably criticism. In 1919, Pierre Chareau, for example, was censured in *Art et décoration* for conflating "style with poverty" in the designs for a doctor's study and a bedroom he displayed at the Salon d'Automne (see fig. 3.7).[18]

Even as the economy continued to struggle through the 1920s, however, the taste among decorative artists for inexpensive interior ensembles faded quickly. In 1922, the critic Yvanhoë Rambosson complained repeatedly in *Art et décoration* about the almost uniform sumptuousness of the interior ensembles presented at the various Paris Salons.[19] With a very few exceptions, notably Francis Jourdain and Chareau, decorative artists lapsed into old habits soon after the war. After having been criticized in 1919 for making things too inexpensive-looking, Chareau found favor with the critic Gaston Varenne in early 1923 for work that "exactly reflects our needs, our tastes, our habits."[20] In the same issue of *Art et déco-*

ration in which Varenne voiced his praise for Chareau, though, René Chavance complained that, among the works displayed at the fourteenth Salon des Artistes Décorateurs, there were only a few, "too few to my tastes," designers whose work was conceived with low cost in mind.[21]

By 1925, with the opening of the Exposition Internationale des Arts Décoratifs et Industriels Modernes, the most prominent decorative artists in France—Maurice Dufrène, Jacques-Emile Ruhlmann, Pierre Selmersheim, and others—concentrated again on areas of traditional French preeminence: opulent settings, rare materials, luxurious finishes (see figs. 4.1, 4.2).[22] Designers and critics who followed more progressive tendencies saw the lavish interiors of these decorative artists as evidence of thoughtlessness and degraded tastes. In *The Decorative Art of Today*, Le Corbusier explained this view, declaring: "In the face of unbroken and continuing evidence, good sense has gradually rejected the tendency to luxuriousness as inappropriate to our needs. Its last popular resort has been the devotion to beautiful materials, which leads to real byzantinism. The final retreat for ostentation is in polished marbles with restless patterns of veining, in paneling of rare woods."[23]

The French *architectes-décorateurs* displayed judicious alternatives to this tendency at the 1925 exposition. Although the Pavillon de l'Esprit Nouveau occupied a dark corner of the grounds, Le Corbusier's offering was certainly the most progressive. Robert Mallet-Stevens contributed a highly visible pavilion in planar concrete for the board of tourism. Francis Jourdain designed a "sober" and "discrete" interior of a passenger railcar for the Compagnie des Chemins de Fer du Paris-Orléans.[24] Mallet-Stevens, Jourdain, and Chareau collaborated on a series of room ensembles for a French embassy, which comprised the pavilion of the Société des Artistes Décorateurs.

Contemporary critics responded most enthusiastically to the embassy project, although some censured the choice of an institutional building program when some sort of housing project would have been more appropriate. Waldemar George, for example, complained that it provided little opportunity to explore current problems of design for the middle and working classes.[25] As members and representatives of the group, Jourdain, Mallet-Stevens, and Chareau could hardly fail to comply with the program, but they resuscitated its progressive atmosphere in the details. Their rooms captured attention not only for an almost complete absence of ornamentation but also for the integration of decor and architecture. As in his domestic work, Jourdain included built-in furniture. He also boldly riv-

4.8 Francis Jourdain, boutique for travel articles, Paris, 1919

eted paneling to the walls or hung it on exposed brackets, an economical means of interior finishing he had been using since the end of the war, as shown, for example, in a 1919 Paris boutique (fig. 4.8). Chareau devised ingenious built-in bookcases and rotating room partitions for the project's study library (fig. 4.9) Mallet-Stevens angered exhibition organizers when he placed Cubist paintings by Robert Delaunay and Fernand Léger prominently in the main hall of the pavilion (fig. 4.10). He was forced to remove the paintings briefly, but he replaced them after the critical press raised an outcry.

Despite its success, the pavilion accentuated growing tensions among members of the Société des Artistes Décorateurs. Although the group had originated as an agent of design reform at the turn of the century, it had become increasingly conservative into the twenties. And in 1929, its "left wing," under the leadership of Francis Jourdain, seceded to form the Union des Artistes Modernes. Founding members of the Union des Artistes Modernes included Mallet-Stevens, Eileen Gray, and Charlotte Perriand (with whom Le Corbusier and Pierre Jeanneret later collaborated to produce the 1929 Salon d'Automne display, Equipment for Living). Chareau

defected from the Société des Artistes Décorateurs in sympathy but did not join the new group until the following year. Le Corbusier and Pierre Jeanneret joined in 1931.

Although these designers were by no means unanimous in their intentions, they tended to undertake more sober and practical analyses of postwar circumstances in France than did their more conservative contemporaries. The work of these *architectes-décorateurs* continued to focus

4.9 Pierre Chareau, study library of the French embassy project, Exposition Internationale des Arts Décoratifs et Industriels Modernes, Paris, 1925

on economic, practical, and ethical requirements of modern furniture and domestic interiors, but it also began to extend these concerns to buildings, streets, and cities. These aims, which had been gaining clarity since before the turn of the century in French decorative art, acquired definition, if not the official status of an architectural movement, by 1925. Gaston Varenne declared that year in *Art et décoration* that "the liaison between architecture and furniture is the most important problem of the moment."[26] Le Corbusier concluded much more forcefully that their work presaged the ascendancy of modern architecture and the demise of the decorative arts: "except for the rising generation of twenty-year olds, all our feet are mired in the agony of the previous age. . . . A new conception has been born. Decoration is no longer possible. Our effusions, our vivid awareness of the beauties and power of nature have found their place within the framework of architecture."[27] Le Corbusier considered this to be a question not so much of a liaison between architecture and furniture but of a change, a change with a single, inevitable conclusion: architecture.

4.10 Robert Mallet-Stevens, hall of the French embassy project, Exposition Internationale des Arts Décoratifs et Industriels Modernes, Paris, 1925, with painting by Robert Delaunay

THE END OF DECORATIVE ART

Le Corbusier's radical program suggested that because "decorative art is no longer possible," the production of furniture and equipment for the home must be left to industry. Designers aspiring to modernism would produce architecture. The Pavillon de l'Esprit Nouveau, despite its presence at the Exposition Internationale des Arts Décoratifs et Industriels Modernes, exemplified this assertion. It was meant to herald the beginning of modern architecture and, ironically, the end of decorative art. *The Decorative Art of Today*, which Le Corbusier published as a companion to the pavilion, reinforced the point.[28] His goal in presenting the pavilion and the book, then, was twofold: first, to expose the fundamental inconsistency of "decorative art" and, second, to show how architecture could accomplish what the decorative arts had failed to achieve.

The visual contrast between the Pavillon de l'Esprit Nouveau and many of the other pavilions in the exposition was remarkable. The pavilion's austerity made it seem not only inharmonious and improper but also expressionless. Auguste Perret, the president of the exposition jury and longtime mentor of Le Corbusier's, declared, "There is no architecture in it!"[29] He might have said, more appropriately, that there was no decorative art in it.

The "error" of the decorative arts was, Le Corbusier argued, that they sought to accommodate the incompatible goals of equipment and art. From a purely practical standpoint, "beautiful tools," as he disparagingly referred to the products of decorative artists, served utilitarian interests less effectively than did highly refined tools, and aesthetic interests less completely than art. "This," he mused, "is the paradox: why should chairs, bottles, baskets, shoes, which are all objects of utility, all *tools*, be called *decorative art*? The paradox of making art out of tools."[30]

To unravel this contradiction, Le Corbusier proposed that designers first reexamine the entrenched habit of decoration:

> We are told that decoration is necessary to our existence. Let us correct that: art is necessary to us, that is to say, a disinterested passion that exalts us.
>
> So to see things clearly, it is sufficient to separate the satisfaction of disinterested emotion from that of utilitarian need. Utilitarian needs call for tools brought in *every respect* to that degree of perfection seen in industry. This then is the great programme for the decorative arts.[31]

The great program of the decorative arts seemed to be that of dismantling themselves and ceding the design of tools to industry and the creation of art to artists.

Le Corbusier had written to Francis Jourdain a decade earlier, praising his Salon d'Automne ensemble as "simple, instinctive, necessary," but he had also expressed a sense of "uneasiness" with it and, more generally, with "the problem of interior decoration" in France.[32] Later, he articulated the source of this discomfiture, explaining that the specially designed piece of art furniture and the unique interior always lack clarity of purpose. They conflate disinterested emotion with utilitarian need. Bemused by this inconsistency, decorative artists created beautiful furniture and unique interiors and paid little attention to the highly refined furniture and utilitarian objects being produced all around them. Even if the interiors of innovators like the *coloristes* or Jourdain could have accommodated such objects, they never quite did so. Ensembles displayed in France before the early 1920s rarely included anything that might be called an ordinary piece of furniture or a ubiquitous piece of household equipment.

In the early 1910s, Le Corbusier had been no less accountable for this "error" than were his contemporaries. Having just moved back to La Chaux-de-Fonds from a long sojourn in Germany and extensive travels abroad, he was busy reestablishing credentials as a decorative artist and architect, designing houses, and training students in the town's decorative arts school. The disquiet he experienced when considering the work of Jourdain and the *coloristes* would have been all the more unsettling since his own interiors at the time were closely modeled on their example.

A decade later, he proposed that architecture would help resolve the paradox of decorative art. Instead of seeking to blend utility and art, architecture would put them in gratifying proximity to each another. The Pavillon de L'Esprit Nouveau, placed as it was amidst the extravagantly ornamental products of Art Deco, provided a vivid demonstration of the point. It brought together highly refined but seemingly ordinary tools (furniture by the manufacturers Kohn, Motté, and Thonet as well as a number of custom-made "standardized" pieces designed to be easily manufactured) and unique pieces of art (paintings and sculptures by Le Corbusier, Juan Gris, Fernand Léger, Amédée Ozenfant, and Jacques Lipschitz) in the architectural framework of an ordinary dwelling unit (see figs. 4.4, 4.5).[33] Although highly composed, the pavilion was meant to indicate one of many possible configurations of the standardized dwelling unit, brought together not by decorative artists or interior designers but by enlightened inhabitants of the modern dwelling (see figs. 1.3, 4.7).

The inhabitant was a crucial protagonist in this arrangement. Le Corbusier emphasized that modern society no longer requires decorative art but demands an architecture that accommodates the occupants' needs and provides them the space in which to express their aspirations. Although he acknowledged a debt to the work of designers over the previous three decades, Le Corbusier emphasized that the new architecture encompassed far more than the creative inspiration of a few innovative individuals. It represented the culmination of a broad cultural change in France, a change

4.11 Le Corbusier, commercial glassware and crockery, *The Decorative Art of Today*, 1925

that had begun to show itself a generation earlier, often subtly, in the evolution of the decorative arts and in the exhibition of domestic interior ensembles. No doubt, an acute housing shortage and the penury of the liberal middle class after the war helped to compel this movement and the ascendancy of architecture in it. To design the hundreds of thousands of new dwelling units needed would be the task of architects, and to arrange them, tastefully or otherwise, was the task of their inhabitants. Industry, not decorative artists, would supply the furniture and equipment; artists, not decorative artists, would supply the works of art on the walls. The ubiquitous products of industry were not only less expensive than those of decorative artists and craftsmen but were often more refined and visually arresting, a point Le Corbusier illustrated abundantly in *The Decorative Art of Today*: office furniture by the Roneo and Ormo corporations, luggage by Innovation, chairs by Thonet, automobiles by Voisin and Peugeot, and commercial glassware and crockery (fig. 4.11). While industry produced the refined utilitarian objects of the new era, a coterie of modern artists—among them Le Corbusier, Gris, Léger, Lipschitz, Ozenfant—would make art suited to the circumstances of an enlightened middle class.

THE HOUR OF ARCHITECTURE IN FRANCE

Even if this new conception of architecture had gestated in France for several decades, there was as yet little outward appearance that it represented a large cultural movement, as Le Corbusier proclaimed in 1925. Unlike Germany, whose tradition of large-scale collaboration in design gave rise to the Deutscher Werkbund and the Bauhaus (which moved from its quarters in the Weimar School of Arts and Crafts to its new buildings in Dessau in 1925), no group that could rival the artistic production of these formidable organizations came together in France. Although *architectes-décorateurs* in France collaborated occasionally during the 1920s as members of exhibiting organizations such as the Société des Artistes Décorateurs and, later, the Union des Artistes Modernes, they usually worked independently of one another. They continued to reject institutional ties and resist collective labels, as their most progressive predecessors had done.[34] The aims of modernist designers in Germany and France were also different. Members of the Bauhaus, unlike the *architectes-décorateurs*, strove to influence the mechanization of craft production. A primary goal of the Bauhaus after 1925 was to develop prototypes for mass production of consumer products. French designers allowed mechanization to proceed on its own.

And in any case, progressive designers in France generally were more interested in the sensual qualities of their work than in technological, economic, political, or intellectual concerns.[35] They dealt more consistently, therefore, with the immediacy of their work than with their metaphysical consequences. This was an attitude endorsed not only by artists but also by the most influential thinkers of early twentieth-century France. Henri Bergson, for example, protested that individual perception, rather than metaphysical speculation, must be the basis of a common understanding of the world. In 1910, he had declared:

> It would greatly astonish a man unaware of the speculations of philosophy if we told him that the object before him, which he sees and touches, exists only in his mind and for his mind or even, more generally, exists only for mind. . . . Such a man would always maintain that the object exists independently of the consciousness which perceives it. But, on the other hand, we should astonish him quite as much by telling him that the object is entirely different from that which is perceived in it, that it has neither the color ascribed to it by the eye nor the resistance found in it by the hand. The color, the resistance, are, for him, in the object: they are not states of our mind; they are part and parcel of an existence really independent of our own. For common sense, then, the object exists in itself, and, on the other hand, the object is, in itself, pictorial, as we perceive it: image it is, but a self existing image.[36]

Bergson's appeal to common sense was especially influential among progressive artists in France because it fortified their interest in problems of

perception and the experiences associated with everyday life. His emphasis on common sense turned attention to practical reality.

Le Corbusier restated this notion in very different terms fifteen years
later. In an essay titled "Type-Needs, Type-Furniture," which he published
in *The Decorative Art of Today*, he declared that the fundamental orientation of contemporary design must be toward the human being. "Since the
crisis has now come to a head," he proclaimed,

> there is no more urgent task than to force ourselves to re-adjust to our
> functions in all fields. . . .
>
> To search for the human scale, for human function, is to define
> human needs.
>
> They are not very numerous; they are similar for all mankind, since
> man has been made out of the same mould from the earliest times
> known to us.[37]

This passage goes on to describe a host of objects that had evolved to accommodate common human needs:

> Thus the cupped hands of Narcissus led us to invent the bottle; the bar-
> rel of Diogenes, already a notable improvement on our natural pro-
> tective organs (our skin and scalp), gave us the primordial cell of the
> house; filing cabinets and copy-letters make good the inadequacies of
> our memory; wardrobes and sideboards are the containers in which
> we put away the auxiliary limbs that guarantee us against cold or heat,
> hunger or thirst, etc. These apparently paradoxical definitions take us
> far from Decorative Art.[38]

If objects defined in this way stray far from decorative art, it would
seem that they also deviate from art.[39] Nevertheless, these "type-objects,"
as Le Corbusier referred to them, could be the subject of careful artistic
analysis. The Purist paintings that Le Corbusier and Amédée Ozenfant produced in the early 1920s examine the highly refined, though decidedly
mundane and simple, objects associated with everyday life (fig. 4.12).[40] Le
Corbusier asserted:

> That is why Purism begins with elements chosen from existing
> objects. . . .
>
> . . . it draws them for preference from among those that serve the
> most direct of human uses; those which are like extensions of man's

limbs, and thus of an extreme intimacy, a banality that makes them barely exist as subjects of interest in themselves, and hardly lend themselves to anecdote.[41]

While he made these objects the subject of rational analysis and carefully regulated composition in his Purist paintings, their underlying fascination for him was their extraordinary humanness.

The appeal of such things to the people who might inhabit modern dwellings like the Pavillon de l'Esprit Nouveau was self-evident. Composed alongside modern paintings, between planar walls, in the vast urban assembly of similarly equipped dwelling units, the Pavillon de l'Esprit Nouveau established the basis not merely for a new way of decorating interiors but for a sweeping new program for architectural design.

In the brief period from 1923 to 1927, Le Corbusier produced four books that describe this program as part of an even more comprehensive vision for modern design: *Towards a New Architecture*, *The Decorative Art of Today*, *The City of Tomorrow and Its Planning* (originally published as *Urbanisme*), and *Modern Painting* (La peinture moderne). In these volumes, Le Corbusier laid out a strategy for design that included everything from works of art, simple tools, and domestic equipment to cities. He placed these on a continuum in relation to human spheres of influence, starting with tools, whose forms are entirely dependent upon direct contact with the body

4.12 Amédée Ozenfant, *Fugue*, oil on canvas, 1922

in the context of particular actions, and ending with cities, which must be geometrically pure in order to function as lucid backdrops to the multitude of human interactions that take place in them. The Pavillon de l'Esprit Nouveau, the prototypical modern dwelling unit, was meant to encapsulate this program.[42]

The pavilion demonstrated that because the house occupies the middle of this continuum, it must accommodate virtually all products of design. The visceral satisfaction of tools and the intellectual purity of cities meet in modern architecture. Art, too, finds a place there, providing emotional complement to the practical satisfaction of physical needs. Like Henri Sauvage, who envisioned the modern dwelling as "an anonymous frame," Le Corbusier proposed that the modern house would create a setting for contemporary life, bringing together tools and art so as to shelter human bodies and enrich human experience.[43] He described just such a scenario in *The Decorative Art of Today*: "We pick up a book or a pen. In this mechanical, discreet, silent, attentive comfort, there is a very fine painting on the wall. Or else: our movements take on a new assurance and precision among walls whose proportions make us happy, and whose colors stimulate us."[44] Visitors to this exhibit at the Exposition Internationale des Arts Décoratifs et Industriels Modernes stepped into a space that challenged all the presumptions of the decorative arts and interior design and proposed a radically innovative kind of architecture. It was not so much an ensemble of more or less beautiful objects but a prototypical yet fully individualized domestic situation.

As visitors passed through the model dwelling into the attached exhibition gallery, they saw a staggering multiplication of this modern domestic scenario: two urban projects, an audacious plan for the insertion of a business center in Paris (the Voisin Plan) and the extraordinary "Plan for a Modern City of Three Million Inhabitants," which had been exhibited three years earlier as Une Cité Industrielle (see fig. 4.6) in the *art urbain* section of the 1922 Salon d'Automne. In the latter plan, 600,000 of the city's 3 million inhabitants were to be housed in huge blocks of standardized dwelling units, or *immeubles-villas*, of which the pavilion was an example.[45] Le Corbusier intended that each of these units would acquire its own particular character according to the tastes of its occupants (see figs. 1.3, 4.7). Standardization facilitates individual expression. Architecture is a frame for living.

In his earlier design for the Maison Citrohan (fig. 4.13), a prototype for standardized mass-produced houses, Le Corbusier envisioned a very flexible kind of building much like the earlier Maison Dom-ino. Speak-

ing of the first version of the house in 1920, he explained that "one dreams
of building this house in any area of the country; the two walls will be
either in brick, or in stone or in the masonry of the local tradesmen."[46]
Although later versions of the Maison Citrohan and other mass-produced
housing schemes left significantly less latitude for different construction
techniques, Le Corbusier contended that they were all malleable enough
to adapt to the individual dispositions of their inhabitants. "Rational construction of cubes does not destroy anyone's initiative," he said. "We only
have to make use of them according to our tastes."[47] He suggested that
within the neutral framework of the standardized modern dwelling unit,
one could make a home by equipping it to suit individual needs and desires.
This implies, of course, that the architectural character of mass-produced
buildings develops from their relationships with decor and the personalities of their inhabitants, a point that is frequently evident in the drawings and interior photographs of Le Corbusier's early buildings.

He was certainly familiar with the importance of furniture choice and
arrangement from his visits to the Salons in Paris before the war and his

work during the war in La Chaux-de-Fonds, where he undertook several interior design commissions and furnished their rooms in the bold, eclectic manner of the *coloristes*. In the modernist projects he built in Paris during the early 1920s, the choice and arrangement of furniture, although far sparer than in his previous projects, was crucial. Many of the photographs he published in *Oeuvre complète* demonstrate this essential quality. A photograph of the interior of the 1922 house of the painter Amédée Ozenfant, for example, shows a Thonet bentwood chair and a violin beyond it on the central axis (fig. 4.14). To the left and right in the foreground are two worktables with the tools of the painter; in the middle ground to the right, a standard easel supports a finished painting. The violin, of course, is out of place in the painting studio. It appears to be not so much a prop for the painting of still life pictures as the symbolic centerpiece of the composition, where tool and art harmonize.

Le Corbusier explained that the program for the Pavillon de l'Esprit Nouveau included "the rejection of decorative art as such, accompanied

4.14 Le Corbusier and Pierre Jeanneret, house of the painter Amédée Ozenfant, 1922

by the affirmation that the sphere of architecture embraces every detail of household furnishing, the street as well as the house, and a wider world still beyond that." And although he might have exaggerated its significance somewhat when he declared it to be "a turning point in the design of modern interiors and a milestone in the evolution of architecture," this dwelling was nevertheless a particularly lucid and comprehensive essay into modern design.[48] It crystallized ideas that had been incipient in France for several decades: the preeminence of ordinary things, the conquest of machine production, the significance of art in the lives of ordinary people, and the coordinating function of architecture. It demonstrated that the fundamental task of architects was to establish the field upon which humans interact not only with objects of use but also with objects of art. Situated in architecture, joined with prosaic human existence, tools and art would assume value appropriate to contemporary life. This was a goal that decorative art had failed to accomplish. But architecture in 1925, Le Corbusier contended, was ideally suited to the task.

THE *ARCHITECTES-DÉCORATEURS*

If Le Corbusier was intent on showing that "architecture embraces every detail of household furnishing," he also emphasized distinctions between mobile equipment (*meuble*) and the immobile structure (*immeuble*) that encompasses it. This served to reinforce the dominance of architecture in the formulation of modernist design: after all, architecture had superseded decorative art as the medium for expressing and accommodating contemporary life. Le Corbusier's modernist contemporaries in France—especially Pierre Chareau, Eileen Gray, Francis Jourdain, and Robert Mallet-Stevens—also accorded architecture an increasingly important role in their work. But they were less willing to relinquish control over the design of household equipment and furniture. Instead, they sought to bring architecture into balance with interior design and the elements of decor without resorting to anachronistic tastes or modes of production. In this regard, their aims sometimes cut against those of Le Corbusier, but the artists shared with him an intense desire to accommodate the needs and express the circumstances of ordinary people in France.[49] And so, during the 1920s, they, too, made the modern house their primary mode of expression.

Chareau aimed to show that rigid distinctions among design disciplines are artificial, that modern architecture and household furnishing are essentially continuous. He designed chairs, tables, bureaus, and other free-

standing pieces of furniture for his interiors, but he also ensured that the boundaries between furniture and building always remained unclear. The mobile fan partition, for example, which he introduced at the Salon d'Automne of 1923 and used in both the French embassy exhibit and the Salon d'Automne of 1925, is both furniture and wall (see fig. 4.9). Marc Vellay and Kenneth Frampton point out that Chareau devised a host of similarly ambiguous fixtures that straddled the limits of architecture and furnishing.[50]

The Maison de Verre is full of such objects (figs. 4.15–4.17). In nearly every space in the house, the limits are either indeterminate or defined only temporarily with a folding screen, sliding wall, rotating panel, or some other mechanism. Moreover, even bathroom fixtures are sometimes not fixed; for example, the bidets shown in figure 4.17 pivot. From 1928 to 1932, Chareau inserted the three-story glass house and office in its very quirky site, a space opened under the upper floor of an eighteenth-century row house in Paris. The new steel frame, left mostly exposed in the house, supported the existing dwelling of "an old lady who didn't want to leave

4.15 Pierre Chareau, Maison de Verre, 1928–32, main hall, dining room, and doctor's study (second floor)

4.16 Pierre Chareau, Maison de Verre, 1928–32, main bedroom (second floor)

4.17 Pierre Chareau, Maison de Verre, 1928–32, bathroom (third floor)

her dingy second floor apartment," in the words of Dr. Dalsace, who along with his wife, Annie, was Chareau's client.[51] Chareau worked closely on the house with the clients, the collaborating architect Bernard Bijvoët, and metalworker André Dalbet. Although certainly "modern" in most regards—in its lack of applied ornamentation, its use of steel and glass, and its mechanical precision, for example—the building always defied categorization as much as it obscured boundaries.

In his analysis of the building, Frampton asks, "Should the Maison de Verre be looked on as architecture or as a furnishing operation on a large scale?"[52] The house is clearly not a discrete building, nor can it properly be called an interior renovation. It is an extraordinarily complex essay on both household equipment and architecture. What makes it particularly fascinating, and problematic, as a work of modern architecture is precisely this resistance to definition. Frampton's question is enough to explain why the house does not fit very comfortably in the historical canon of modern architecture. He declares that "it has in the main been left out of general works which discuss the Modern Movement."[53] It is unquestionably modern but difficult to classify as architectural.

The Maison de Verre resists definition in a number of other respects. It blurs functional boundaries between working and living: the doctor's office and examining rooms occupy the ground floor, and the waiting room is continuous spatially with the living quarters above, while the main stairway links the living room of the house with the reception area of the office. Its material qualities are also indeterminate; it simultaneously demonstrates the structural and ornamental potential of steel, for example, as well as the revealing and obscuring functions of glass. In its precise organization and in the industrialized appearance of its hand-produced furniture and fittings, it also comments on the virtues of modularity and mechanical refinement. In this way, the Maison de Verre proclaims the merits of standardization while also emphasizing the essential role of handicraft. Above all, it exemplifies the sensory emphasis of modern French design without eliminating the practical and aesthetic values of purity and functional clarity.

In these regards, the Maison de Verre is similar in spirit to the Pavillon de l'Esprit Nouveau, although it is less clearly delimited as *architecture*. If, for Le Corbusier, modern architecture was the natural and definitive successor to decorative art, for Pierre Chareau, modern domestic architecture merely expanded decorative art to the scale of buildings. Both designers might very well have claimed that the spirit of modern architecture "was first enlisted under the banner of decorative art," but

4.18 Eileen Gray
and Jean Badovici,
E.1027, Roquebrune-
Cap-Martin, France,
1926–29, exterior
view

whereas Le Corbusier asserted that architecture superseded and destroyed
the decorative arts, Chareau clearly believed otherwise. For Chareau, modern architecture and modern decorative arts were simply complementary
responses to the same set of circumstances.

The work of Eileen Gray demonstrates a similar view. Having worked
for many years as a decorator of exorbitant, luxurious interiors (which
almost invariably included unique, meticulously handcrafted lacquer
pieces), her interpretation of architecture in the mid 1920s was bound with
surprising firmness to the practical realities of everyday life played out
among the furnishings and walls of modest domestic environments. In a
description of her first major architectural work, E.1027 (figs. 4.18–4.20), a
small vacation house she designed for herself with Jean Badovici, she
strongly criticized recent efforts to create a modern architecture independent of interior design. "External architecture," Gray and Badovici protested, "seems to have absorbed avant-garde architecture at the expense
of the interior. As if a house should be conceived for the pleasure of the
eye more than for the well-being of its inhabitants."[54] Much of Gray's decorative arts production and interior design work up to the mid 1920s had

defied such distinctions. Each of her designs adjusted domestic space in ways that obscured boundaries between decor and architecture. In later projects, E.1027 in particular, she demonstrated the broader applicability of the idea at the scale of whole buildings.

One of Gray's first large-scale interior designs involved extraordinarily elegant and eccentric alterations to the apartment of Mme. Mathieu-Lévy in Paris (1918–22). In the salon of the apartment, Gray inserted a series of lacquered panels that reconfigured contours of the room (eliminating, in particular, a ceiling molding that Gray disliked).[55] The deeply reflective black lacquer surfaces, inlaid with sweeping plane figures and lines of silver, adjusted the plane of the wall itself, making the sense of space "visually elusive," in the words of Caroline Constant.[56] In other rooms, Gray used handwoven fabrics to alter ceiling heights, obscure moldings, and hide spatial irregularities. When Gray later redesigned a hallway in the same apartment (1922–24), she introduced freestanding lacquer screens that paralleled the walls on either side and then turned inward to meet each other two or three paces before Mme. Lévy's bedroom door (fig. 4.21). These screens—composed of hundreds of individually lacquered blocks joined with metal rods, which allowed them to pivot—veiled the boundaries between fixed and movable portions of the room. Placed as they were to subdivide the original hallway into a passage and entry foyer for the bedroom, they also established new limits for the space without formally delimiting new rooms.

Whereas the built-in cabinetry Francis Jourdain had designed ten years earlier merged furniture with wall, Gray's screens made walls out of freestanding pieces of furniture. These pieces constructed an elegant play on the perception of the French building interior, where the movable piece of furniture (*meuble*) merges with the static building (*immeuble*). While Le Corbusier sometimes sought to maintain these distinctions, his terminology reveals similar ambiguity. In his urban project of 1922 for 3 million inhabitants, Une Ville Contemporaine, furniture (*meuble*) merges with building (*immeuble*), which merges with apartment-house (*immeuble-villa*), which merges with city (*ville*).[57]

In the work of the *architectes-décorateurs* of the 1920s, the co-extension of interior, architecture, and city derived from a serious assessment of contemporary living conditions, not merely an intellectual and spatial legerdemain. "It is not a matter of only constructing beautiful arrangements of lines," Gray declared, "but above all, *dwellings for people*."[58] Even as Gray and other *architectes-décorateurs* continued to appeal to this sense of the human orientation of design, brutal economic necessity demanded the

4.19 Eileen Gray and Jean Badovici, E.1027, Roquebrune-Cap-Martin, France, 1926–29, bedroom

4.20 Eileen Gray and Jean Badovici, E.1027, Roquebrune-Cap-Martin, France, 1926–29, living room

radical simplification of domestic arrangements and the standardization and mechanized production of household equipment. The apartment of Mme. Lévy might have been a model for progressive design, but it was anything but frugal. As Gray turned her attention to the housing of the "new poor" of the *rentier* class in the late 1920s—with unbuilt designs for an engineer, two sculptors, a professor, and an artists' cooperative, in addition to "minimal" dwellings for herself and Badovici—economy, simplification, and an attendant functional logic were indispensable. All of these projects bore strong outward similarities in form and appearance to the modernist buildings that were appearing throughout Europe in the late 1920s; however, they were by no means formalist in principle. Each was highly idiosyncratic and placed primary emphasis on the character and needs of its occupants. In E.1027, particularly, this concern showed itself

4.21 Eileen Gray, apartment of Mme. Mathieu-Lévy, Paris, 1922–24, hallway

in the complex integration of the interior walls and the furniture, and in the delimitation of space according to Badovici's and Gray's own patterns of dwelling.

Like Francis Jourdain and Pierre Chareau, Gray sought to obscure distinctions between decor and building; she also strove to eliminate traditional subdivisions among rooms. In E.1027, salon and dining room combine to make a larger living room (see fig. 4.20). Here, however, the living room includes a large divan/bed and an area for serving drinks. The exterior wall spanning the length of this multifunctional space further emphasizes the spatial diffusion of the house. It consists entirely of sliding glass panels, which open onto a wide terrace and, beyond that, the Mediterranean. These extend the room, effectively, from glass wall, to railing, to horizon.

While the functions and spatial limits of virtually every area in E.1027 remain unfixed, Gray and Badovici were careful not to allow a sense of expansiveness to eliminate the possibility for enclosure and inward focus. The house therefore sets aside private spaces, tucking them behind bookshelves or isolating them in shadows. Much of the furniture is mobile, following "the 'camping' method," as they called it, so that a desk table that usually inhabits some private corner might be brought out into the main space and joined with others, pulled out from the recesses of the house, and "made into a very large dining table that is lightweight but perfectly stable."[59] The house expands and contracts with the moods and activities of its inhabitants. Rather than relying on a formal plan to order its spaces, the spaces shape themselves according to the particular domestic scenario playing out from one moment to the next.

Although all of the houses Gray designed exhibited a sense of formal purity in their smooth white walls, strip windows, and flat roofs, their spatial organization was always intuitive. This made each acutely responsive to its situation in the landscape and to the personalities of its occupants. In a dialogue with Gray, which Badovici published in 1929, he asked, "Don't you fear that this return to fundamentals, this systematic simplification that seems to dictate modern art, will only end by grounding this art in general, and architecture in particular, in a purely theoretical pursuit that is too intellectual to satisfy the demands of both our minds and our bodies?" Gray responded in a characteristically nuanced fashion, blending both sides of the argument:

> You are right. This return to essential elements, this emancipation from
> all that was inessential, responded to a need. It is necessary to liberate

oneself from such oppression in order to experience freedom anew. But this state of intellectual coldness that we have reached, which corresponds only too well to the harsh laws of modern mechanization, can be no more than a passing phase. We must rediscover the human being in plastic expression, the human intention that underlies material appearance and the pathos of this modern life.[60]

E.1027, the most complete of Gray's houses, straddled these issues. Gray described her own approach to design as one that anticipated human action. The building and its furniture become extensions of these potential actions, not rational solutions to questions of form or even of economic necessity. "The object should be given a form," Gray declared, "that is most suited to the spontaneous gesture or instinctive reflex which corresponds to its purpose."[61] This statement recalls Le Corbusier's notion of the human-limb object, which also takes its form in response to human actions. Although the highly idiosyncratic furniture Gray designed for E.1027 and the products of mechanical selection Le Corbusier chose for his own interiors resulted from different processes of design, the underlying motivation for their presence in the dwelling was very similar. It reverted in both cases to what Henri Bergson called "common sense," or an understanding of things as they appear to be. Common sense demands, Bergson declared, that "the objects which surround my body reflect its possible action upon them."[62] Just as Bergson's definition of common sense could not abide pure theoretical speculation, Gray's houses emphasized that "theory is insufficient for life and does not answer to all its requirements." So it was to the gesture and to the senses—to the human being—that she turned her attention in the design of spaces for living. "Formulas are nothing," she declared, "life is everything."[63]

Thus, while Gray designed the spaces of her houses in response to the gestures that accompany work, rest, and entertaining, she also articulated their surfaces to bring the senses into play. Caroline Constant suggests that this was especially true in E.1027, where, for example, "in the tile flooring underfoot that radiates heat from the sun or the cork-covered tea and dining table that muffle sound. . . . Gray relied on materials to suggest degrees of bodily contact."[64] Even as her attention shifted from the luxurious and exquisitely crafted lacquerwork of her early interiors to the more mundane materials of E.1027, the sensual appeal of her work remained central to the aim of designing for human life rather than adhering to formal, theoretical principles.

Gray's work is often contrasted with that of Le Corbusier on these grounds; however, their intentions were remarkably consistent.[65] Although Le Corbusier's polemics during the 1920s shaded toward formalism far more than did Gray's, they always gravitated back to the human being. Far from establishing rigid, formulaic parameters for modern architecture, Le Corbusier suggested that architecture should be about balance. "When one factor in our technico-cerebro-emotional equation grows disproportionately, a crisis occurs," he states. "The compass will save us from this disturbance; the compass in this case is ourselves: a man, a constant, the fixed point that is in truth the only object of our concern." Architecture, Le Corbusier suggested, is an art of relationships predicated on human action, human thought, and human feeling: "Architecture is there, concerned with our home, our comfort, and our heart. Comfort and proportion. Reason and aesthetics. Machine and plastic form. Calm and beauty."[66]

The oft-cited formal "rules" for architecture that Le Corbusier introduced in the mid 1920s are not so much about architectural form as they are about balance.[67] The first is his "three reminders to architects," which reiterate the significance of (1) the play of architectural masses in sunlight, (2) the contribution of surface characteristics to this effect, and (3) the crucial importance of the plan, which "carries in itself the essence of feeling."[68] The second rule is "regulating lines," which Le Corbusier described in *Towards a New Architecture* as deriving from a primitive desire to give order to dwelling spaces, to make them "comfortable" and "on the human *scale*" but also to make them intellectually satisfying by equating human creations to natural "rhythms, rhythms apparent to the eye."[69] Le Corbusier ridiculed the architects of his day who had "forgotten that great architecture is rooted in the very beginnings of humanity," and he warned that formalism leads only to absurdity and inhumanity. "The regulating line," he admonished, "is a means to an end; it is not a recipe."[70] The third rule consists of "five points for a new architecture," which are similarly balanced. In point 1 (*Les pilotis*), Le Corbusier and Pierre Jeanneret explain that the *pilotis*, made possible with the advent of concrete, place the house between sky and garden; this is especially good for localities that are often dark and humid, as in much of France. In point 2 (*Les toits-jardins*), they declare that "reasons of technique, reasons of economy, reasons of comfort and sentimental reasons lead us to adopt the roof garden." Point 3 (*Le plan libre*) notes that the free plan eliminates the paralysis instilled by heavy walls while it saves money and material. In point 4 (*La fenêtre en longueur*), they note that the strip window brightens the house. Point 5 (*La façade libre*) covers the free facade, which essentially makes the strip window possible.[71]

Le Corbusier showed that even standardized housing could accommodate human sensibilities as long as it provided a framework, or plan, flexible enough to serve individual lifestyles and to harmonize with the objects that accompanied them. Conceived in this way, the mass-produced house, the prototypical modern house, would become less threatening. Le Corbusier argued that standardization of the house would not destroy the creative, emotional individual, as many people feared, because it would also cater to individual choice. In 1929, Gray similarly asserted:

> I think that most people are mistaken in the meaning that they have agreed to give this word "type." For them "type" is synonymous with a creation that is simplified in the extreme and destined to be reproduced in series. But I understand it otherwise. *For me a* maison type *is only a house whose construction has been carried out according to the best and least costly technical procedures, and whose architecture attains the maximum of perfection for a given situation; that is to say, it is like a model not to be infinitely produced, but that will inspire the construction of other houses in the same spirit.*[72]

The work of Robert Mallet-Stevens also attested to this rather flexible conception of standardization in the design of houses.[73] Although he made use of modern production methods for his furniture and building elements, Mallet-Stevens was not particularly interested in the systematization of architectural form. He asserted that "detail is the only real thing which benefits from standardization. . . . In the house, certain parts such as doors, locks, switches, etc. could also be standardized after in-depth studies and be widely used thereafter but the whole, the overall concept, this will always be the work of an individual."[74] D. Deshoulières and H. Jeanneau characterize the oeuvre of Mallet-Stevens as the "work of an individual" whose buildings "relate to their environment and prevailing production conditions."[75] There is a notable—and frequently noted—consistency among his designs, but there is also great variety in scale, venue, and audience. Although Mallet-Stevens often worked for an elite clientele, he was by far the most effective of his contemporaries in promoting modernist sensibilities to the wider public.

This was largely because the range of his work was so extensive. In the brief period between 1920 and 1925, for example, Mallet-Stevens's oeuvre included many pieces of furniture, interior ensembles at the Salon d'Automne (one or more each year) and the Salon des Artistes Décorateurs, four interior remodels, film sets for five cinema productions, three villas (one of which also served as a set for the 1924 short film *Les mystères du*

Chateau de Dé [The mysteries of the Castle of Dice], by Man Ray), and a project for a modern city (published as a folio with an introduction by Frantz Jourdain) in addition to several other published and unpublished building design projects, two clothing retail showrooms, and a garage and showroom for Alfa Romeo. His was also the most visible modernist work at the Exposition Internationale des Arts Décoratifs et Industriels Modernes in 1925; he designed two pavilions, one of which was the Tourism Pavilion (fig. 4.22), a film studio, and the principal hall for the French embassy project submitted by the Société des Artistes Décorateurs (see fig. 4.10). After 1925, he was, along with Le Corbusier, one of the most prolific designers of modernist buildings in France. But even if Le Corbusier considered the problems that concerned working-class people and members of the *rentier* class more seriously than did Mallet-Stevens, it was through the design of houses for film sets and highly visible constructions at the Exposition Internationale des Arts Décoratifs et Industriels Modernes that Mallet-Stevens captured popular attention.

The great range of Mallet-Stevens's design interests and a hint of their popular appeal appeared first in a folio of drawings for *Une Cité Moderne,* which he began to develop before the war and continued in earnest after 1917. Unlike the comprehensive city planning projects that Tony Garnier and Le Corbusier developed at about the same time, *Une Cité Moderne* does not present a city plan. However, in their consistency of scale, detail, and relationship to the street, the building projects nevertheless "reveal a feeling for urbanism not immediately evident," to use the words of Deshoulières and Jeanneau.[76] If less sophisticated and thorough than its companions, *Une Cité Moderne* also exhibits a similarly broad scope. The drawings in the 1911 folio include a series of stylized interior and exterior perspectives representing institutional and residential buildings and spaces—a school, a cinema (fig. 4.23), a town hall, two shops along with their interiors, a hotel, an apartment block, several houses, a dining room, a bedroom, and so on. Almost all of the buildings in the 1922 folio are simple (although none is completely devoid of ornamentation) and of relatively modest scale; most recall some vernacular or other historical model. A notable addition to the earlier drawings is a project for workers' housing (fig. 4.24). The buildings in the postwar version of *Une Cité Moderne* thus seem distinctively up-to-date, but they clearly do not suggest a radical departure from the realm of the familiar. The drawings are lively and appealing, and one gets the impression that they are intended for an audience with modest aspirations toward modernism—for potential inhabitants, perhaps—rather than for critics or colleagues.

TOURISME
RENSEIGNE
MENTS DE
TOURISME·
AVIATION·
BILLETS·
DE CH·DE
FER NAVI
GATION·

4.22 Robert Mallet-
Stevens, Tourism
Pavilion, Exposition
Internationale des
Arts Décoratifs et
Industriels Modernes,
Paris, 1925

Mallet-Stevens undertook, but did not publish, a series of building sketches on the same theme in 1924 that all but dispenses with ornamentation and vernacular references. What remains is a series of buildings consistently detailed with smooth walls, flat roofs, expansive windows, and dramatic, often symmetrical massings. These correspond closely in appearance with his influential built works—houses for the Vicomte de Noailles and Paul Poirot—and his film sets of the mid 1920s.

The film sets in particular put the modernist attributes of Mallet-Stevens's houses very much in the public eye. For his first big-budget film collaboration, *L'inhumaine* (The heartless woman), Mallet-Stevens designed two houses, each of which was to exemplify one of the two principal characters, an imperious diva and an eccentric engineer. The house of the singer, for example, is aggressively large. Its immense prismatic volumes dominate the hillside from which it overlooks Paris. The house of the engineer, by contrast, is a diminutive although by no means a penurious dwelling of the impoverished *rentier* class (fig. 4.25). Its overlapping volumes mount up to support a massive laboratory tower, whose fantastic interior was designed by Fernand Léger. If, as Michel Louis asserts in a recent analysis of the film set, "the composition and handling of the façades presages the deliberately modern character of the occupants," it also reveals their idiosyncrasies.[77] As modernist as they appear, the houses are anything but rational in their intended effects. There is, however, a note of practicality in the use of modern houses for the sets of the film,

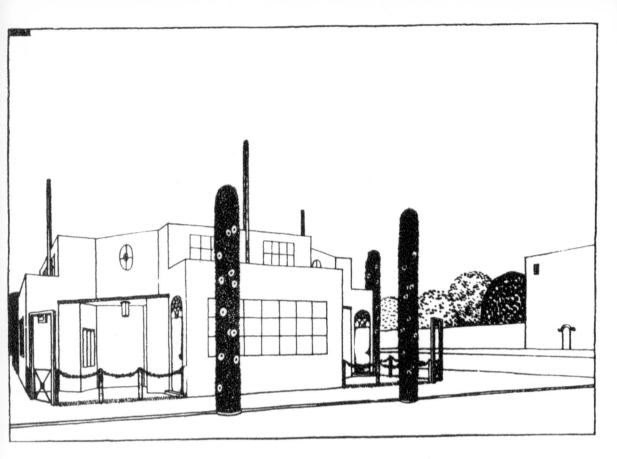

4.24 Robert Mallet-Stevens, worker's house, *Une Cité Moderne*, 1922

as Louis points out: "If the sobriety of the sets resulted from a desire for strict balance, it was also motivated by the need to produce an inexpensive product in a very short space of time. As far as the film's director was concerned, modern art also derived from the need for the economical use of Time."[78]

While it would not be judicious to associate the character of Mallet-Stevens's architectural work too closely with his highly stylized film sets, there are certainly some points to be taken away from them. First, the rational and purist aspects of modern houses, at least as Mallet-Stevens conceived them, were less consequential than their ability to express the personalities of their inhabitants. In 1925, Mallet-Stevens explained that the film set "must present the character before he appears, must indicate his social position, his tastes, his habits, his lifestyle, his personality."[79] Two of his built works from the mid 1920s emphasized how the cinematic personality of modern architecture extended to reality: the Tourism Pavilion at the 1925 Exposition Internationale des Arts Décoratifs et Industriels Modernes and the 1923 villa for the Vicomte Charles and Marie-Laure de Noailles at Hyères, France.

In the Tourism Pavilion, four interlocking planes of concrete thrust upward to support a simple, elegant clock (see fig. 4.22). Visitors weaving among the concrete planes at the ground level passed through the sun-lit concrete facade into a deep exhibition hall. There, they followed a frenetic exhibit of French history, "whose truncated images in stained glass of France's most glorious moments jostled each other 'like those on the retina of a tourist hurtling along at 100 kilometres an hour in an automobile.'"[80] Time, movement, tourism—the Tourism Pavilion sought to capture the escapist mood of the twenties. But unlike the lavish pavilions of the department stores farther along the esplanade, and much more like contemporary cinema, Mallet-Stevens's pavilion invited ordinary people in, not merely to witness the tastes of the *haute bourgeois*, but to participate in the spectacle of everyday life in France.

It is hardly surprising that Mallet-Stevens's first house should have played a role in French cinema (figs. 4.26, 4.27). The Vicomte de Noailles was, after all, an ardent supporter of film, and soon after the building was finished, he had avant-garde director Marcel L'Herbier film a documen-

4.25 Robert Mallet-Stevens, house of the engineer, film set for *L'inhumaine*, 1923

tary about the building. Several years later, he commissioned dadaist filmmaker Man Ray to shoot a short work of fiction there. In both productions, the house itself becomes a protagonist, even as it serves as the backdrop for the action that takes place in the film.

The villa functioned similarly in the quotidian task of housing the Noailles—as the setting for their modernist lifestyle and tastes. It included a small room designed by Theo van Doesburg, furniture by a host of important modernist designers such as Marcel Breuer, Pierre Chareau, Eileen Gray, and Francis Jourdain, and a garden by Gabriel Guévrékian. Also, in its manner of contending with its own setting, the house was cinematic. Man Ray was intrigued by the way its austere gray volumes, perched high on a hill overlooking the village of Hyères, cloaked the rich possibilities of its interior. For Ray, the house conjured an image of dice—so simple, yet so pregnant with possibilities—and thus the title of the film: *The Mysteries of the Castle of Dice*.

4.26 Robert Mallet-Stevens, villa of the Vicomte de Noailles, Hyères, France, 1923, exterior view

For all its cinematic appeal, though, the villa at Hyères is remarkably sympathetic to its setting. It is a frank and austere building but nevertheless very sensitive to the contours of the site and to the ruins of the old monastery on which it sits. A contemporary critic, Léon Deshairs, conveyed an impression of his visit there in 1928, saying, "The trees, masterpieces of time and the soil, have been respected to the utmost . . . seen from the plain, this new building fits in so well with the ruins that it seems like an offshoot of the defunct chateau, an offshoot in reinforced concrete not intended for defensive purposes, but for the greatest amount of hospitality."[81] Although certainly at ease with the collaborative effort of other modernist designers, its appeal is personal and its configuration very specific to the adjacent landscape and its vegetation. Even as Mallet-Stevens continued to construct characteristically plain, white volumes in the great many buildings he produced after 1925, the sense of poise and personality continually made his work difficult to categorize as "modern" in any orthodox sense.

FRENCH MODERN ARCHITECTURE

4.27 Robert Mallet-Stevens, villa of the Vicomte de Noailles, Hyères, France, 1923, interior view

Le Corbusier talked often about the flexibility of his designs for mass-produced houses rather than their uniformity. Like the regulating line, standardization was a means to an end, and that end was the human being. As Le Corbusier described it in the mid 1920s, the goal of architecture was to accommodate people, to extend their capabilities and to appeal to their sentiments. In their own ways, the French *architectes-*

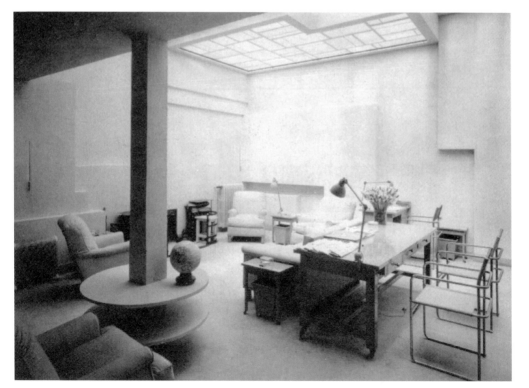

décorateurs of the time—Pierre Chareau, Eileen Gray, Francis Jourdain, and Robert Mallet-Stevens—pursued the same end. The Pavillon de l'Esprit Nouveau demonstrated the setting for a modern domestic scenario among smooth walls, discrete, effective equipment, and excellent modern art. One could just as well envision this scenario unfolding in the Maison de Verre, in E.1027, or in the villa at Hyères.

The flexible accommodation of life had, in fact, been a hallmark of progressive French design since at least 1911, when *coloriste* designers proposed interiors composed of disparate objects selected from a stock of well-established French examples. The study that André Mare had displayed in the 1911 Salon d'Automne was intended as a space to be lived in, not merely an art ensemble. At about the same time, Francis Jourdain marketed his interchangeable and built-in furniture for the "living-rooms" of the middle class.

For the progressive *architectes-décorateurs* of France, modern design at all scales was fundamentally responsible to human life, to human action and human aspiration, to work and leisure. They recognized that life unfolds unpredictably in the special conditions that surround it, and they sought to design buildings and rooms that were well suited to the unique conditions of contemporary life.

AFTERWORD

There is, first, a new conception of architecture as volume rather than as mass. Secondly, regularity rather than axial symmetry serves as the chief means of ordering design. These two principles, with a third proscribing arbitrary applied decoration, mark the productions of the international style.

—HENRY-RUSSELL HITCHCOCK AND PHILIP JOHNSON,
THE INTERNATIONAL STYLE

After Henry-Russell Hitchcock and Philip Johnson published *The International Style* in 1932, architectural critics and historians tended to emphasize the aesthetic and formal aspects of early modern architecture. Because of their clarity and overt simplicity, modern buildings lent themselves to this kind of analysis, but excessive focus on formalism obscured other intentions. Le Corbusier showed in the Pavillon de l'Esprit Nouveau that a modern work of architecture presents a synthesis of contemporary sensibilities. These appear in the building and also in the objects used to equip it for day-to-day living; some accommodate human needs, others amplify human aspirations—equipment and art. Furthermore, the relationships that develop among these things and the building make possible the expression of individual personalities. According to Le Corbusier, these relationships, which originated from "the material, sentimental, and spiritual demands of present-day life," were based only minimally on aesthetic considerations.[1]

Buildings similar in intention to the Pavillon de l'Esprit Nouveau appeared throughout Europe. Hitchcock and Johnson described these efforts as "parallel experiments," which seems an appropriate characterization. However, the authors of *The International Style* concluded that similar results necessarily implied the development of a uniform style. "Today a single new style has come into existence," they declared. "The aesthetic conceptions on which its disciplines are based derive from the experimentation of individualists. . . . The international style has become evident and definable only gradually as different innovators throughout the world have successfully carried out parallel experiments."[2] This was inconsistent with what contemporary architects said about their work.

A visual examination of the modern houses at the 1927 Deutscher Werkbund exhibition The Dwelling, held in Stuttgart, Germany (see fig. 1.4), which was the most comprehensive gathering of modernist architects to date, seems to justify Hitchcock's and Johnson's assumption. Clearly, there was much uniformity among the work of architects throughout Europe in the late 1920s.[3] Lost to this view, though, was a very different project that the many contributors to the exposition espoused. Form was not its goal. According to Ludwig Mies van der Rohe, who organized the exhibit,

> Form as a goal always ends in formalism. For this striving is not towards an inside, but towards an outside. But only a living inside has a living outside.
>
> Only intensity of life has intensity of Form. . . . Real form presupposes real life. . . . Life is for us the decisive factor. In all its fullness, in its spiritual and real commitments.[4]

Contemporary life—not style, not form, not aesthetics—was the foundation of modern architecture in the late 1920s. To see this, it was essential to understand architecture, interiors, furnishings, and equipment as essential and intertwined. Early modern architects, including most of those who exhibited houses in Stuttgart, hoped to show that a new, modern architecture would emerge out of a new way of living, especially domestic living. In an assessment of the Dwelling exhibition for *L'architecture vivante*, Jean Badovici reasserted this point: "The extraordinary transformations of European life call for a new expression."[5] Modern life was central to the intentions of early modern architects throughout Europe. However, inasmuch as life (and economics, politics, environments, and so on) varied in Europe, it followed that architecture, too, would vary.

With the formation of the Congrès Internationaux d'Architecture Moderne (CIAM) in 1928, it became possible for modern architects to state explicitly, for the first time, a set of common intentions. Formal and aesthetic considerations were conspicuously absent from their declarations. In the year following the Werkbund Dwelling exhibition in Stuttgart, CIAM convened in La Sarraz, Switzerland. At this first meeting, its members, who represented Austria, Belgium, France, Germany, Italy, the Netherlands, Spain, and Switzerland, drafted a founding document stating:

> The undersigned architects, representing the national groups of modern architects, affirm their uniformity of viewpoint regarding the fundamental conceptions of architecture and their professional obligations towards society.
>
> They insist particularly on the fact that "building" is an elementary activity of man intimately linked with evolution and the development of human life. The destiny of architecture is to express the orientation of the age. Works of architecture can spring only from the present time.
>
> They therefore refuse categorically to apply in their working methods means that may have been able to illustrate past societies; they affirm today the need for a new conception of architecture, which will fulfill the material, sentimental, and spiritual demands of present-day life.[6]

The La Sarraz declaration made it clear that modern architects from virtually every nation in Europe saw their common task to be "of an economic and sociological order, dedicated solely to the service of the human being."[7] But their uniformity of viewpoint never demanded uniformity of style. Although the signatories at La Sarraz agreed about the fundamental conception of modern architecture, and the role it was to play in society, they vehemently denied allegiance to a particular, international style of architecture. Sigfried Giedion, a founding member of CIAM, repudiated this claim in 1928. He protested that "there is nothing more ridiculous than continually asserting that modern architecture is international. It is clear that, for purely economic reasons, one builds differently in a region rich in iron than in a region rich in wood. The region, the climate and customs impose themselves on every organic construction."[8] This view was characteristic of many members of CIAM, and up until at least the 1940s, they continued to maintain that modern architecture is concerned primarily with human beings and the circumstances in which they find themselves. In an introduction to CIAM's Athens Charter of 1941, for example, Le Corbusier continued to ascribe the origins of contemporary architecture to contemporary dwellings: "There came into view, slowly but surely, a statute for the human abode which, pursuant to climates, customs, and races, allows for every diversity of form, but submits each of them to those vital precepts which must dictate the law for every undertaking: a sound notion of the human scale and a profound respect for individuality."[9] He could have pointed to significant and well-known differences in attitude toward housing in the early twentieth century to support this view: the predominance of the family house in England, the social basis of housing in Holland, the persistence of aristocratic biases in Austria, German efforts to unite industrial production with design, and French attempts to accommodate the idiosyncratic needs of individuals. These circumstances contributed to somewhat different conceptions of modern architecture.

The formalism of International Style modern architecture disregarded subtle differences among architects in Europe, which often manifested themselves most clearly in house interiors. In the 1940s, after the International Style of modern architecture was well entrenched, Eileen Gray lamented, "The poverty of modern architecture stems from the atrophy of sensuality. Everything is dominated by reason in order to create amazement without proper research. The art of the engineer is not enough if it is not guided by the primitive needs of men. Reason without instinct. We must mistrust merely pictorial elements if they are not assimilated by instinct."[10]

In recent years, the International Style, and, all too often, modern architecture with it, has come to be seen as ill-considered, narrow-minded, and inhumane. Critics of modern architecture protest that it did not take into account environmental, social, and individual circumstances, that it sought to articulate universal values rather than local conditions, that it, like many other disciplines, failed because it took seriously the untenable project of Universal Modernism handed down by the autocrats of Enlightenment thought. But what makes the work of the early modern architects, particularly the French *architectes-décorateurs* of the mid 1920s, particularly compelling even today is that it established architecture as an art of relationships dependent on situations—usually domestic situations—rather than on rules.[11] The form of a building therefore could not be simply "appropriate to its meaning," as had been true of architecture in the past, because in modern architecture, meaning emerged in the context of the lives of the people who inhabited the building.[12] It could not be merely "composed in accordance with precedent" as classical notions of architecture demanded, because circumstances exert control over the significance of a work of modern architecture.[13] Nor could it be a matter of personal choice alone, because modern buildings had to reflect broad cultural circumstances.[14] The *architectes-décorateurs* established that the center of all considerations "is ourselves: man, a constant, the fixed point that in truth is the only object of our concern."[15] And they determined the characteristics of modern architecture by first developing solutions to "the problem of the house," along with the circumstances of life it implied. Their aim for modern architecture extended beyond considerations of form or beauty because it was concerned primarily with *people* and their relationships with the world. The *architectes-décorateurs* of the 1920s, the designers of the first modern houses in France, showed that architecture was equal to the task.

NOTES

INTRODUCTION

1. Le Corbusier, *The City of Tomorrow and Its Planning*, trans. Frederick Etchells (New York: Dover Publications, 1987), 231, n. 2.

2. Le Corbusier and Pierre Jeanneret, *Oeuvre complète*, vol. 1, *1910–1929*, 14th ed. (Zurich: Les Editions d'Architecture [Artemis], 1995), 98.

3. Le Corbusier, *The Decorative Art of Today*, trans. James I. Dunnett (Cambridge, Mass.: The MIT Press, 1987), 132. Le Corbusier's emphasis.

4. Le Corbusier, *Towards a New Architecture*, trans. Frederick Etchells, 13th ed. (New York: Dover Publications, 1986), 227.

5. Le Corbusier cites this statement in the introduction to *The Decorative Art of Today* and attributes it to "the President of the Jury (a great Frenchman)" of the exposition. The president of the jury was Auguste Perret. Le Corbusier, *Decorative Art of Today*, xv.

6. Ibid., 84.

7. Le Corbusier and Jeanneret, *Oeuvre complète*, 98.

8. Le Corbusier, *Decorative Art of Today*, 131–37.

9. See ibid., xiii.

10. When he published *Towards a New Architecture* in 1923, Le Corbusier could declare, "The problem of the house is a problem of the epoch." It was, however, a problem as yet ill defined: "The problem of the house has not yet been formulated." Le Corbusier, *Towards a New Architecture*, 227, 107.

11. Ibid., 120. Le Corbusier's emphasis.

12. For an example of the use of this term, see Gaston Varenne, "L'esprit nouveau de Pierre Chareau," *Art et décoration* 43 (January–June 1923): 129.

13. Ludwig Mies van der Rohe, "On Form in Architecture," in *Programs and Manifestoes on 20th-Century Architecture*, ed. Ulrich Conrads, trans. Michael Bullock (Cambridge, Mass.: The MIT Press, 1970), 102.

14. Major contributors to the exhibition include Peter Behrens, Victor Bourgeois, Le Corbusier, Richard Döcker, Josef Frank, Walter Gropius, Ludwig Hilberseimer, Pierre Jeanneret, Ludwig Mies van der Rohe, J. J. P. Oud, Hans Poelzig, Adolf Rading, Hans Scharoun, Adolf G. Schneck, Mart Stam, Bruno Taut, and Max Taut.

15. Sigfried Giedion, *Mechanization Takes Command: A Contribution to Anonymous History* (New York: W. W. Norton, 1969), 526.

16. See, for example, Richard Pommer and Christian F. Otto, *Weissenhof 1927 and the Modern Movement in Architecture* (Chicago: University of Chicago Press, 1991). Mark Wigley also comments on this variety, particularly in the coloration of the walls in the various houses, in Mark Wigley, *White Walls, Designer Dresses: The Fashioning of Modern Architecture* (Cambridge, Mass.: The MIT Press, 1995), 302–30.

17. Congrès Internationaux d'Architecture Moderne (CIAM), "The La Sarraz Declaration," 1928, in Le Corbusier, *The Athens Charter* (New York: Grossman Publishers, 1973), 6. Signatories include H. P. Berlage, V. Bourgeois, P. Chareau, J. Frank, G. Guévrékian, M. E. Haefeli, H. Häring, H. Hoste, P. Jeanneret, Le Corbusier, A. Lurçat, E. May, A. G. Mercadal, Hannes Meyer, W. M. Moser, E. C. Rava, G. Rietveld, A. Sartoris, Hans Schmidt, Mart Stam, R. Steiger, H. R. von der Mühll, and Juan de Zavala.

18. On the role of fashion in the shaping of modern design, see Wigley, *White Walls, Designer Dresses*, and Nancy J. Troy, *Couture Culture: A Study in Modern Art and Fashion* (Cambridge, Mass.: The MIT Press, 2003). The role played by mass culture and consumerism in the development of modern architecture is discussed in Beatriz Colomina, *Privacy and Publicity: Modern Architecture as Mass Media* (Cambridge, Mass.: The MIT Press, 1994); Frederic J. Schwartz, *The Werkbund: Design Theory and Mass Culture before the First World War* (New Haven, Conn.: Yale University Press, 1996); and Kathleen James-Chakraborty, *German Architecture for a Mass Audience* (New York: Routledge, 2000). On the subject of the ambivalent but necessary relationship that developed between avant-garde art and popular culture early in the twentieth century, see Arthur C. Danto, *The Transfiguration of the Commonplace: A Philosophy of Art* (Cambridge, Mass.: Harvard University Press, 1981); Christine Poggi, *In Defiance of Painting: Cubism, Futurism, and the Invention of Collage* (New Haven, Conn.: Yale University Press, 1992); and Jeffrey Weiss, *The Popular Culture of Modern Art: Picasso, Duchamp, and Avant-Gardism* (New Haven, Conn.: Yale University Press, 1994).

19. Christopher Reed, ed., *Not at Home: The Suppression of Domesticity in Modern Art and Architecture* (New York: Thames and Hudson, 1996).

20. Ibid., 8.

21. Witold Rybczynski, *Home: A Short History of an Idea* (New York: Viking, 1986), 190.

22. See, for example, Wigley, *White Walls, Designer Dresses*, and Troy, *Couture Culture*.

23. Wigley, *White Walls, Designer Dresses*, 144.

24. Ibid., 102.

25. Ibid., 111.

26. Ibid., 216.

27. Tag Gronberg, "Making Up the Modern City: Modernity on Display at the 1925 International Exposition," in *L'Esprit Nouveau: Purism in Paris, 1918–1925*, ed. Carol S. Eliel (Los Angeles: Los Angeles County Museum of Art in association with Harry N. Abrams, 2001), 123.

28. Alice Friedman, *Women and the Making of the Modern House: A Social and Architectural History* (New York: Abrams, 1998), 16. This subject is also treated in more general terms under the heading "The Feminist Movement and the Rational Household," in Giedion, *Mechanization Takes Command*, 512–26.

29. See Reed, *Not at Home*.

30. See Reyner Banham, *Theory and Design in the First Machine Age*, 2nd ed. (Cambridge, Mass.: The MIT Press, 1980). This understanding of modern architecture

dates back at least to the early 1930s. Henry-Russell Hitchcock and Philip Johnson argued in 1932, for example, that modern architecture distinguished itself from the eclectic architecture of the nineteenth century primarily by embodying rational design principles and incorporating standardized architectural elements, which led almost inevitably to the abstraction of architectural forms. See Henry-Russell Hitchcock and Philip Johnson, *The International Style* (New York: W. W. Norton, 1995). These forms characterized a "rationalist wing" of architects, to use the words Spiro Kostof penned fifty years later, who developed a "distinctive language of design" that emphasized "the free plan; new building techniques based on materials like concrete and steel; the visual precedent of Loos' stark white cubes; the functional tradition of the architecture of industry." Spiro Kostof, *A History of Architecture: Settings and Rituals*, 2nd ed. (New York: Oxford University Press, 1995), 701. In 1983, Alberto Pérez-Gómez asserted similarly that modern architecture expressed a strongly rationalist view that was indifferent to human concerns: "the geometry of the Bauhaus, the International Style, and the Modern Movement . . . ," he declared, "was essentially the undifferentiated product of a technological world view. As part of a theory that cast off metaphysical speculation, the simple and anonymous geometry of most contemporary architecture speaks only to technological process, not to the world of man." Alberto Pérez-Gómez, *Architecture and the Crisis of Modern Science* (Cambridge, Mass.: The MIT Press, 1983), 311. If this view formed the background to a necessary reevaluation of the ethical and practical goals of architecture, it did so partly by overemphasizing the dehumanizing qualities of modern architecture. The tactic elicited a vigorous defense of modernism that continues even now, but which met at first with "howls of protest," to quote Hilton Kramer, because, during the early 1980s, "In the academy, in the museums, and in the media, modernism was in the process of being unmasked and 'deconstructed' as either a bourgeois plot or an outmoded aesthetic idea or both. . . ." Hilton Kramer, "The First Five Years: An Introduction," in *The New Criterion Reader: The First Five Years* (New York: The Free Press, 1988), xiii. The defense of modernism gained many adherents, however, and a rich scholarship has since developed to show that modern architecture was very much involved with humanity.

31. For an explanation of the academic origins of rational modern architecture, see Joseph Rykwert, *The First Moderns: The Architects of the Eighteenth Century* (Cambridge, Mass.: The MIT Press, 1991). See also Anthony Vidler, *The Writing of the Walls: Architectural Theory in the Late Enlightenment* (Princeton, N.J.: Princeton Architectural Press, 1987). For an account of the scientific orientation of rational modern architecture, see Pérez-Gómez, *Architecture*. Steven Toulmin gives a more general account of the modernist project in *Cosmopolis: The Hidden Agenda of Modernity* (Chicago: University of Chicago Press, 1990).

32. In addition to the contributions of seventeen architects and fifty-five designers to the full-scale housing exhibit, the exposition also included a huge display of work by architects throughout the world (including 531 projects) and a very large display of household products from German industries. See Karin Kirsch, *The Weissenhofsiedlung: Experimental Housing Built for the Deutscher Werkbund, Stuttgart, 1927* (New York: Rizzoli, 1989), 17–31.

33. Hermann Muthesius, *Style-Architecture and Building-Art: Transformations of Architecture in the Nineteenth Century and Its Present Condition*, trans. Stanford Anderson (Santa Monica, Calif.: Getty Center for the History of Art and the Humanities, 1994), 95.

34. Hermann Muthesius, "Aims of the Werkbund," in *Programs and Manifestoes on 20th-Century Architecture*, ed. Ulrich Conrads (Cambridge, Mass.: The MIT Press, 1970), 26–27.

35. See W. R. Lethaby, "Modern German Architecture and What We May Learn from It," in *Form in Civilization: Collected Papers on Art and Labour*, 2nd ed. (London: Oxford University Press, 1957), 81. He is referring here to several works on English architecture that Muthesius produced in the early 1900s. These include a general work on contemporary English architecture, *Die englische Baukunst der Gegenwart: Beispiele neuer englisher Profanbauten* (Leipzig, Germany: Cosmoz, 1900); a more specialized study of religious architecture, *Die neuer kirchliche Baukunst in England: Entwicklung, Bedingungen und Grundzüge des Kirchenbaues der englischen Staatskirche und der Secten* (Berlin: W. Ernst & Sohn, 1901); and a minutely detailed study on the English house, *Das englische Haus: Entwicklung, Beingungen, Anlage, Aufbau, Einrichtung und Innenraum*, 3 vols. (Berlin: Ernst Wasmuth, 1904–5).

36. Lethaby, "Modern German Architecture," 81.

37. Ibid., 80.

38. See Lucius Burckhardt, ed., *The Werkbund: History and Ideology 1907–1933*, trans. Pearl Sanders (New York: Barron's, 1980).

39. See Charles L'Eplattenier et al., *Un mouvement d'art à La Chaux-de-Fonds à propos de la Nouvelle Section de l'Ecole d'Art* (La Chaux-de-Fonds, Switzerland: Imprimerie Georges Dubois, 1914).

40. Ch.-E. Jeanneret, *Etude sur le mouvement d'art décoratif en Allemagne* (La Chaux-de-Fonds, Switzerland, 1912), 3.

41. Hector Guimard, letter to Henri Bopp-Boillot, March 28, 1914. Reprinted in L'Eplattenier et al., *Un mouvement d'art*, 35.

42. See Wigley, *White Walls, Designer Dresses*, 180.

43. Jeanneret, *Etude*, 13.

44. Walter Gropius, "Bauhaus Dessau—Principles of Bauhaus Production," reprinted in Hans M. Wingler, *The Bauhaus*, trans. Wolfgang Jabs and Basil Gilbert, ed. Joseph Stein (Cambridge, Mass.: The MIT Press, 1969), 109.

45. Le Corbusier published three texts on design between 1923 and 1929: *Towards a New Architecture, The Decorative Art of Today*, and *The City of Tomorrow and Its Planning* (originally published under the title *Urbanisme*).

46. That France had little to contribute to modern architecture is a consistent presumption in many of the standard histories of the subject. In *Pioneers of Modern Architecture*, for example, Nikolaus Pevsner asserts that "the contribution of France to the Modern Movement before the war consists exclusively in the work of two architects: Auguste Perret and Tony Garnier." Nikolaus Pevsner, *Pioneers of Modern Design from William Morris to Walter Gropius*, Pelican ed. (Harmondsworth, England: Penguin Books, 1975), 179. Similarly, in *Space, Time and Architecture*, which was first published in 1939 and went through five editions over the next

twenty-five years, Sigfried Giedion asserts that "the new architecture had first to develop out of those elements that had remained sound: iron and ferro-concrete. But by 1930 the new means of expression had been attained. Now it was possible to strive for further development and to dare the leap from the rational-functional to the irrational-organic." Sigfried Giedion, *Space, Time and Architecture: The Growth of a New Tradition*, 5th ed. (Cambridge, Mass.: Harvard University Press, 1967), 620. Reyner Banham follows the same line of thinking, stating, "Outside the contribution of engineers like Freyssinet, France gave to the developing practice of a new architecture before 1914 only the work of two members of the academic secession to Gaudet: . . . Auguste Perret and Tony Garnier." Banham, *Theory and Design*, 35. Kenneth Frampton takes a similar view in his 1985 study *Modern Architecture: A Critical History*, 3rd ed. (New York: Thames and Hudson, 1992), chapters 10 and 11, as does Hanno-Walter Kruft in his more recent book, *A History of Architectural Theory from Vitruvius to the Present*, trans. Ronald Taylor, Elsie Callander, and Antony Wood (London: Zwemmer; Princeton, N.J.: Princeton Architectural Press, 1994), 393–402.

47. William Logue, *From Philosophy to Sociology: The Evolution of French Liberalism, 1870–1914* (De Kalb: Northern Illinois University Press, 1983), 9.

48. Even if some progressive artists in the 1910s and 1920s were openly antagonistic to the decidedly bourgeois interests of the Third Republic, as Jeffrey Weiss points out, their work was nevertheless compelled by bourgeois interests. In his recent study of French avant-garde art before World War I, Weiss argues that Cubism, and Cubist collage in particular, commented upon not only the interests of the liberal middle class but also its inability to comprehend this avant-garde commentary. "Collage," he states, "almost symbolizes the tension between popular culture and incomprehension in modern art of the pre-war period. Further, possessed of an iconography that could hardly have been more familiar, the works existed in their time at a considerable remove from popular consumption." Weiss, *Popular Culture of Modern Art*, xviii.

1 RAISING UP THE BOURGEOIS HOME

1. Although this was certainly the primary intention of structures such as the 300-meter tower that Gustave Eiffel designed for the 1889 Exposition Universelle, as well as the Gallery of Machines constructed under the direction of Charles-Louis-Ferdinand Dutert for the same exposition, French engineers were developing solutions to practical problems at the time. New modes of transportation and production of goods along with increasingly large public spectacles demanded long-span structures—rail stations, railway bridges, warehouses, large public venues for theater and sport, etc. The rational basis of the solution to these problems derived directly from Enlightenment thinking, which resulted in the systematization of statics. However, it is essential to note that the motivations for engineered works of the nineteenth century in France sprang largely from the needs and aspirations of the middle and working classes. Indeed, given the widespread

reaction against these engineered structures that occurred after 1900 and the consequent resurgence of the decorative arts, it would appear that a modernist project was not of so much interest at the time as was the potential for applying its discoveries in contemporaneous circumstances. In Germany, a similar preoccupation with the application of new technologies to the creation of furniture and equipment for the home superseded interest in the intellectual basis (rational, lawful, universal) of these technologies.

2. Le Corbusier, *Towards a New Architecture*, trans. Frederick Etchells, 13th ed. (New York: Dover Publications, 1986), 6.

3. Auguste Choisy, *Histoire de l'architecture* (Paris: Editions Vincent Fréal & Cie, 1964), 2:593.

4. The tower was reviled by the contemporary artistic community. For an account, see Caroline Mathieu, ed., *1889: La Tour Eiffel et l'Exposition Universelle* (Paris: Editions de la Réunion des Musées Nationaux, 1989).

5. Emile Zola, quoted in an interview with Frantz Jourdain, "Que pensez-vous de l'architecture moderne?" *Revue des arts décoratifs* 16 (1896): 95. See Debora L. Silverman, *Art Nouveau in Fin-de-Siècle France: Politics, Psychology and Style* (Berkeley: University of California Press, 1989), 7.

6. Zola, quoted in "Souvenirs des Goncourts," *La revue encyclopédique* 153 (August 8, 1896): 552. This passage quoted in Silverman, *Art Nouveau in Fin-de-Siècle France*, 7.

7. See Silverman, *Art Nouveau in Fin-de-Siècle France*, 5.

8. Ibid., 10.

9. For two rather different accounts of the development of household technologies, see Sigfried Giedion, *Mechanization Takes Command: A Contribution to Anonymous History* (New York: W. W. Norton, 1969), and Witold Rybczynski, *Home: A Short History of an Idea* (New York: Viking, 1986).

10. Emile Zola quoted in "Souvenirs des Goncourts," *La revue encyclopédique* 153 (August 8, 1896): 552.

11. According to Silverman, "French art nouveau provided a visual language for this modern psychological discovery, as modern in its way as the Eiffel Tower." *Art Nouveau in Fin-de-Siècle France*, 10.

12. See Mathieu, *1889*, 40.

13. "Rapport de la Commission Consultative," *Le génie civil*, 4.21 (March 21 and 28, 1885). This passage quoted in Mathieu, *1889*, 13. My translation.

14. These were subdivided into nine categories and eighty-three subcategories. For a more thorough account of these categories, see Mathieu, *1889*, 31, 40.

15. Charles Garnier, letter, *L'illustration* 2437 (November 9, 1889): 399. Excerpted in Mathieu, *1889*, 42. My translation.

16. Before the exhibition and his appointment as architectural adviser, Garnier was one of a number of influential artists who signed a letter protesting the tower.

17. There were many historical inaccuracies in this exhibit, resulting in part from a lack of sufficient archaeological information. Garnier admitted that many of the house ensembles were purely his own creations. See Mathieu, *1889*, 139.

18. For an account of the insinuation of electricity into the home, see Rybczynski, *Home*, 151.

19. This passage quoted in Philippe Julian, *The Triumph of Art Nouveau: Paris Exhibition 1900*, trans. Stephen Hardman (London: Phaidon Press, 1974), 98. Original source not cited.

20. Ibid., 99.

21. Ibid., 26.

22. This passage quoted in ibid., 99–100. Original source not cited.

23. Much of this work was also recorded and disseminated in another nineteenth-century innovation: illustrated design journals. These became increasingly important mouthpieces for designers, design theorists, and critics into the twentieth century. Among the more important of these were *The Studio*, *Hobby Horse*, *Ver Sacrum*, *Art et décoration*, *Cahiers d'aujourd'hui*, and *Dekorative Kunst* and later *De Stijl*, *L'esprit nouveau*, *L'architecture d'aujourd'hui*, and *L'architecture vivante*.

24. Eugène-Emmanuel Viollet-le-Duc, *Lectures on Architecture*, trans. Benjamin Bucknall (New York: Dover Publications, 1987), 2:250.

25. Ibid., 2:144.

26. Ibid., 2:271.

27. Ibid., 2:247.

28. William Logue, *From Philosophy to Sociology: The Evolution of French Liberalism, 1870–1914* (De Kalb: Northern Illinois University Press, 1983), 75.

29. Logue discusses the motivations and development of the public education system under the Third Republic in ibid., 73–94.

30. On the subject of the increasing artistic authority of the bourgeoisie in France, see Lisa Tiersten, "The Chic Interior and the Feminine Modern: Home Decorating as High Art in Turn-of-the-Century Paris," in *Not at Home: The Suppression of Domesticity in Modern Art and Architecture*, ed. Christopher Reed (New York: Thames and Hudson, 1996), 18–32.

31. Tiersten, "Chic Interior," 18.

32. Neither of these could be characterized as "compliant" students, however, as each maintained tumultuous relationships with the Academy of Fine Arts.

33. See, for example, Reyner Banham, *Theory and Design in the First Machine Age*, 2nd ed. (Cambridge, Mass.: The MIT Press, 1980), 35.

34. Tony Garnier, *Une Cité Industrielle*, ed. Riccardo Mariani, trans. Andrew Ellis (New York: Rizzoli, 1990), 43.

35. Ibid., 43.

36. Ibid., 47.

37. Giedion states that "Tony Garnier made reinforced concrete the basis of all his work." *Space, Time and Architecture: The Growth of a New Tradition*, 5th ed. (Cambridge, Mass.: Harvard University Press, 1967), 332. Although it certainly figures into his work, concrete can hardly be said to be its basis, particularly in the Cité Industrielle.

38. Tony Garnier, *Une Cité Industrielle*, 47.

39. See ibid., 13, 29–32.

40. At least since the publication of Peter Collins, *Concrete: The Vision of a New*

Architecture: A Study of Auguste Perret and His Precursors (New York: Horizon Press, 1959).

41. Karla Britton, *Auguste Perret* (New York: Phaidon Press, 2001), 8.

42. Auguste Perret, "Architecture" [1933], reprinted in ibid., 238–43.

43. See Britton, *Auguste Perret*, 25–26.

44. See ibid., 23.

45. Kenneth Frampton, *Modern Architecture: A Critical History*, 3rd ed. (New York: Thames and Hudson, 1992), 106.

46. Britton, *Auguste Perret*, 142.

47. Giedion, *Space, Time and Architecture*, 328. The tone of Giedion's comment here is slightly pejorative, the message being that the apartment is not quite "modern."

48. The courtyards were a notable innovation at the time. For an account of contemporary reaction, see Roberto Gargiani, *Auguste Perret: La théorie et l'oeuvre* (Paris: Gallimard/Electa 1994), 222.

49. For an account of these buildings and their apparent banality, see Britton, *Auguste Perret*, 104–33. See also Gargiani, *Auguste Perret*, 60–95.

50. Jean Dubuffet, letter to Auguste Perret, 2 August 1946, AA, Box 535 AP 321. This passage quoted in Britton, *Auguste Perret*, 107.

51. Perret, "Architecture," 243.

52. In his analysis of the Maison Cubiste, David Cottington discusses Perret's association with the group, noting that Raymond Duchamp-Villon in particular shared Perret's enthusiasm for steel and concrete. Although this was no doubt one result of Perret's presence, I believe his influence was subtler. As his later studio-houses suggest, Perret was capable of developing superb interior compositions that were very much to the tastes of his artist collaborators. See David Cottington, "The Maison Cubiste and the Meaning of Modernism in Pre-1914 France," in *Architecture and Cubism*, ed. Eve Blau and Nancy J. Troy (Cambridge, Mass.: The MIT Press, 1997), 19–20.

53. Prominent members of these groups include Guillaume Apollinaire, Raymond Duchamp-Villon, André Gide, Chana Orloff, Amédée Ozenfant, Pablo Picasso, Paul Poiret, Maurice Ravel, and Paul Valéry.

54. This group included, among others, Raymond Duchamp-Villon, André Mare, and Amédée Ozenfant and, later, in its postwar reincarnation, Le Corbusier. For an account of their activities, see chapter 2.

55. Frampton, *Modern Architecture*, 101.

56. For a discussion of the British contribution to the Exposition Universelle of 1855 and later, see Patricia Mainardi, *Art and Politics of the Second Empire: The Universal Expositions of 1855 and 1867* (New Haven, Conn.: Yale University Press, 1987), 103–7.

57. Marius Vachon, *La guerre artistique avec l'Allemagne: L'organisation de la victoire* (Paris: Payot, 1916), 153–54.

58. Clearly, the matter of aesthetic reform in industry was no less serious in France than in England; however, the liberal politics of the Second Empire and,

later, of the Third Republic precluded the kind of direct federal intervention in aesthetic matters that had reinforced reform efforts in England. William Logue argues: "That (major) aspect of liberalism which insists on the limitation of government, on the careful definition of its legitimate authority, and on the constitutional structure most likely to ensure the respect for those limits received a powerful impetus from the Napoleonic experience." Logue, *From Philosophy to Sociology*, 4.

59. Silverman, *Art Nouveau in Fin-de-Siècle France*, 111.

60. Tiersten, "Chic Interior," 21.

61. Gustave Geffroy, "La vie artistique," *Les temps nouveaux* 1, no. 2 (1895). This passage quoted in Eugenia W. Herbert, *The Artist and Social Reform: France and Belgium, 1885–1898* (New Haven, Conn.: Yale University Press, 1961), 157.

62. Tiersten, "Chic Interior," 23–24.

63. See ibid., 19. See also Nancy J. Troy, *Modernism and the Decorative Arts in France: Art Nouveau to Le Corbusier* (New Haven, Conn.: Yale University Press, 1991), 58–59, which quotes one anonymous commentator who complained that industry "makes tinsel for the bourgeoisie and junk for the masses"; and J., "L'art industriel," *L'art décoratif* 1 (March 1899): 253.

64. De Goncourt recommended that decorative artists revive styles, particularly the rococo, representative of France's aristocratic past. See Silverman, *Art Nouveau in Fin-de-Siècle France*, 23.

65. In purely economic terms, the hesitancy of French furniture producers to respond to demands of the middle-class market made them vulnerable to competition from abroad. Between 1873 and 1889, to cite one measure, exports of furniture from France dropped by a third, while imports of furniture increased at an even greater rate. See ibid., 54.

66. Among Bing's most important contributions was to bring Japanese and American crafts to the attention of French collectors. For a full accounting of Siegfried Bing's contribution to the decorative arts in France, see Gabriel P. Weisberg, *Art Nouveau Bing: Paris Style 1900* (New York: Harry N. Abrams, 1986).

67. Siegfried Bing and Georges Lemmen, *L'Art Nouveau* (1895), reprinted in Weisberg, *Art Nouveau Bing*, 91, fig. 88.

68. Exhibits included Japanese prints as well as work by the English designers William Benson, Frank Brangwyn, and Charles Conder, the Belgian designers Henri van de Velde and Henri Jaeger, and American designer Louis Comfort Tiffany, among others.

69. Siegfried Bing, "L'Art Nouveau," trans. unknown, *The Architectural Record* 12 (1902): 279–85. Reprinted in Siegfried Bing, *Artistic America, Tiffany Glass and Art Nouveau* (Cambridge, Mass.: The MIT Press, 1970), 222.

70. Siegfried Bing, "L'Art Nouveau," trans. Irene Sargent, *The Craftsman* 5, no. 1 (October 1903). Reprinted in Bing, *Artistic America*, 229.

71. Bing visited La Maison d'Art in 1895 with the prominent young art critic from Germany Julius Meier-Graefe, and it was evidently on Meier-Graefe's advice that Bing decided to arrange L'Art Nouveau in this way. Like Bing, Meier-Graefe

had argued for the need to eliminate distinctions among the arts. See Kenworth Moffett, *Meier-Graefe as Art Critic* (Munich: Prestel Verlag, 1973), 13.

72. See, for example, Arsène Alexandre, "L'Art Nouveau," from *Le Figaro*, December 28, 1895, reprinted in Victor Champier, "Les expositions de L'Art Nouveau," *Revue des arts décoratifs* 16 (1896): 4. For a full treatment of the reactions to Bing's gallery in the press, see Weisberg, *Art Nouveau Bing*, 77–95.

73. See Siegfried Bing, introduction, *Salon annuel des peintures japonaises*, première année (Paris: Pillet & Demoulin, 1883), 5. For an account of the influence of the Far East on French court styles, see Joseph Rykwert, *The First Moderns: The Architects of the Eighteenth Century* (Cambridge, Mass.: The MIT Press, 1991).

74. Bing, "L'Art Nouveau" (1902), 222.

75. Ibid. (1903), 230.

76. Gabriel Mourey, "L'Art Nouveau at Paris," *Art Journal* 59 (1897): 89–90.

77. For an account of the influence of decorating handbooks and journal articles on home interiors, see Tiersten, "Chic Interior," 21, 27.

78. Bing, "L'Art Nouveau" (1903), 231.

79. Quoted by Bing from an unknown prospectus in Bing, "L'Art Nouveau" (1902), 215.

80. Vachon, *La guerre artistique avec l'Allemagne*, 153–54; Geffroy, "La vie artistique," quoted in Herbert, *Artist and Social Reform*, 157.

81. Clausen notes that Jourdain was animated and vociferous. He was influential, but hotheaded enough that he sometimes met with bemusement. See Meredith L. Clausen, *Frantz Jourdain and the Samaritaine: Art Nouveau Theory and Criticism* (Leiden, Netherlands: E. J. Brill, 1987), 14–16.

82. Léon Bourgeois was premier of France from November 1895 to April 1896, after having served as minister of public instruction and fine arts. Jourdain, like Bourgeois, was influenced by the socialist tendencies of William Morris, but, as Silverman notes, the popularization of French art was different from that of the Arts and Crafts movement in England. The creation of artworks remained the province of a select few in France, even as its inspiration and appeal was broadened. In France, art could never be by the people so much as for them. Silverman argues that, in France, the artist was "by definition different from other people," but he "could heal the split between self and others by internalizing the ideology of debt, duty, and solidarity. Continual contact with 'communal sources' would discharge the debt to society while this duty to the whole would enliven the artist's creative spirit." Silverman, *Art Nouveau in Fin-de-Siècle France*, 139.

83. Frantz Jourdain, "Le Salon d'Automne," *Excelsior*, September 29, 1911. This passage quoted in Arlette Barré-Despond and Suzanne Tise, *Jourdain* (New York: Rizzoli, 1991), 85.

84. Elie Faure, preface, *Le Salon d'Automne*, exh. cat., October 15, 1905. This passage quoted in Barré-Despond and Tise, *Jourdain*, 105.

85. See Faure, preface.

86. Herbert argues that most nineteenth-century artists, whether conservative or liberal, thought of themselves as external observers of contemporary society. They also believed, however, that they were powerful agents for the

expression and formation of culture. This was particularly true of the 1890s in France. The virulent events of that decade—workers strikes and the Dreyfus affair especially—inaugurated an important change in this relationship. Artists depicted these events vividly in their work as they had done for several decades; however, they also got involved in them. Emile Zola's explosive participation in the Dreyfus affair, to cite a particularly vivid example, indicates the extent to which the artistic world had descended into the fray of contemporary experience. Rather than elevating the masses, which had been the goal of early reform movements, artists began to engross themselves in the concerns of ordinary people. See Herbert, *Artist and Social Reform*, xiv; see also Mainardi, *Art and Politics*, 1.

87. Mainardi argues that the 1867 Exposition Universelle in Paris, which closely followed the death of Jean-Auguste-Dominique Ingres, the most prominent of the academic history painters, marked an important turning point for French painting. It was at that time that genre painting garnered serious consideration even among members of the Academy of Fine Arts. See Mainardi, *Art and Politics*, 89, 154–77.

88. See Gabriel P. Weisberg, ed., *The European Realist Tradition* (Bloomington: Indiana University Press, 1982), vii.

89. See Mainardi, *Art and Politics*, 172–73.

90. Recent studies of the Realist movement in painting have shown that aside from its social consciousness, Realism was not very unified. In fact, Realism was driven by two widely different intentions. These are made evident in the response that various Realist artists received. Painters, who maintained a relatively uncritical view of the living conditions of the working class, generally received support from social conservatives. Indeed, Napoleon III had an aggressive policy of rewarding these artists, in order to disseminate a sense of goodwill between the government and the populace, which, as he was well aware, posed a potentially great threat to his position. Other painters, Courbet in particular, used painting as a vehicle for social criticism; their reception in official circles was generally quite cool during the Second Empire. For a concise description of the different motivations within Realism, see Robert Bezucha, "Being Realistic about Realism: Art and the Social History of Nineteenth-Century France," in *The European Realist Tradition*, ed. Gabriel P. Weisberg (Bloomington: Indiana University Press, 1982), 1–14. For a description of Napoleon III's role in promoting some Realist painters, see Albert Boime, "The Second Empire's Official Realism," in *European Realist Tradition*, 31–123, and Mainardi, *Art and Politics*, 123–27. Geneviève Lacambre notes the connection between the Second Republic and Realist painters with left-leaning tendencies; see Geneviève Lacambre, "Toward an Emerging Definition of Naturalism in French Nineteenth-Century Painting," in *European Realist Tradition*, 231.

91. Lacambre, "Toward an Emerging Definition," 231–32.

92. This is Henri Bergson's terminology. See Henri Bergson, *Matter and Memory*, trans. N. M. Paul and W. S. Palmer (New York: Zone Books, 1991), 11. See also Mark Antliff, "Bergson and Cubism: A Reassessment," *Art Journal* 47 (Winter 1988): 341–49.

93. Bergson, *Matter and Memory*, 10.

94. George Heard Hamilton, *Painting and Sculpture in Europe, 1880–1940* (New York: Penguin Books, 1972), 76.

95. Robert Goldwater, *Symbolism* (New York: Harper & Row, 1979), 32.

96. See Hamilton, *Painting and Sculpture*, 75.

97. Maurice Denis, "Définition du néotraditionnisme," *Art et critique* 23 and 30 (August 1890). This passage quoted in Hamilton, *Painting and Sculpture*, 107, and also in Goldwater, *Symbolism*, 18. Denis was a Symbolist painter and a decorative muralist. He contributed a number of murals to Siegfried Bing's L'Art Nouveau gallery in 1895.

98. The emerging emphasis on the decorative function of painting after 1890 has been the frequent subject of discussion. See, for example, David Cottington, *Cubism in the Shadow of War: The Avant-Garde and Politics in Paris, 1905–1914* (New Haven, Conn.: Yale University Press, 1998), 67–68; and Christine Poggi, *In Defiance of Painting: Cubism, Futurism and the Invention of Collage* (New Haven, Conn.: Yale University Press, 1992), 138–40.

99. Albert Aurier, "Le Symbolisme en peinture, Paul Gauguin," *Mercure de France* 2, no. 15 (March 1891): 163. Quoted in Poggi, *In Defiance of Painting*, 138.

100. Henri Matisse, "Notes d'un peintre," *La grande revue* (Paris, December 25, 1908). This passage quoted in Hamilton, *Painting and Sculpture*, 169. My italics.

101. The Fauves were perhaps the first artists to insist that their work was purely compositional and, by implication, intended to be viewed by everyone on equal terms. Since their effect was immediate and direct, they required no previous understanding. See Hamilton, *Painting and Sculpture*, 34–57. This distinguishes them from earlier proponents of "effect" in art. Degas, Monet, and Seurat, who all achieved similar results in terms of compositional effect, for example, never denied that their paintings were also didactic. Mallarmé, who in 1861 recommended that the primary value of a work of architecture should lie in the effect that it produces, always assumed that effect had transcendent implications, intending that it would somehow carry one beyond the work (into poetic sentiments, for example). See ibid., 157.

102. Jack D. Flam, ed., *Matisse on Art* (Berkeley: University of California Press, 1994), 49.

103. Leo Steinberg, "The Algerian Women and Picasso at Large," in *Other Criteria: Confrontations with Twentieth-Century Art* (New York: Oxford University Press, 1972), 159.

104. Colin Rowe and Robert Slutzky, "Transparency: Literal and Phenomenal," in *The Mathematics of the Ideal Villa, and Other Essays*, by Colin Rowe (Cambridge, Mass.: The MIT Press, 1976), 161. This is based on a quote taken from Lásló Moholy-Nagy, *Vision in Motion* (Chicago: P. Theobald, 1947), 157.

105. Poggi, *In Defiance of Painting*, 153.

106. Jeffrey Weiss, *The Popular Culture of Modern Art: Picasso, Duchamp, and Avant-Gardism* (New Haven, Conn.: Yale University Press, 1994), xviii.

107. Poggi asserts that "the practice of collage techniques indicates a denial of the precious, fine art status of traditional works of art as well as an attempt to

subvert the seemingly inevitable process by which art becomes a commodity in the modern world." It was difficult for the art market to ascribe value to works composed of the cast-off fragments of mundane materials. Thus, Cubist collage approaches commonplace experience on one level by accepting materials drawn from mass culture as its constitutive material, yet, on another, it distances itself from direct experience by requiring a difficult act of interpretation to understand its complex and circumstantial intentions. "The Cubists," she declares, "found their public in the extremely restricted circle of other avante-garde artists, poets, critics, dealers and a few bourgeois amateurs. But within these narrowed margins, there was a positive identification with the degraded pleasures of popular mass culture." Poggi, *In Defiance of Painting*, 128, 141, 157. On the offense to bourgeois sensibilities, see Weiss, *Popular Culture of Modern Art*, 20–36.

108. Mare and his collaborators sought to capitalize on bourgeois aspirations to prosperity, using Salon exhibition displays to market their work directly to middle-class French consumers. See Tiersten, "Chic Interior," 23–24. See also Troy, *Modernism and the Decorative Arts*, 86–88.

2   DESIGN AND DOMESTIC SETTINGS: THE SALONS D'AUTOMNE OF 1910 TO 1913

Epigraph from Robert Mallet-Stevens, quoted in Yvonne Brunhammer, "Robert Mallet-Stevens as Interior Architect," in *Rob Mallet-Stevens, Architecte*, ed. D. Deshoulières and H. Jeanneau, trans. Susan Day (Brussels: Archives d'Architecture Moderne, 1980), 113–14.

1. Lethaby suggested that this was largely due to the efforts of Hermann Muthesius: "For five or six years, round about the year 1900, the German Government had attached to its Embassy in London an expert architect, Herr Muthesius, who became the historian (in German) of the English free architecture. All the architects who at that time did any building were investigated, sorted, tabulated, and, I must say, understood. . . . It is equally true or even more true that the German advances in industrial design have been founded on the English arts and crafts. They saw the essence of our best essays in furniture, glass, textiles, printing, and all the rest, and, laying hold on them, coined them into money." W. R. Lethaby, "Modern German Architecture and What We May Learn from It," in *Form in Civilization: Collected Papers on Art and Labour*, 2nd ed. (London: Oxford University Press, 1957), 81.

2. Ch-E. Jeanneret, *Etude sur le mouvement d'art décoratif en Allemagne* (La Chaux-de-Fonds, Switzerland, 1912), 25. Jeanneret also mentions that designers of objects produced in these factories received commissions on the sale of their pieces. For a more detailed account of the economic motivations of these workshops, see Frederic J. Schwartz, *The Werkbund: Design Theory and Mass Culture before the First World War* (New Haven, Conn.: Yale University Press, 1996), 160.

3. Jeanneret, *Etude*, 43.

4. Total sales of German goods in France rose by more than 50 percent

between 1909 and 1913, while sales of French goods in Germany rose by only 20 percent during the same period.

5. The German incursion onto this French terrain continued to rankle the French for many years and was still the subject of vehement discussion as late as 1925. See Kenneth E. Silver, *Esprit de Corps: The Art of the Parisian Avant-Garde and the First World War, 1914–1925* (Princeton, N.J.: Princeton University Press, 1989), 368.

6. See Jeanneret, *Etude*, 13.

7. The delegation included, among others, Frantz Jourdain, president of the Salon d'Automne; Victor Prouvé, president of the Union Provinciale des Arts Décoratifs; Senator Charles Couyba; and the spokesman for the delegation, Rupert Carabin. Their primary purpose had been to attend the Congress of the Union Provinciale des Arts Décoratifs, which coincided with the Munich exhibition.

8. Municipal Council of Paris, Report on the Second Congress of the Union Provinciale des Arts Décoratifs held in Munich [1908], in *L'art et les métiers d'art*, January 1919. This passage quoted in Arlette Barré-Despond and Suzanne Tise, *Jourdain* (New York: Rizzoli, 1991) 111–13.

9. See Jeanneret, *Etude*, 12.

10. M.-P. Verneuil, "Le Salon d'Automne," *Art et décoration* 28 (July–December 1910): 130.

11. Charles Saunier, "Le 5me Salon de la Société des Artistes Décorateurs," *Art et décoration* 27 (January–June 1910): 112.

12. M.-P. Verneuil, "L'architecture aux Salons," *Art et décoration* 28 (July–December 1910): 53.

13. *Guide officiel, Exposition des Arts Décoratifs de Munich, Salon d'Automne*, Paris, 1910, 2.

14. Kenneth Silver refers to the exhibit as "a major cultural event of the pre-war years." Its immediate effects were "enormous" and continued to affect French design well into the next decade. See Silver, *Esprit de Corps*, 171–74, 368.

15. For descriptions of the interiors and objects displayed in this and subsequent Salon d'Automne exhibits, see Nancy J. Troy, *Modernism and the Decorative Arts in France: Art Nouveau to Le Corbusier* (New Haven, Conn.: Yale University Press, 1991), 52–158.

16. See, for example, Verneuil, "Le Salon d'Automne," 129–60.

17. M.-P. Verneuil, "Supplément," *Art et décoration* (October 1910): 2.

18. Verneuil, "Le Salon d'Automne," 160. Verneuil's emphasis. See also Barré-Despond and Tise, *Jourdain*, 114.

19. François Monod, "L'enseignement de l'art décoratif en Allemagne et en France à propos d'un congrès recent," *Art et décoration* 34 (August 1913, supplément 3): 3.

20. Verneuil, "Le Salon d'Automne," 136.

21. Saunier, "VIᵉ Salon de la Société des Artistes Décorateurs au Pavillon de Marsan," *Art et décoration* 29 (January–June 1911): 78, 97.

22. Saunier, "VIᵉ Salon," 77.

23. Frantz Jourdain, "Les écoles regionals d'architecture," manuscript, Jourdain Archives. This passage quoted in Barré-Despond and Tise, *Jourdain*, 111.

24. M.-P. Verneuil, "Un intérieur moderne," *Art et décoration* 31 (January–June 1913): 58–59.

25. For clarity, I add their first names here. In the first group: Maurice Dufrène, Léon Jallot, Eugène Gaillard, Thomas Gallerey, Louis Majorelle, and Tony Selmersheim. In the second: André Groult, Paul Huillard, Gustave-Louis Jaulmes, André Mare, and Louis Suë. M.-P. Verneuil, "L'ameublement au Salon d'Automne," *Art et décoration* 35 (January–June 1914): 2.

26. Many of the *constructeurs*—Maurice Dufrène, Léon Jallot, Louis Majorelle, and others—were closely associated with the Art Deco movement after the war.

27. Léandre Vaillat, "L'art décoratif au Salon d'Automne," *L'art et les artistes* 14 (November 1911): 82. This passage quoted in Troy, *Modernism and the Decorative Arts*, 67. This is remarkably similar to the design strategy encouraged by decoration handbooks for middle-class householders, which encouraged them to assemble a wide range of objects but with the aim of achieving a unified effect. See Lisa Tiersten, "The Chic Interior and the Feminine Modern: Home Decorating as High Art in Turn-of-the-Century Paris," in *Not at Home: The Suppression of Domesticity in Modern Art and Architecture*, ed. Christopher Reed, 18–32 (New York: Thames and Hudson, 1996).

28. Cottington suggests that the favorable critical reception the room received had much to do with the self-consciously provincial origins of the furniture. See David Cottington, "The Maison Cubiste and the Meaning of Modernism in Pre-1914 France," in *Architecture and Cubism*, ed. Eve Blau and Nancy J. Troy (Cambridge, Mass.: The MIT Press, 1997), 27.

29. This relationship between the *coloriste* décor and Cubist painting has been a matter of debate. Troy suggests that the juxtaposition of colors and forms in the ensembles parallels that of the paintings the Puteaux Cubists were doing at the time; Cottington argues that there is little evidence from the correspondence of the artists involved that this was the case. See Troy, *Modernism and the Decorative Arts*, 83–88, 94–96; and Cottington, "Maison Cubiste," 28. The fact that these ensembles were self-consciously equivalent to contemporary bourgeois interiors, if perhaps ironically so, suggests that the composition comments on the prevailing trend, just as did Cubist paintings and collages. This seems to support Troy's supposition.

30. Cottington notes that individual objects in the ensemble were "not inexpensive everyday ware suitable for mass production." However, they did sell rather well. See David Cottington, *Cubism in the Shadow of War: The Avant-Garde and Politics in Paris 1905–1914* (New Haven, Conn.: Yale University Press, 1998), 175.

31. Louis Hourticq, "Chronique d'un project d'Exposition Internationale des Arts Décoratifs," *Art et décoration* (August 1911, supplément): 1–2.

32. Ibid., 1.

33. See, for example, ibid., 2. The exhibit did not take place until 1925.

34. In many cases, these objects were drawn from a range of sources representing all levels of the culture. Maurice Guillemot, "Logis d'ouvriers," *Art et décoration* 32 (July–December 1912): 79.

35. Gabriel Mourey, "VIIᵉ Salon de la Société des Artists Décorateurs au Pavillon de Marsan," *Art et décoration* 31 (January–June 1912): 105.

36. M.-P. Verneuil, "L'art décoratif aux Salons de 1912," *Art et décoration* 32 (July–December 1912): 177.

37. Thirteen artists contributed to Un Salon Bourgeois. André Mare directed the entire project, and Raymond Duchamp-Villon designed the facade. Marcel Duchamp, Albert Gleizes, Roger de La Fresnaye, Fernand Léger, Jean Metzinger, Paul Vera, and Jacques Villon contributed paintings. Richard Desvallières, Jean-Louis Gampert, Marie Laurencin, and Maurice Marinot produced decorative artworks. For a detailed description of the objects in the exhibit, see Troy, *Modernism and the Decorative Arts*, 80–90.

38. Emile Sedeyn, "Au Salon d'Automne," *Art et décoration* 32 (July–December 1912): 160.

39. André Mare, letter to Maurice Marinot, February 20, 1912 (collection Michel Mare, Paris). This passage quoted in Troy, *Modernism and the Decorative Arts*, 72. Clearly, Mare was reacting to a number of tendencies that had dominated the decorative arts in France since before the turn of the century, but the overtly nationalist tone of his statements requires some qualification: The political situation in France was becoming increasingly tense and was exacerbated by continued commercial pressure from Germany, particularly in the decorative arts. Most decorative artists working in France were understandably cautious about acknowledging any affinity with Germany, and this often translated into either pointed repudiation of German design or assertions of France's indisputably good taste. However, it was certainly clear to Mare, and to many others at the time, that whether French designers emulated German designers or not, they could easily assert that they were only perpetuating an already well established French tradition. For example, *coloriste* designers employed brilliant colors in their interior ensembles and were consequently criticized for emulating a technique that a number of *munichois* designers had used in 1908 and 1910; however, a similar sensibility had appeared as early as 1905 in the Salon d'Automne. Fauve and Nabis painters had exhibited such color combinations for a decade and had, moreover, applied them in their canvases to decidedly French interiors.

40. Reyner Banham, *Theory and Design in the First Machine Age*, 2nd ed. (Cambridge, Mass.: The MIT Press, 1980), 203.

41. Raymond Duchamp-Villon, letter to Walter Pach, January 16, 1913. This passage quoted in Troy, *Modernism and the Decorative Arts*, 92–93.

42. Tiersten, "Chic Interior," 25–26. See also Henri de Noussane, *Le goût dans l'ameublement* (Paris: Frimin-Didot et Cie, 1896), 150–51. The source for the Emmeline Raymond quotation is not cited.

43. Verneuil, "Un intérieur moderne," 58–59.

44. Sedeyn, "Au Salon d'Automne," 156.

45. See "Supplément," *Art et décoration* (December 1912): 1–3.

46. Adolphe Cadot, 15^{em} *Salon d'Automne: 1 Novembre–20 Decembre 1922*, exh. cat., 69.

47. Olivier Cinqualbre suggests, nevertheless, that the geometrical ornamentation of the facade was innovative enough to influence other modern architects,

particularly Robert Mallet-Stevens, whose work after the war, especially his film sets, recalls Un Salon Bourgeois. See Olivier Cinqualbre, "Mésaventures d'un modèle grandeur," in Centre Georges Pompidou, *Duchamp-Villon* (Paris: Editions du Centre Pompidou et Réunion des Musées Nationaux, 1998), 22–27.

48. Henri Verne and René Chavance, *Pour comprendre l'art décoratif moderne en France* (Paris: Librairie Hachette, 1925), 99. Verne and Chavance continue, stating, "One can say that architecture has passed into the interior. It is frequently the case that architects become decorators who concern themselves with the furnishing of 'the home' as much as with its construction." As I demonstrate below, Le Corbusier contended that the flow of influence worked primarily in the opposite direction during the 1910s and 1920s: the interior passed into architecture, and many decorators began to concern themselves with architecture.

49. See Lethaby, "Modern German Architecture," 80–82.

50. Robert Mallet-Stevens, "Le Salon d'Automne," *Tekhné* 34 (November 16, 1911). This passage quoted in Brunhammer, "Robert Mallet-Stevens as Interior Architect," 113–14.

51. See "Supplément," 2.

52. Barré-Despond and Tise, *Jourdain*, 122. The included quotation is from *Le radical*, November 30, 1913.

53. Verneuil, "L'ameublement au Salon d'Automne," 15.

54. Ibid., 20.

55. See ibid., 12.

56. Ibid.

57. In 1922, Jourdain discussed some of the intentions behind these interiors in an interview with René Chavance, "Notre enquête sur le mobilier moderne—Francis Jourdain," *Art et décoration* 41 (January–June 1922): 53.

58. Léon Werth, advertisement for Les Ateliers Modernes in *Cahiers d'aujourd'hui* 5 (June 1913).

59. Designers frequently used the English term "living room" in the 1920s to describe a flexible room that would replace or expand the French salon.

60. Sauvage's emphasis. I have translated Sauvage's term *pièce à usages diverses* as "multipurpose room." Later in the passage, Sauvage uses the English term "living-room." This and the next passage by Sauvage are in response to Guillaume Janneau's survey question: "Que sera demain le logis?" in Guillaume Janneau, *L'art décoratif moderne: Formes nouvelles et programmes nouveaux* (Paris: Bernheim Jeune, 1925), 20–21.

61. Henri Sauvage in Janneau, *L'art décoratif moderne*, 17.

62. Guillaume Janneau, "Introduction à l'Exposition des Arts Décoratifs: Considerations sur l'esprit moderne," *Art et décoration* 47 (January–June 1925): 146. Janneau uses the English term "living room" here.

63. Francis Jourdain, Les Ateliers Modernes advertisement, *Cahiers d'aujourd'hui* 5 (June 1913).

64. M.-P. Verneuil, "L'ameublement au Salon d'Automne," 2.

65. Gabriel Mourey, "Une villa de Charles Plumet," *Art et décoration* 30 (July–

December 1911): 277. This was also the theme of another essay in the same issue of *Art et décoration;* see Maurice Guillemot, "Habitations d'employés," *Art et décoration* 30 (July–December 1911): 209–16.

66. Chavance, "Notre enquête sur le mobilier moderne," 50.

67. Francis Jourdain, Les Ateliers Modernes advertisement.

68. Léon Werth, "Meubles modernes," *Cahiers d'aujourd'hui* (1912). Jourdain used passages from this text for his advertising brochures. Compare this to Loos's own assessment of his work in "Architecture," which he wrote in 1910. Adolf Loos, "Architecture 1910," in *The Architecture of Adolf Loos: An Arts Council Exhibition,* trans. Wilfred Wang (London: Arts Council of Great Britain, 1985).

69. Barré-Despond and Tise, *Jourdain,* 386.

70. Guillaume Janneau, "L'art décoratif au Salon d'Automne," *Art et décoration* 37 (July–December 1920): 159.

71. See Adolf Loos, "Ornament et crime," trans. Marcel Ray, *Cahiers d'aujourd'hui* 5 (June 1913): 247–56.

72. Adolf Loos, *Spoken into the Void: Collected Essays 1897–1900,* trans. Jane O. Newman and John H. Smith (Cambridge, Mass.: The MIT Press, 1982), viii.

73. Barré-Despond and Tise, *Jourdain,* 244.

74. See, for example, Le Corbusier, *Decorative Art of Today,* 85, 134.

75. Troy explains that while visiting the exhibition, Jeanneret concentrated his attention almost entirely on the ensembles of the *coloristes.* Only after he returned to La Chaux-de-Fonds did he begin to reconsider the significance of Jourdain's work. Troy, *Modernism and the Decorative Arts,* 120.

76. Charles-Edouard Jeanneret, letter to Francis Jourdain, December 21, 1913 (Jourdain Archives). This passage quoted in Troy, *Modernism and the Decorative Arts,* 140.

77. For a reproduction of this letterhead, see Geoffrey H. Baker, *Le Corbusier— The Creative Search: The Formative Years of Charles-Edouard Jeanneret* (New York: Van Nostrand Reinhold, 1996), 192.

3 THE WAR, HOUSE RECONSTRUCTION, AND FURNITURE PRODUCTION

Epigraph by Robert de la Sizeranne. This passage quoted in Romy Golan, *Modernity and Nostalgia: Art and Politics in France between the Wars* (New Haven, Conn.: Yale University Press, 1995), 14.

1. Robert de la Sizeranne, *L'art pendant la guerre 1914–1918* (Paris, 1919), 229. This passage quoted in Golan, *Modernity and Nostalgia,* 14.

2. Not all of these plans appear in the *Oeuvre complète.* They include Cité jardin aux Crétets, La Chaux-de-Fonds (1914); Maison Dom-ino (1914–15); Maisons ouvrières, Saintes, France (1917); Cité ouvrière, Saint-Nicolas d'Aliermont, France (1917); Maison Monol (1919); Cité ouvrière du Vouldy à Troyes, France (1919); Maisons ouvrières, Grand-Couronne, France (1920); Le Pont-Vert, near Ecouen, France (1920); Maison ouvrière en série (1922); Cité contemporaine pour trois millons d'habitants

(1922); Maison Citrohan (1922); Immeubles-villas (1922–25); Maisons en série pour artisans (1924); Cité Audincourt, France (1924); Cité universitaire pour étudiants (1925); Pessac, France (designed 1925); "Plan Voisin" de Paris (1925); and the Pavillon de l'Esprit Nouveau (1925). See Le Corbusier and Pierre Jeanneret, *Oeuvre complète,* vol. 1, *1910–1929,* 14th ed. (Zurich: Les Editions d'Architecture [Artemis], 1995).

3. This, at least, is how Le Corbusier described it in 1929. See ibid., 104.

4. See ibid.

5. Octave Mirbeau, preface, in Léon Werth, *Meubles modernes* (Paris: Les Ateliers Moderns, 1912), 1. From a facsimile copy in Arlette Barré-Despond and Suzanne Tise, *Jourdain* (New York: Rizzoli, 1991), 386–89.

6. Le Corbusier and Jeanneret, *Oeuvre complète,* 23–24.

7. Ibid. Le Corbusier's ellipsis. Le Corbusier managed a factory that made conglomerate blocks for building construction, the Briueterie d'Alfortmille, from 1917 to 1921.

8. Ibid., 26.

9. Geoffrey H. Baker, *Le Corbusier—The Creative Search: The Formative Years of Charles-Edouard Jeanneret* (New York: Van Nostrand Reinhold, 1996), 221–22.

10. Tony Garnier, letter to Charles-Edouard Jeanneret, December 13, 1915, FLC B1–20, 86–87.

11. Jeanneret later visited Garnier's house near Lyon, in the fall of 1916, dedicating a page in his sketchbook to its plan and exterior aspect. Brooks points out that several of Jeanneret's working-class housing projects of the early 1920s were even more strongly influenced by Garnier, whom Jeanneret met and with whom he actively corresponded during the last half of 1919 and the first half of 1920. See H. Allen Brooks, *Le Corbusier's Formative Years* (Chicago: University of Chicago Press, 1997), 409, 497.

12. Kenneth E. Silver, *Esprit de Corps: The Art of the Parisian Avant-Garde and the First World War, 1914–1925* (Princeton, N.J.: Princeton University Press, 1989), 25–26.

13. The price for these ensembles was 460 and 348 francs, respectively (about $1,450 and $1,100 in 2006 dollars), comparable to what one might spend on similar furnishings at Ikea. Barré-Despond and Tise, *Jourdain,* 261.

14. See ibid., 262.

15. Tony Garnier, *Une Cité Industrielle,* ed. Riccardo Mariani, trans. Andrew Ellis (New York: Rizzoli, 1990), 47.

16. Golan, *Modernity and Nostalgia,* 5.

17. For a complete accounting of the devastation of northern France during World War 1, see Hugh Clout, *After the Ruins: Restoring the Countryside of Northern France after the Great War* (Exeter, U.K.: University of Exeter Press, 1996), 19–58.

18. See Leonard V. Smith, Stéphane Audoin-Rouzeau, and Annette Becker, *France and the Great War, 1914–1918* (Cambridge: Cambridge University Press, 2003), 96. Of the 8.4 million French soldiers mobilized, 16.8 percent were killed and about 42.8 percent were wounded.

19. See Golan, *Modernity and Nostalgia,* 12.

20. Silver, *Esprit de Corps,* 369.

21. Ibid., 33.

4 THE END OF DECORATIVE ART,
THE HOUR OF ARCHITECTURE

1. Le Corbusier, *The Decorative Art of Today,* trans. James Dunnett (Cambridge, Mass.: The MIT Press, 1987), 141–42.

2. For an account of how this collective nostalgia played out in French painting particularly, see Romy Golan, *Modernity and Nostalgia: Art and Politics in France between the Wars* (New Haven, Conn.: Yale University Press, 1995).

3. Le Corbusier, *Decorative Art of Today,* 142.

4. Ibid., 129–32.

5. Ibid., 131–35.

6. Guillaume Janneau, *L'art décoratif moderne: Formes nouvelles et programmes nouveaux* (Paris: Bernheim Jeune, 1925), 17. This is quoted from Henri Sauvage's response to the question "Que sera demain le logis?" which Janneau asked of a number of other designers (Pierre Chareau, Paul Hillard, Francis Jourdain, Robert Mallet-Stevens, Pierre Patout, Auguste Perret, André Ventre). Many of these designers were called *architectes-décorateurs* in the press. For example, Gaston Varenne declared in 1923: "Pierre Chareau is, among today's *architectes-décorateurs,* one of the most interesting to study." Gaston Varenne, "L'esprit nouveau de Pierre Chareau," *Art et décoration* 43 (January–June 1923): 129.

7. By the end of the war, 729,000 houses had been destroyed or nearly destroyed. See Kenneth E. Silver, *Esprit de Corps: The Art of the Parisian Avant-Garde and the First World War, 1914–1925* (Princeton, N.J.: Princeton University Press, 1989), 187.

8. The quoted passages represent the words of Gustave Geffroy, Elie Faure, Siegfried Bing, and André Mare, respectively. Gustave Geffroy, "La vie artistique," *Les temps nouveaux* 1, no. 2 (1895), quoted in Eugenia W. Herbert, *The Artist and Social Reform: France and Belgium, 1885–1898* (New Haven, Conn.: Yale University Press, 1961), 157; Elie Faure, preface, *Le Salon d'Automne,* exh. cat., October 15, 1905, quoted in Arlette Barré-Despond and Suzanne Tise, *Jourdain* (New York: Rizzoli, 1991), 105; Siegfried Bing, "L'Art Nouveau," trans. Irene Sargent, *The Craftsman* 5, no. 1 (October 1903), in *Artistic America, Tiffany Glass and Art Nouveau* (Cambridge, Mass.: The MIT Press, 1970), 229; and André Mare, letter to Maurice Marinot, February 20, 1912 (collection Michel Mare, Paris), in *Modernism and the Decorative Arts in France: Art Nouveau to Le Corbusier,* by Nancy J. Troy (New Haven, Conn.: Yale University Press, 1991), 72.

9. Le Corbusier advertised similar *immeubles-villas* for 180,000 francs, or 209,000 francs for a freestanding version. This corresponds to about $95,000 and $110,000, respectively, in 2006 dollars. In both cases, the prices quoted do not include the cost of the land. See Collection de "L'Esprit Nouveau," *Almanach d'architecture moderne* (Paris: Les Editions G. Crès et Cie, 1926), 218–20.

10. Le Corbusier, *Decorative Art of Today,* 186. Le Corbusier's emphasis. This view is confirmed in the historical analysis of the period. Philippe Bernard and Henri Dubief remark that "the war had a truly revolutionary effect in that it encouraged in the country an awareness of new needs for comfort, culture and progress."

Philippe Bernard and Henri Dubief, *The Decline of the Third Republic, 1914–1938*, trans. Anthony Forester (Cambridge: Cambridge University Press, 1985), 142.

11. Bernard and Dubief, *Decline of the Third Republic*, 157.

12. Louis Hourticq, "Au Salon des Artistes Décorateurs," *Art et décoration* 36 (July 1914–December 1919): 44–46.

13. Ibid., 46.

14. H. M. Magne, "L'architecture et les matériaux nouveaux," *Art et décoration* 36 (July 1914–December 1919): 90.

15. The increasing presence of department stores in the home furnishings market helped to enforce this attitude. The department stores had access to a tremendous amount of capital and so were able to weather financial crises better than could small firms and independent artists. For this reason, they managed to acquire the services of some of the most exclusive designers after the war. And, because their markets included the "new poor," they sought to offer the kinds of designs that formerly had been exhibited only in the Paris boutiques and decorative art Salons. The alliance of department stores with artists such as Jacques Rhulmann and Maurice Dufrène carried the refined tastes of the wealthy bourgeois into lower strata of society. See Yvonne Brunhammer, *Art Deco Style* (London: Academy Editions, 1983), 18.

16. Jean-Louis Vaudoyer, "Le Salon d'Automne, II—l'art décoratif," *Art et décoration* 36 (July 1914–December 1919): 180. Vaudoyer's view parallels closely the critique of Jugendstil interiors that Adolf Loos sets forth in "The Poor Little Rich Man" two decades earlier. See Adolf Loos, *Spoken into the Void: Collected Essays 1897–1900*, trans. Jane O. Newman and John H. Smith (Cambridge, Mass.: The MIT Press, 1982), 125–27.

17. Nevertheless, their influence on progressive design was limited after the war. While *coloriste* designers and collaborators in the 1912 Un Salon Bourgeois provided an alternative to the luxurious, unified style of the *constructeurs* before the war—by absorbing historical French furnishings, contemporary works of art, and even decidedly middle-class objects—their work after the war was very different. For example, André Mare's ensembles, which could be typified as "robust" and "informal" in 1911 and 1912, were lavish and expensive in 1925. The extravagant interiors that he and Louis Süe exhibited for the Compagnie des Arts Français at the 1925 Exposition Internationale des Arts Décoratifs et Industriels Modernes, along with the interiors of a number of designers against whom they had formerly competed, were widely criticized for ignoring middle-class needs.

18. Vaudoyer, "Le Salon d'Automne," 183.

19. See Yvanhoë Rambosson, "Le XIIᵉ Salon des Artistes Décorateurs," *Art et décoration* 41 (January–June 1922): 112. See also Yvanhoë Rambosson, "Les artistes décorateurs au Salon des Artistes Français," *Art et décoration* 41 (January–June 1922): 185.

20. Gaston Varenne, "L'Exposition des Arts Décoratifs: Le mobilier français," *Art et décoration* 48 (July–December 1925): 1.

21. René Chavance, "Le XIVᵉ Salon des Artistes Décorateurs," *Art et décoration* 43 (January–June 1923): 183–86.

22. Kenneth Silver gives a particularly vivid account of this trend in his *Esprit de Corps,* 362–68.

23. Le Corbusier, *Decorative Art of Today,* 96.

24. See Barré-Despond and Tise, *Jourdain,* 314.

25. Waldemar George, "L'Exposition des Arts Décoratifs et Industriels de 1925," *L'amour de l'art* (1925): 285–86.

26. Varenne, "L'Exposition des Arts Décoratifs," 1.

27. Le Corbusier, *Decorative Art of Today,* 135–36. Most of his progressive contemporaries who contributed to the modernist movement in France were in their thirties or forties, not their twenties. Le Corbusier was nearly forty, and Jourdain turned fifty in 1925.

28. It is worth noting here that *The Decorative Art of Today* has received relatively scant attention from historians of twentieth-century architecture. One indication of this neglect is that the book was not translated into English until 1987, whereas *Towards a New Architecture* has been available to English readers since 1927, and *The City of Tomorrow and Its Planning* (originally published as *Urbanisme*) since 1929. This is no doubt partly because of the apparent irrelevance (to architecture) of the title *The Decorative Art of Today,* which hardly inspires the same level of passion in architects that has been stimulated by *Towards a New Architecture. The Decorative Art of Today* is, nevertheless, an important book in Le Corbusier's oeuvre. In a letter to Takamasa Yosizaka in 1954, Le Corbusier declared that it was the best book in the *Esprit Nouveau* series (Le Corbusier, letter to Takamasa Yosizaka, 8 November 1954, Le Corbusier Archives [R3-09-40], Paris). It is, in fact, central to his early theory of architecture. That a theorist and historian of modern architecture such as Reyner Banham could dismiss *The Decorative Art of Today* as "a polemical work of only local interest" is particularly egregious. Reyner Banham, *Theory and Design in the First Machine Age,* 2nd ed. (Cambridge, Mass.: The MIT Press, 1960), 248. The work is thoroughly tied to Le Corbusier's other important works: like *Towards a New Architecture* and *The City of Tomorrow and Its Planning,* it is largely a compilation of articles from *L'Esprit Nouveau.* It should be seen not as independent of them but as the central portion of these related essays, which Le Corbusier published at the beginning of his architectural career. He indicated the breadth of the theory that he had been formulating in these essays when he wrote in *The City of Tomorrow and Its Planning,* "we can say that the further human creations are removed from our immediate grasp, the more they tend to pure geometry; a violin or a chair, things which come into close contact with the body are of a less pure geometry; but a town is pure geometry." Le Corbusier, *The City of Tomorrow and Its Planning,* trans. Frederick Etchells (New York: Dover Publications, 1987), 22. Le Corbusier asserted repeatedly that modern architecture was inextricably linked to a continuum of design that rested fundamentally in common sense, ordinary things, and everyday actions: "We must specify clearly that if we are to bring together into one formidable array the various means which our own age has placed in our hands—that is to say, the equipment with which we must set up our framework for the work itself. We shall become conscious then of a feeling which is set free, and arising out of our small and fixed daily occupations, a

sensibility which can lead them in the direction of an ideal form—towards a *style* (for style is a state of mind)—toward a culture, that is. These are the many-sided efforts of a society which feels it is ready for the crystallization of a new attitude after one of the most fruitful periods of preparation that mankind has ever known." Le Corbusier, *City of Tomorrow,* 34.

29. Le Corbusier cites this statement in the introduction to *The Decorative Art of Today* and credits it to "the President of the Jury (a great Frenchman)"; Auguste Perret was the president of the jury. Le Corbusier, *Decorative Art of Today,* xv.

30. Ibid., 84. Le Corbusier's emphasis.

31. Ibid., 81.

32. Charles-Edouard Jeanneret, letter to Francis Jourdain, December 21, 1913. This passage quoted in Nancy J. Troy, *Modernism and the Decorative Arts in France: Art Nouveau to Le Corbusier* (New Haven, Conn.: Yale University Press, 1991), 140.

33. For a discussion of the "standard-cabinets" in the pavilion, see Carol S. Eliel, "Purism in Paris, 1918–1925," in *L'Esprit Nouveau: Purism in Paris, 1918–1925* (New York: Harry N. Abrams, 2001), 51–53, 69, n. 106.

34. Until recently, even assimilating these designers into the history of modern architecture has proved difficult. Eileen Gray is indicative of the problem: Beatriz Colomina declares that "[her] name does not figure into most histories of modern architecture, including the most recent and, presumably, critical ones." Beatriz Colomina, *Privacy and Publicity: Modern Architecture as Mass Media* (Cambridge, Mass.: The MIT Press, 1994), 80–84, 335, n. 13. In *Modern Architecture: A Critical History,* for example, Kenneth Frampton mentions Gray only in passing and does not cite her work. He treats Mallet-Stevens similarly; Chareau and Jourdain do not appear at all. See Kenneth Frampton, *Modern Architecture: A Critical History,* 3rd ed. (New York: Thames and Hudson, 1992), 333–34. Sigfried Giedion mentions neither Gray, Mallet-Stevens, nor Jourdain and states only that Chareau was a "friend" of Le Corbusier's. Sigfried Giedion, *Space, Time and Architecture: The Growth of a New Tradition,* 5th ed. (Cambridge, Mass.: Harvard University Press, 1967), 696. The situation has changed somewhat in recent years with the publication of architectural monographs treating these designers, as well as general histories that incorporate some of their work.

35. For an extensive analysis of surface qualities in early modernist architecture, especially that of Le Corbusier, see Mark Wigley, *White Walls, Designer Dresses: The Fashioning of Modern Architecture* (Cambridge, Mass.: The MIT Press, 1995).

36. Henri Bergson, *Matter and Memory,* trans. N. M. Paul and W. S. Palmer (New York: Zone Books, 1991), 10.

37. Le Corbusier, *Decorative Art of Today,* 71–72. Le Corbusier's emphasis.

38. Ibid., 72.

39. The presence of such objects in self-consciously avant-garde French art during the 1910s—in Cubist collage and in the work of Marcel Duchamp, for example—emphasized how difficult the relationship between ordinary objects and art had been.

40. For an extensive analysis of these paintings, see Eliel, *L'Esprit Nouveau,* 11–69. See also Silver, *Esprit de Corps,* 378–91.

41. This passage quoted in Banham, *Theory and Design,* 211; specific reference not cited.

42. See *Decorative Art of Today,* vii.

43. In this, Le Corbusier and Pierre Jeanneret were emulating closely, but with very different materials, the work of the *coloristes* whom Le Corbusier had admired before 1913. While the work of the *coloristes* was stylistically eclectic, Le Corbusier and Jeanneret's was eclectic but ostensibly indifferent to style. One may also detect a parallel here with Loos's distaste for "stylishness" and his desire to accommodate the style of a family. See, for example, "Interiors in the Rotunda" in Loos, *Spoken into the Void,* 23–27. The Pavillon de l'Esprit Nouveau was clearly intended to be a very flexible prototype—a framework open to the lives that might occupy it.

44. Le Corbusier, *Decorative Art of Today,* 77.

45. Aside from the 600,000 people in the *immeubles-villas,* 400,000 people would occupy high-rise buildings in the center of the city, and the remaining 2 million inhabitants would live in outlying garden cities.

46. Le Corbusier and Pierre Jeanneret, *Oeuvre complète,* vol. 1, *1910–1929,* 14th ed. (Zurich: Les Editions d'Architecture [Artemis], 1995), 31.

47. Ibid., 47, 69.

48. Ibid., 104.

49. Although these designers executed major commissions for wealthy, middle-class patrons, they each proposed or built projects for people of modest means, often developing their most innovative work in these contexts. These projects are discussed further on in the chapter.

50. Marc Vellay and Kenneth Frampton, *Pierre Chareau: Architect and Craftsman, 1883–1950* (New York: Rizzoli, 1984), 62–64.

51. From a letter from Pierre Chareau to René Herbst, quoted in Vellay and Frampton, *Pierre Chareau,* 239.

52. Vellay and Frampton, *Pierre Chareau,* 242.

53. Ibid., 242. Frampton notes that the French edition of *Modern Architecture: A Critical History* was an exception in that it did include discussion of the Maison de Verre. He does not explain why it did so only in the 1980 French edition and not in the English editions.

54. Eileen Gray and Jean Badovici, "Description," *L'architecture vivante* (Winter 1929): 23–38. Reproduced and translated in Caroline Constant, *Eileen Gray* (London: Phaidon Press, 2000), 240–45.

55. See Constant, *Eileen Gray,* 37.

56. Ibid., 38.

57. Le Corbusier explains that in the *immeuble-villa,* "each house is actually a little house with a garden, situated at any level of an apartment block." Le Corbusier and Jeanneret, *Oeuvre complète,* 41.

58. Gray and Badovici, "Maison en bord de mer," quoted in Constant, *Eileen Gray,* 240. The original source, *L'architecture vivante* (Winter 1929), does not list "Maison en bord de mer" in its table of contents, but the text is found on pages 17–38. Constant provides a translation of the entire essay in *Eileen Gray.*

59. Constant, *Eileen Gray,* 243.

60. Ibid., 238.

61. Ibid., 239.

62. Bergson, *Matter and Memory,* 21.

63. Constant, *Eileen Gray,* 239, 240.

64. Ibid., 113.

65. Constant frequently mentions the critical dialogue Gray maintained, through her work, with Le Corbusier. See for example, ibid., 72.

66. Le Corbusier, *Decorative Art of Today,* 70–71, 137.

67. Le Corbusier introduced the "three reminders to architects" and "regulating lines" in 1923; the "five points for a new architecture" were articulated by Le Corbusier and Pierre Jeanneret in 1926.

68. Le Corbusier and Jeanneret, *Oeuvre complète,* 33.

69. Le Corbusier, *Towards a New Architecture,* trans. Frederick Etchells, 13th ed. (New York: Dover Publications, 1986), 71–72. Le Corbusier's emphasis.

70. Ibid., 67.

71. Le Corbusier and Jeanneret, *Oeuvre complète,* 128–29.

72. Eileen Gray and Jean Badovici, "De l'eclecticisme au doute," *L'architecture vivante* (Winter 1929): 17–21. Gray and Badovici's emphasis. Reproduced and translated in Constant, *Eileen Gray,* 21.

73. D. Deshoulières and H. Jeanneau, "The Demands of Architecture," in *Rob Mallet-Stevens, Architecte,* trans. Susan Day (Brussels: Archives d'Architecture Moderne, 1980), 51.

74. Robert Mallet-Stevens, in *Extraits des sept arts,* 1923. This passage quoted in Deshoulières and Jeanneau, "Demands of Architecture," 51; original page not cited.

75. Deshoulières and Jeanneau, "Demands of Architecture," 51.

76. Ibid., 39.

77. Michel Louis, "Mallet-Stevens and the Cinema, 1919–1929," in Deshoulières and Jeanneau, *Rob Mallet-Stevens, Architecte,* 151.

78. Louis, "Mallet-Stevens and the Cinema," 151.

79. Robert Mallet-Stevens, "Le cinema et les arts: L'architecture," *Les cahiers du mois,* nos. 16–17 (1925). Excerpted in *Film Architecture: Set Designs from Metropolis to Blade Runner,* ed. Dietrich Neumann (New York: Prestel Verlag, 1999), 200.

80. Deshoulières and Jeanneau, "Demands of Architecture," 48. The quotation is from an unidentified critic of the exhibit.

81. Léon Deshairs, "Une villa moderne à Hyères," *Art et décoration* 54 (July–December 1928). Quoted in Deshoulières and Jeanneau, "Demands of Architecture," 42; original page not cited.

AFTERWORD

1. Congrès Internationaux d'Architecture Moderne (CIAM), "The La Sarraz Declaration," 1928, in *The Athens Charter,* ed. Le Corbusier (New York: Grossman, 1973), 6. Historical analysis of Le Corbusier's work, and indeed of most modern work, from this same period makes scant mention of their concerns for "demands

of present-day life"; see, for example, Kenneth Frampton, *Modern Architecture: A Critical History,* 3rd ed. (New York: Thames and Hudson, 1992), and Reyner Banham, *Theory and Design in the First Machine Age,* 2nd ed. (Cambridge, Mass.: The MIT Press, 1960).

2. Henry-Russell Hitchcock and Philip Johnson, *The International Style* (New York: W. W. Norton, 1995), 35, 36.

3. This uniformity was highly choreographed, however. The selection process for architects who might work to present a unified exposition was long and rather bitter. See Richard Pommer and Christian F. Otto, *Weissenhof 1927 and the Modern Movement in Architecture* (Chicago: University of Chicago Press, 1991).

4. Ludwig Mies van der Rohe, "On Form in Architecture," in *Programs and Manifestoes on 20th-Century Architecture,* ed. Ulrich Conrads, trans. Michael Bullock (Cambridge, Mass.: The MIT Press, 1964), 102.

5. Jean Badovici, "A propos du Stuttgart," *L'architecture vivante* (Spring and Summer 1928): 5.

6. CIAM, "La Sarraz Declaration," 6.

7. Ibid., 6.

8. Sigfried Giedion, "La leçon de l'Exposition du 'Werkbund' Stuttgart 1927," *L'architecture vivante* (Spring and Summer 1928): 38.

9. Le Corbusier, *The Athens Charter,* 5.

10. Peter Adam, *Eileen Gray: Architect/Designer* (New York: Harry N. Abrams, 1987), 216. Adams cites this passage from a personal conversation with Gray.

11. "And how will this atmosphere be created," asks Le Corbusier, "except by architecture, whose objective is to create relationships?" Le Corbusier, *The Decorative Art of Today,* trans. James Dunnett (Cambridge, Mass.: The MIT Press, 1987), 126. For a more recent discussion of this concept, see Dalibor Vesely, "Architecture and the Poetics of Representation," *Daidalos* 25 (September 1987): 24–36.

12. J. J. Pollitt, *The Ancient View of Greek Art: Criticism, History, and Terminology* (New Haven, Conn.: Yale University Press, 1974), 343.

13. Vitruvius, *De Architectura,* I, c. 2, 5, trans. F. Granger (Cambridge: Harvard University Press, 1983), 27–29.

14. Alberti had advised this long before: "I firmly believe that any person of sense would not want to design his private house very differently from those of others, and would be careful not to incite envy through extravagance or ostentation." Leon Battista Alberti, *On the Art of Building in Ten Books,* trans. Joseph Rykwert, Neil Leach, and Robert Tavernor (Cambridge, Mass.: The MIT Press, 1988), 292.

15. Le Corbusier, *Decorative Art of Today,* 71. Bergson had reached a similar conclusion more than a decade earlier: "The objects which surround my body reflect its possible action upon them." Henri Bergson, *Matter and Memory,* trans. N. M. Paul and W. S. Palmer (New York: Zone Books, 1991), 21. According to Le Corbusier, beauty in an object resulted from its performance in a given situation. "The only possible objects are *objects with a function.*" Le Corbusier, *Decorative Art of Today,* 188, Le Corbusier's emphasis. Objects could be beautiful only in the context of human activity.

BIBLIOGRAPHY

Adam, Peter. *Eileen Gray: Architect/Designer.* New York: Harry N. Abrams, 1987.

Alberti, Leon Battista. *On the Art of Building in Ten Books.* Trans. Joseph Rykwert, Neil Leach, and Robert Tavernor. Cambridge, Mass.: The MIT Press, 1988.

Alexandre, Arsène. "L'Art Nouveau." *Le figaro*, December 28, 1895, 1. Reprinted in Champier, "Les expositions."

Antliff, Mark. "Bergson and Cubism: A Reassessment." *Art Journal* 47 (Winter 1988): 341–49.

Augé, Marc. *Non-Places: Introduction to an Anthropology of Supermodernity.* Trans. John Howe. New York: Verso, 1995.

Aurier, Albert. "Le symbolisme en peinture, Paul Gauguin." *Mercure de France* 2, no. 15 (March 1891): 163. Quoted in Poggi, *In Defiance of Painting.*

Badovici, Jean. "A propos du Stuttgart." *L'architecture vivante* (Spring and Summer 1928): 5–8.

Baker, Geoffrey H. *Le Corbusier—The Creative Search: The Formative Years of Charles-Edouard Jeanneret.* New York: Van Nostrand Reinhold, 1996.

Banham, Reyner. *Theory and Design in the First Machine Age.* 2nd ed. Cambridge, Mass.: The MIT Press, 1960.

Barré-Despond, Arlette, and Suzanne Tise. *Jourdain.* New York: Rizzoli, 1991.

Benjamin, Walter. "The Work of Art in the Age of Mechanical Reproduction." In *Illuminations: Essays and Reflections*, ed. Hannah Arendt, trans. Harry Zohn, 217–51. New York: Schocken Books, 1969.

Berger, Georges. "Rapport de M. Georges Berger." *Revue des arts décoratifs* 12 (1891–92): 360–61.

Bergson, Henri. *Matter and Memory.* Trans. N. M. Paul and W. S. Palmer. New York: Zone Books, 1991.

Bernard, Philippe, and Henri Dubief. *The Decline of the Third Republic, 1914–1938.* Trans. Anthony Forester. Cambridge: Cambridge University Press, 1985.

Bezucha, Robert. "Being Realistic about Realism: Art and the Social History of Nineteenth-Century France." In *The European Realist Tradition*, ed. Gabriel P. Weisberg, 1–14. Bloomington: Indiana University Press, 1982.

Bing, Siegfried. *Artistic America, Tiffany Glass and Art Nouveau.* Cambridge, Mass.: The MIT Press, 1970.

———. Introduction. *Salon annuel des peintures japonaises*, première année. Paris: Pillet & Demoulin, 1883.

———. *La culture artistique en Amérique.* Paris, 1896.

———. "L'Art Nouveau." Trans. unknown. *The Architectural Record* 12 (1902): 279–85. Reprinted in Bing, *Artistic America.*

———. "L'Art Nouveau." Trans. Irene Sargent. *The Craftsman* 5, no. 1 (October 1903). Reprinted in Bing, *Artistic America*.

Bing, Siegfried, and Georges Lemmen. *L'Art Nouveau*. Brochure, 1895. Reprinted in Weisberg, *Art Nouveau Bing*.

Blau, Eve, and Nancy J. Troy, eds. *Architecture and Cubism*. Montreal: Canadian Center for Architecture; Cambridge, Mass.: The MIT Press, 1997.

Boime, Albert. "The Second Empire's Official Realism." In *The European Realist Tradition*, ed. Gabriel P. Weisberg, 31–123. Bloomington: Indiana University Press, 1982.

Borgmann, Albert. *Technology and the Character of Contemporary Life: A Philosophical Inquiry*. Chicago: University of Chicago Press, 1984.

Borsi, Franco. *The Monumental Era: European Architecture and Design, 1929–1939*. New York: Rizzoli, 1987.

Britton, Karla. *Auguste Perret*. New York: Phaidon Press, 2001.

Brooks, H. Allen. *Le Corbusier's Formative Years*. Chicago: University of Chicago Press, 1997.

Brunhammer, Yvonne. *Art Deco Style*. London: Academy Editions, 1983.

———. "Robert Mallet-Stevens as Interior Architect." In D. Deshoulières and H. Jeanneau, *Rob Mallet-Stevens, Architecte*.

Burckhardt, Lucius, ed. *The Werkbund: History and Ideology, 1907–1933*. Trans. Pearl Sanders. New York: Barron's, 1980.

Casey, Edward S. *Getting Back into Place: Toward a Renewed Understanding of the Place-World*. Bloomington: Indiana University Press, 1993.

———. *Remembering: A Phenomenological Study*. Bloomington: Indiana University Press, 1987.

Centre Georges Pompidou. *Duchamp-Villon*. Paris: Centre Georges Pompidou et Réunion des Musées Nationaux, 1998.

Certeau, Michel de. *The Practice of Everyday Life*. Trans. Steven Rendall. Berkeley: University of California Press, 1984.

Champier, Victor. "Les expositions de L'Art Nouveau." *Revue des arts décoratifs* 16 (1896): 1–6.

Chavance, René. "Le XIVe Salon des Artistes Décorateurs." *Art et décoration* 43 (January–June 1923): 161–92.

———. "Notre enquête sur le mobilier moderne—Francis Jourdain." *Art et décoration* 41 (January–June 1922): 49–56.

Choisy, Auguste. *Histoire de l'architecture*. 2 vols. Paris: Editions Vincent Fréal & Cie, 1964.

Cinqualbre, Olivier. "Mésaventures d'un modèle grandeur." In Centre Georges Pompidou, *Duchamp-Villon*. Paris: Editions au Centre Pompidou et Réunion des Musées Nationaux, 1998.

———, ed. *Pierre Chareau: Architecte, un art interieur*. Paris: Centre Georges Pompidou, 1993.

Clausen, Meredith L. *Frantz Jourdain and the Samaritaine: Art Nouveau Theory and Criticism*. Leiden, Netherlands: E. J. Brill, 1987.

Clout, Hugh. *After the Ruins: Restoring the Countryside of Northern France after the Great War*. Exeter, U.K.: University of Exeter Press, 1996.

Collection de "L'Esprit Nouveau." *Almanach d'architecture moderne*. Paris: Les Editions G. Crès et Cie, 1926.

Collins, Peter. *Concrete: The Vision of a New Architecture; A Study of Auguste Perret and His Precursors*. New York: Horizon Press, 1959.

Colomina, Beatriz. *Privacy and Publicity: Modern Architecture as Mass Media*. Cambridge, Mass.: The MIT Press, 1994.

Colquhoun, Alan. *Modernity and the Classical Tradition*. Cambridge, Mass.: The MIT Press, 1989.

Congrès Internationaux d'Architecture Moderne (CIAM). "The La Sarraz Declaration." 1928. In Le Corbusier, *The Athens Charter*.

Conrads, Ulrich, ed. *Programs and Manifestoes on 20th-Century Architecture*. Trans. Michael Bullock. Cambridge, Mass.: The MIT Press, 1970.

Constant, Caroline. "E.1027: The Nonheroic Modernism of Eileen Gray." *Journal of the Society of Architectural Historians* (September 1994): 265–79.

———. *Eileen Gray*. London: Phaidon Press, 2000.

Cottington, David. *Cubism in the Shadow of War: The Avant-Garde and Politics in Paris, 1905–1914*. New Haven, Conn.: Yale University Press, 1998.

———. "The Maison Cubiste and the Meaning of Modernism in Pre-1914 France." In *Architecture and Cubism*, ed. Eve Blau and Nancy J. Troy. Cambridge: The MIT Press, 1997.

Culot, Maurice, et al., eds. *Les frères Perret: L'oeuvre complète*. Paris: Editions NORMA, 2000.

Dal Co, Francesco. *Figures of Architecture and Thought: German Architecture Culture, 1880–1920*. New York: Rizzoli, 1990.

Danto, Arthur C. *The Transfiguration of the Commonplace: A Philosophy of Art*. Cambridge, Mass.: Harvard University Press, 1981.

Denis, Maurice. "Définition du néotraditionnisme." *Art et critique* 23 and 30 (August 1890). Quoted in Hamilton, *Painting and Sculpture*, and in Goldwater, *Symbolism*.

Deshairs, Léon. "Une villa moderne à Hyères." *Art et décoration* 54 (July–December 1928). Quoted in Deshoulières and Jeanneau, "Demands of Architecture."

Deshoulières, D., and H. Jeanneau. "The Demands of Architecture." In *Rob Mallet-Stevens, Architecte*.

———. *Rob Mallet-Stevens, Architecte*. Trans. Susan Day. Brussels: Archives d'Architecture Moderne, 1980.

Dubuffet, Jean. Letter to Auguste Perret. August 2, 1946. AA, Box 535 AP 321. Quoted in Britton, *Auguste Perret*.

Duchamp-Villon, Raymond. Letter to Walter Pach. January 16, 1913. Quoted in Troy, *Modernism and the Decorative Arts*.

Ecole d'Art. "Prospectus." La Chaux-de-Fonds, Switzerland: Haefel & Co., 1912.

————. *Rapport de la Commission, 1910–1911.* La Chaux-de-Fonds, Switzerland, 1911.

Eichmuller, V. "Trois Villas." *Art et décoration* 29 (January–June 1911): 60–64.

Eliel, Carol S. *L'Esprit Nouveau: Purism in Paris, 1918–1925.* New York: Harry N. Abrams, 2001.

L'Eplattenier, Charles, Georges Albert, Charles-Edouard Jeanneret, and Léon Perrin. *Un mouvement d'art à La Chaux-de-Fonds à propos de la Nouvelle Section de l'Ecole d'Art.* La Chaux-de-Fonds, Switzerland: Imprimerie Georges Dubois, 1914.

Etlin, Richard A. *Frank Lloyd Wright and Le Corbusier: The Romantic Legacy.* New York: Manchester University Press, 1994.

Facos, Michelle. *Nationalism and the Nordic Imagination: Swedish Art of the 1890s.* Berkeley: University of California Press, 1998.

Faure, Elie. Preface. *Le Salon d'Automne.* Exhibition catalog. October 15, 1905. Quoted in Barré-Despond and Tise, *Jourdain.*

Flam, Jack D., ed. *Matisse on Art.* Berkeley: University of California Press, 1994.

Frampton, Kenneth. *Modern Architecture: A Critical History.* 3rd ed. New York: Thames and Hudson, 1992.

Friedman, Alice. *Women and the Making of the Modern House: A Social and Architectural History.* New York: Abrams, 1998.

g. "Französisches Mobiliar." *Decorative Kunst* 2 (1898): 104–6.

Gallagher, Shaun. "Lived Body and Environment." *Research in Phenomenology* 16 (1986): 139–70.

Gargiani, Roberto. *Auguste Perret: La théorie et l'oeuvre.* Trans. Odile Ménégaux. Milan: Gallimard/Electa, 1994.

Garnier, Charles. Letter. *L'illustration* 2437 (November 9, 1889). Excerpted in Mathieu, *1889.*

Garnier, Tony. Letter to Charles-Edouard Jeanneret. December 13, 1915. FLC B1–20, 86–87.

————. *Une Cité Industrielle.* Ed. Riccardo Mariani. Trans. Andrew Ellis. New York: Rizzoli, 1990.

Geffroy, Gustave. "La vie artistique." *Les temps nouveaux* 1, no. 2 (1895). Quoted in Herbert, *The Artist and Social Reform.*

George, Waldemar. "L'Exposition des Arts Décoratifs et Industriels de 1925." *L'amour de l'art* (1925): 395–98.

Georgiadis, Sokratis. *Sigfried Giedion: An Intellectual Autobiography.* Edinburgh: Edinburgh University Press, 1993.

Giedion, Sigfried. *Building in France, Building in Iron, Building in Ferroconcrete.* Trans. Duncan J. Berry. Santa Monica, Calif.: Getty Center for the History of Art and the Humanities, 1995.

————. "La leçon de l'exposition du 'Werkbund' Stuttgart 1927." *L'architecture vivante* (Spring and Summer 1928): 37–43.

————. *Mechanization Takes Command: A Contribution to Anonymous History.* New York: W. W. Norton, 1969.

————. *Space, Time and Architecture: The Growth of a New Tradition.* 5th ed. Cambridge, Mass.: Harvard University Press, 1967.

Golan, Romy. *Modernity and Nostalgia: Art and Politics in France between the Wars.* New Haven, Conn.: Yale University Press, 1995.

Golding, John. *Cubism: A History and an Analysis, 1907–1914.* 3rd ed. Cambridge, Mass.: Belknap Press of Harvard University Press, 1988.

Goldwater, Robert. *Symbolism.* New York: Harper and Row, 1979.

Gray, Eileen, and Jean Badovici. "De l'eclecticisme au doute." *L'architecture vivante* (Winter 1929): 17–21. In Constant, *Eileen Gray*, 238–40.

———. "Description." *L'architecture vivante* (Winter 1929): 23–38. In Constant, *Eileen Gray*, 240–45.

Greenhalgh, Paul, ed. *Modernism in Design.* London: Reaktion Books, 1990.

Gronberg, Tag. "Making Up the Modern City: Modernity on Display at the 1925 International Exposition." In Eliel, *L'Esprit Nouveau: Purism in Paris, 1918–1925.*

Guide officiel, Exposition des arts décoratifs de Munich, Salon d'Automne. Paris, 1910.

Guiheux, Alain, et al., eds. *Tony Garnier: L'oeuvre complète.* Paris: Centre Georges Pompidou, 1989.

Guillemot, Maurice. "Habitations d'employés." *Art et décoration* 30 (June–December 1911): 209–16.

———. "Logis d'ouvriers." *Art et décoration* 32 (July–December 1912): 79–88.

Guimard, Hector. Letter to Charles L'Eplattenier. March 28, 1914. Reprinted in L'Eplattenier et al., *Un mouvement d'art.*

Hamilton, George Heard. *Painting and Sculpture in Europe, 1880–1940.* New York: Penguin Books, 1972.

Herbert, Eugenia W. *The Artist and Social Reform: France and Belgium, 1885–1898.* New Haven, Conn.: Yale University Press, 1961.

Herbst, René, ed. *Un inventeur, l'architecte Pierre Chareau.* Paris, 1954.

Hitchcock, Henry-Russell, and Philip Johnson. *The International Style.* New York: W. W. Norton, 1995.

Hourticq, Louis. "Au Salon des Artistes Décorateurs." *Art et décoration* 36 (July 1914–December 1919): 35–46.

———. "Chronique d'un project d'Exposition Internationale des Arts Décoratifs." *Art et décoration* (August 1911, Supplément): 1–2.

Hugo, Victor. *Notre Dame de Paris.* Paris, 1832.

J. "L'art industriel." *L'art décoratif* 1 (March 1899): 253.

James-Chakraborty, Kathleen. *German Architecture for a Mass Audience.* New York: Routledge, 2000.

Janneau, Guillaume. "Introduction à l'Exposition des Arts Décoratifs: Considerations sur l'esprit moderne" *Art et décoration* 47 (January–June 1925): 146.

———. "L'art décoratif au Salon d'Automne." *Art et décoration* 37 (July–December 1920): 141–60.

———. *L'art décoratif moderne: Formes nouvelles et programmes nouveaux.* Paris: Bernheim Jeune, 1925.

Jeanneret, Ch-E. *Etude sur le mouvement d'art décoratif en Allemagne.* La Chaux-de-Fonds, Switzerland, 1912.

Jeanneret, Charles-Edouard. Card to his parents (M. and Mme. Jeanneret-Perret). Berlin, June 13, 1910. (LCms 54).

————. Card to his parents (M. and Mme. Jeanneret-Perret). Weimar, June 21,
    1910. (LCms 55).

————. Letter to Charles L'Eplattenier. Berlin, January 16, 1911.

————. Letter to Francis Jourdain. December 21, 1913. Jourdain Archives. Quoted
    in Troy, *Modernism and the Decorative Arts*.

————. Letter to his parents. Vienna, December 5, 1907. (LCms 23).

————. Letter to his parents. Vienna, March 8, 1908. (LCms40).

————. Letter to his parents. Munich, April 18, 1910. (LCms 49).

————. Letter to his parents. Munich, June 29, 1910. (LCms 56).

Jourdain, Francis. Les Ateliers Modernes advertisement. *Cahiers d'aujourd'hui* 5
    (June 1913).

Jourdain, Frantz. *Des choses et d'autres*. Paris, 1902.

————. "Le Salon d'Automne." *Excelsior*, September 29, 1911. Quoted in Barré-
    Despond and Tise, *Jourdain*.

————. "Les écoles regionals d'architecture." Manuscript. Jourdain Archives.
    Quoted in Barré-Despond and Tise, *Jourdain*.

Judex. "Chronique du mois." *Revue des arts décoratifs* 16 (1896): 398.

————. "L'initiative d'une nouvelle monnaie." *Revue des arts décoratifs* 15 (1894–
    95): 568.

————. "Roger Marx: La réforme de la monnaie." *Revue des arts décoratifs* 12
    (1891–92).

Julian, Philippe. *The Triumph of Art Nouveau: Paris Exhibition 1900*. Trans. Stephen
    Hardman. London: Phaidon Press, 1974.

Kahn, Gustave. "La réalisation d'un ensemble d'architecture et de décoration."
    L'art décoratif 29 (February 1913): 89–102.

Kallir, Jane. *Viennese Design and the Wiener Werkstätte*. New York: George Braziller
    in association with Galerie St. Etienne, 1986.

Kirsch, Karin. *The Weissenhofsiedlung: Experimental Housing Built for the Deutscher
    Werkbund, Stuttgart, 1927*. New York: Rizzoli, 1989.

Kostof, Spiro. *A History of Architecture: Settings and Rituals*. 2nd ed. New York:
    Oxford University Press, 1995.

Kramer, Hilton. "The First Five Years: An Introduction." In *The New Criterion
    Reader: The First Five Years*. New York: The Free Press, 1988.

Kruft, Hanno-Walter. *A History of Architectural Theory from Vitruvius to the Present*.
    Trans. Ronald Taylor, Elsie Callander, and Antony Wood. London: Zwem-
    mer; Princeton, N.J.: Princeton Architectural Press, 1994.

Lacambre, Geneviève. "Toward an Emerging Definition of Naturalism in French
    Nineteenth-Century Painting." In *The European Realist Tradition*, ed. Gabriel P.
    Weisberg, 229–41. Bloomington: Indiana University Press, 1982.

Larroumet, Gustave. "L'art décoratif et les femmes." *Revue des arts décoratifs* 16
    (1896).

Le Corbusier. *The Athens Charter*. New York: Grossman, 1973.

————. *The City of Tomorrow and Its Planning*. Trans. Frederick Etchells. New
    York: Dover Publications, 1987.

———. *The Decorative Art of Today*. Trans. James I. Dunnett. Cambridge, Mass.:
   The MIT Press, 1987.

———. Letter to Takamasa Yosizaka. November 8, 1954. Le Corbusier Archives
   (R3–09–40), Paris.

———. *Towards a New Architecture*. Trans. Frederick Etchells. 13th ed. New York:
   Dover Publications, 1986.

——— (Ch-E. Jeanneret). *Les voyages d'Allemagne, Carnets*. 5 vols. New York:
   Monacelli Press and Fondation Le Corbusier, 1995.

Le Corbusier and Pierre Jeanneret. *Oeuvre complète*. Vol. 1: *1910–1929*. 14th ed.
   Zurich: Les Editions d'Architecture [Artemis], 1995.

Leatherbarrow, David. "Adjusting Architectural Premises." Typescript. 1995.

Leder, Drew. *The Absent Body*. Chicago: The University of Chicago Press, 1990.

Lethaby, W. R. *Form in Civilization: Collected Papers on Art and Labour*. 2nd ed.
   London: Oxford University Press, 1957.

Logue, William. *From Philosophy to Sociology: The Evolution of French Liberalism,
   1870–1914*. De Kalb: Northern Illinois University Press, 1983.

Loos, Adolf. "Architecture 1910." In *The Architecture of Adolf Loos: An Arts Council
   Exhibition*, trans. Wilfred Wang. London: Arts Council of Great Britain, 1985.

———. "Ornament et crime." Trans. Marcel Ray. *Cahiers d'aujourd'hui* 5 (June
   1913): 247–56.

———. *Spoken into the Void: Collected Essays 1897–1900*. Trans. Jane O. Newman
   and John H. Smith. Cambridge, Mass.: The MIT Press, 1982.

Louis, Michel. "Mallet-Stevens and the Cinema, 1919–1929." In Deshoulières
   and Jeanneau, *Rob Mallet-Stevens, Architecte*.

Lucan, Jacques dir. *Le Corbusier, une encyclopédie*. Paris: Editions du Centre
   Pompidou/CCI, 1987.

Magne, H. M. "L'architecture et les matériaux nouveaux." *Art et décoration* 36
   (July 1914–December 1919): 85–96.

Mainardi, Patricia. *Art and Politics of the Second Empire: The Universal Expositions
   of 1855 and 1867*. New Haven, Conn.: Yale University Press, 1987.

Mallet-Stevens, Robert. *Extraits des sept arts*, 1923. Quoted in Deshoulières and
   Jeanneau, "Demands of Architecture."

———. "Le cinema et les arts: L'architecture." *Les cahiers du mois*, nos. 16–17
   (1925). Excerpted in Neuman, *Film Architecture*.

———. "Le Salon d'Automne." *Tekhné* 34 (November 16, 1911). Quoted in
   Brunhammer, "Robert Mallet-Stevens as Interior Architect."

Mare, André. Letter to Maurice Marinot. February 20, 1912. Collection Michel
   Mare, Paris. Quoted in Troy, *Modernism and the Decorative Arts*.

Margoulis, Ivan. *Cubism in Architecture and the Applied Arts: Bohemia and France
   1910–1914*. London: David & Charles, 1979.

Marx, Roger. *L'art social*. Paris: Fasquelle, 1913.

———. Preface. The Salon d'Automne. Exhibition catalog. October 1906.

Mathieu, Caroline, ed. *1889: La Tour Eiffel et l'Exposition Universelle*. Paris: Editions de la Réunion des Musées Nationaux, 1989.

Matisse, Henri. "Notes d'un peintre." *La grande revue* (Paris), December 25, 1908. Quoted in Hamilton, *Painting and Sculpture.*

Merleau-Ponty, Maurice. *The Visible and the Invisible.* Ed. John Wild. Trans. Alphonso Lingis. Evanston, Ill.: Northwestern University Press, 1968.

Mies van der Rohe, Ludwig. "The New Era." In Conrads, *Programs and Manifestoes on 20th-Century Architecture.*

———. "On Form in Architecture." In Conrads, *Programs and Manifestoes on 20th-Century Architecture.*

———. "Technology and Architecture." In Conrads, *Programs and Manifestoes on 20th-Century Architecture.*

Mirbeau, Octave. Preface. In *Meubles Modernes,* by Léon Werth. Paris: Les Ateliers Modernes, 1912. Facsimile copy in Barré-Despond and Tise, *Jourdain.*

Moffett, Kenworth. *Meier-Graefe as Art Critic.* Munich: Prestel Verlag, 1973.

Moholy-Nagy, Lásló. *Vision in Motion.* Chicago: P. Theobald, 1947.

Monod, François. "L'enseignement de l'art décoratif en Allemagne et en France à propos d'un congrès recent." *Art et décoration* 34 (August 1913, supplément 3): 1–4.

Morris, William. *News from Nowhere and Other Writings.* Ed. Clive Wilmer. New York: Penguin Books, 1993.

Mourey, Gabriel. "L'Art Nouveau at Paris." *Art Journal* 59 (1897): 89–90.

———. "VIIᵉ Salon de la Société des Artistes Décorateurs au Pavillon de Marsan." *Art et décoration* 31 (January–June 1912): 101–22.

———. "Une villa de Charles Plumet." *Art et décoration* 30 (July–December 1911): 277–88.

Municipal Council of Paris. Report on the Second Congress of the Union Provinciale des Arts Décoratifs in Munich 1908. *L'art et les métiers d'art,* January 1919. Quoted in Barré-Despond and Tise, *Jourdain.*

Muthesius, Hermann. "Aims of the Werkbund." In Conrads, *Programs and Manifestoes on 20th-Century Architecture.*

———. *The English House.* Ed. Dennis Sharp. Trans. Janet Seligman. New York: Rizzoli, 1987.

———. *Style-Architecture and Building-Art: Transformations of Architecture in the Nineteenth Century and Its Present Condition.* Trans. Stanford Anderson. Santa Monica, Calif.: Getty Center for the History of Art and the Humanities, 1994.

———. "Wo stehen wir?" Speech to the 1911 Werkbund Congress.

Neumann, Dietrich, ed. *Film Architecture: Set Designs from Metropolis to Blade Runner.* New York: Prestel Verlag, 1999.

Norberg-Schulz, Christian. *Genius Loci: Towards a Phenomenology of Architecture.* New York: Rizzoli, 1979.

Noussane, Henri de. *Le goût dans l'ameublement.* Paris: Frimin-Didot et Cie, 1896. Quoted in Tiersten, "Chic Interior."

Oechslin, Werner. "Influences, confluences et reniements." In Lucan, *Le Corbusier, une encyclopédie,* 33–39.

Ortega y Gasset, Jose. *The Revolt of the Masses.* Trans. Anthony Kerrigan. Ed. Kenneth Moore. Notre Dame, Ind.: University of Notre Dame Press, 1985.

Ozenfant, Amédée. *Foundations of Modern Art*. Trans. John Rodker. New York: Dover Publications, 1952.

Pach, Walter. *Raymond Duchamp-Villon, Sculpture 1876–1918*. Ed. Jacques Povolozky. Paris: John Quinn et Ses Amis, 1924.

Paret, Peter. *The Berlin Secession: Modernism and Its Enemies in Imperial Germany*. Cambridge, Mass.: Belknap Press of Harvard University Press, 1980.

Pérez-Gómez, Alberto. *Architecture and the Crisis of Modern Science*. Cambridge, Mass.: The MIT Press, 1983.

Perret, Auguste. "Architecture" [1933]. Reprinted in Britton, *August Perret*, 238–43.

———. *Contribution à une théorie de l'architecture*. [1952].

Pevsner, Nikolaus. *High Victorian Design: A Study of the Exhibits of 1851*. London: Architectural Press, 1951.

———. *Pioneers of Modern Design from William Morris to Walter Gropius*. Pelican ed. Harmondsworth, England: Penguin Books, 1975.

Poggi, Christine. *In Defiance of Painting: Cubism, Futurism, and the Invention of Collage*. New Haven, Conn.: Yale University Press, 1992.

Pollitt, J. J. *The Ancient View of Greek Art: Criticism, History, and Terminology*. New Haven, Conn.: Yale University Press, 1974.

Pommer, Richard, and Christian F. Otto. *Weissenhof 1927 and the Modern Movement in Architecture*. Chicago: University of Chicago Press, 1991.

Rambosson, Yvanhoë. "La renaissance des arts appliqués." *Revue bleu* 9 (1922): 270–76.

———. "Le XIIᵉ Salon des Artistes Décorateurs." *Art et décoration* 41 (January–June 1922): 97–128.

———. "Les artistes décorateurs au Salon des Artistes Français." *Art et décoration* 41 (January–June 1922): 181–92.

"Rapport de la Commission Consultative." *Le génie civil*, 4.21 (March 21 and 28, 1885). Quoted in Mathieu, *1889*.

Reed, Christopher, ed. *Not at Home: The Suppression of Domesticity in Modern Art and Architecture*. New York: Thames and Hudson, 1996.

Roberts, John M. *Europe 1880–1945*. London: Longmans, Green and Co., 1967.

Rowe, Colin, and Robert Slutzky. "Transparency: Literal and Phenomenal." In Rowe, *The Mathematics of the Ideal Villa, and Other Essays*. Cambridge, Mass.: The MIT Press, 1976.

Ruskin, John. *The Seven Lamps of Architecture*. New York: Dover Publications, 1989.

———. *The Stones of Venice*. Ed. J. G. Links. New York: Da Capo Press, 1960.

Rybczynski, Witold. *Home: A Short History of an Idea*. New York: Viking, 1986.

Rykwert, Joseph. "Eileen Gray, Pioneer of Design." *Architectural Review* (December 1972): 357–61.

———. *The First Moderns: The Architects of the Eighteenth Century*. Cambridge, Mass.: The MIT Press, 1991.

———. *The Necessity of Artifice*. New York: Rizzoli, 1982.

Saunier, Charles. "Le 5me Salon de la Société des Artistes Décorateurs." *Art et décoration* 27 (January–June 1910): 109–40.

———. "VIᵉ Salon de la Société des Artistes Décorateurs au Pavillon de Marsan." *Art et décoration* 29 (January–June 1911): 77–100.

Scruton, Roger. *The Aesthetics of Architecture*. Princeton, N.J.: Princeton University Press, 1979.

Schwartz, Frederic J. *The Werkbund: Design Theory and Mass Culture before the First World War*. New Haven, Conn.: Yale University Press, 1996.

Sedeyn, Emile. "Au Salon d'Automne." *Art et décoration* 32 (July–December 1912): 141–60.

Sedlmyr, Hans. *Art in Crisis: The Lost Center*. Trans. Brian Battershaw. London: Hollis & Carter, 1957.

Semper, Gottfried. *Klien Schriften*. Eds. M. Semper and H. Semper. Berlin, 1884.

———. "Pottery." In *Der stil in den technischen un tektonischen künstne, oder praktische aesthetik*. Munich, 1879.

Silver, Kenneth E. *Esprit de Corps: The Art of the Parisian Avant-Garde and the First World War, 1914–1925*. Princeton, N.J.: Princeton University Press, 1989.

Silverman, Debora L. *Art Nouveau in Fin-de-Siècle France: Politics, Psychology and Style*. Berkeley: University of California Press, 1989.

Simmel, Georg. "The Metropolis and Mental Life." (1903). In *The Sociology of Georg Simmel*, ed. H. Wolf. New York: Free Press, 1950.

Sizeranne, Robert de la. *L'art pendant la guerre, 1914–1918*. Paris, 1919. Quoted in Golan, *Modernity and Nostalgia*.

Smith, Leonard V., Stéphane Audoin-Rouzeau, and Annette Becker. *France and the Great War, 1914–1918*. Cambridge: Cambridge University Press, 2003.

Solomon R. Guggenheim Museum. *Jacques Villon, Raymond Duchamp-Villon, Marcel Duchamp*. Exhibition catalog. January 8–February 17, 1957. N.p.

Steinberg, Leo. *Other Criteria: Confrontations with Twentieth-Century Art*. New York: Oxford University Press, 1972.

Storez, M. "Que seront l'architecture et l'art decoratif après la guerre?" *Grande revue* (October 1915): 492–521.

"Supplément." *Art et décoration* (December 1912).

Tiersten, Lisa. "The Chic Interior and the Feminine Modern: Home Decorating as High Art in Turn-of-the-Century Paris." In Reed, *Not at Home: The Suppression of Domesticity in Modern Art and Architecture*, 18–32.

Toulmin, Stephen. *Cosmopolis: The Hidden Agenda of Modernity*. Chicago: University of Chicago Press, 1990.

Tournikiotis, Panayotis. *Adolf Loos*. Princeton, N.J.: Princeton Architectural Press, 1994.

Troy, Nancy J. *Couture Culture: A Study in Modern Art and Fashion*. Cambridge, Mass.: The MIT Press, 2003.

———. *Modernism and the Decorative Arts in France: Art Nouveau to Le Corbusier*. New Haven, Conn.: Yale University Press, 1991.

Turner, Paul Venable. *The Education of Le Corbusier*. New York: Garland Publishing, 1977.

Vachon, Marius. *La guerre artistique avec l'Allemagne: L'organisation de la victoire*. Paris: Payot, 1916.

Vaillat, Léandre. "L'art décoratif au Salon d'Automne." *L'art et les artistes* 14 (November 1911): 80–85. Quoted in Troy, *Modernism and the Decorative Arts*.

Valéry, Paul. *Aesthetics*. Trans. Ralph Manheim. New York: Bollingen Foundation, Pantheon Books, 1964.

Varenne, Gaston. "L'esprit nouveau de Pierre Chareau." *Art et décoration* 43 (January–June 1923): 129–38.

———. "L'Exposition des Arts Décoratifs: Le mobilier français." *Art et décoration* 48 (July–December 1925): 1–44.

Vaudoyer, Jean-Louis. "Le Salon d'Automne, II—l'art décoratif." *Art et décoration* 36 (July 1914–December 1919): 173–92.

Vellay, Marc, and Kenneth Frampton. *Pierre Chareau: Architect and Craftsman, 1883–1950*. New York: Rizzoli, 1984.

Verne, Henri, and René Chavance. *Pour comprendre l'art décoratif moderne en France*. Paris: Librairie Hachette, 1925.

Verneuil, M.-P. "L'ameublement au Salon d'Automne." *Art et décoration* 35 (January–June 1914): 1–32.

———. "L'architecture aux Salons," *Art et décoration* 28 (July–December 1910): 53–56.

———. "L'art décoratif aux Salons de 1912." *Art et décoration* 32 (July–December 1912): 177–86.

———. "Le Salon d'Automne." *Art et décoration* 28 (July–December 1910): 129–60.

———. "Supplément." *Art et décoration* (October 1910): 2.

———. "Un intérieur moderne." *Art et décoration* 31 (January–June 1913): 53–62.

Vesely, Dalibor. "Architecture and the Poetics of Representation." *Daidalos* 25 (September 1987): 24–36.

Vidler, Anthony. *The Writing of the Walls: Architectural Theory in the Late Enlightenment*. Princeton, N.J.: Princeton Architectural Press, 1987.

Viollet-le-Duc, Eugène-Emmanuel. *Lectures on Architecture*. 2 vols. Trans. Benjamin Bucknall. New York: Dover Publications, 1987.

Vitruvius, *De Architectura*. Translated by F. Granger. Cambridge, Mass.: Harvard University Press, 1983.

Von Moos, Stanislaus, and Arthur Rüegg, eds. *Le Corbusier before Le Corbusier: Applied Arts, Architecture, Painting, Photography, 1907–1922*. New Haven, Conn.: Yale University Press, 2002.

Wagner, Otto. *Modern Architecture: A Guidebook for His Students to This Field of Art*. Trans. Harry Francis Mallgrave. Santa Monica, Calif.: Getty Center for the History of Art and the Humanities, 1988.

Wehler, Hans-Ulrich. *The German Empire 1871–1918*. Trans. Kim Traynor. Dover, N.H.: Berg Publishers, 1985.

Weisberg, Gabriel P. *Art Nouveau Bing: Paris Style 1900*. New York: Harry N. Abrams, 1986.

———, ed. *The European Realist Tradition*. Bloomington: Indiana University Press, 1982.

Weiss, Jeffrey. *The Popular Culture of Modern Art: Picasso, Duchamp, and Avant-Gardism*. New Haven, Conn.: Yale University Press, 1994.

Werth, Léon. *Meubles modernes*. Paris: Les Ateliers Modernes, 1912. Facsimile copy in Barré-Despond and Tise, *Jourdain*, 386–89.

Wigley, Mark. *White Walls, Designer Dresses: The Fashioning of Modern Architecture*. Cambridge, Mass.: The MIT Press, 1995.

Wilson, Richard Guy. "International Style: The MoMA Exhibition." *Progressive Architecture* (February 1982): 92–105.

Windsor, Alan. *Peter Behrens: Architect and Designer*. New York: Whitney Library of Design, 1981.

Wingler, Hans M. *The Bauhaus*. Trans. Wolfgang Jabs and Basil Gilbert. Ed. Joseph Stein. Cambridge, Mass.: The MIT Press, 1969.

Wolfe, Tom. *From Bauhaus to Our House*. New York: Farrar, Straus and Giroux, 1981.

Zola, Emile. Interview by Frantz Jourdain. "Que pensez-vous de l'architecture moderne?" *Revue des arts décoratifs* 16 (1896): 95.

———. Interview. "Souvenirs des Goncourts." *La revue encyclopédique* 153 (August 8, 1896): 55. Quoted in Silverman, *Art Nouveau in Fin-de-Siècle France*.

INDEX

Academic rationalism, 20

Academy of Art, 59

Academy of Fine Arts, 33–34, 48

Aestheticism, 123

Aesthetics, 163–64, 177*n58*

Albert, Prince, 49

Alberti, Leon Battista, 194

Alfa Romeo, 155

Allgemeine Elektricitäts-Gesellschaft
   (AEG), 70

Alsace, 117

Apollinaire, Guillaume, 117, 176*n53*

Architectes-décorateurs, 8, 20, 124, 137,
   143–61, 166–67, 188*n6*

Architecture: Academy of Fine Arts'
   effect on, 33–34; color in, 13;
   cubism in, 20, 22, 86, 87*fig*, 88; in
   England, 8, 17, 166; fashion and,
   11–13, 123; first duty of, 3, 8, 25,
   161–62; formalism in, 164, 166;
   France's hour of, 7, 136–43; in
   Germany, 8, 17, 166, 174*n1*; International Style, 10, 163–66; Le
   Corbusier's rules for, 153; life as
   foundation for, 164–67; middle
   class focus for, 92–100; modern,
   3–8, 124, 139–40, 161–62, 171*n30*;
   nineteenth century, 23, 25–32,
   171*n1*; painting and, 92; in the
   post-war era, 124; rational modernism, 38–39, 171*n30*; revolution
   in, 4, 6; rise over decorative art,
   121–22, 133, 142–43; uniformity in
   international viewpoint, 164–65,
   194*n3*

Architecture and Cubism (Troy and
   Blau), 22

Art: academic, 33; Belgian influence,
   32; elimination of distinctions
   within, 177*n71*; fine, 58–67; in
   nineteenth-century France,
   178*n86*; political liberalization
   and, 59; popularization in France
   of, 178*n82*; reform of, 55–58; tools
   as, 134; urban, 92. *See also* Decorative art; Integrated ensembles;
   Painting

Art Deco, 11, 122

Art et Décoration, 129–30, 133

Art et Liberté, 46

Art Nouveau: Bing's gallery, 52–55,
   56*fig*, 57*fig* 58, 177*n71*; origin of,
   52–53; as products for everyday
   use, 31–33, 174*n11*; waning of, 55

*Art Nouveau in Fin-de-Siècle France:
   Politics, Psychology and Style*
   (Silverman), 22, 26

Arts and Crafts Movement (England),
   68, 93

Association Général de Hygiénistes
   et Techniciens Municipaux, 114

Athens Charter (*1941*), 165–66

Aurier, Albert, 61

Austria, 8, 17, 165–66

Bachelot, Melle, 111

Badovici, Jean, 147, 148*fig*, 151, 164

Baker, Geoffrey, 22

Banham, Reyner, 14, 86, 173*n46*,
   190*n28*

Barré-Despond, Arlette, 22, 95

Bauhaus (Dessau, Germany), 19,
   136–37

Beauty, 83, 123, 194*n15*

Behrens, Peter: as AEG artistic direc-
    tor, 70; as domestic designer, 16;
    The Dwelling exhibition, 169*n14*;
    electric teakettle, 70*fig*
Belgium, 32, 165
Benson, William, 177*n68*
Bergson, Henri, 24, 60, 137–38, 152
Berlage, H. P., 170*n17*
Bernard, Philippe, 127, 188*n10*
Berndl, Richard, 74*fig*
Besnard, Albert, 52, 63
Besson, Georges, 101–2
Bijvoët, Bernard, 146
Bing, Siegfried: art gallery of, 52–53,
    55, 58, 177*n71*; art's effect on the
    masses, 188*n8*; Japanese and
    American art introduced to
    France by, 52, 177*n66*; painting
    and domestic space, 63
Blau, Eve, 22
Bonhommé, François, 62*fig*
Bonnard, Pierre, 52
Bonnier, Louis, 53; L'Art Nouveau
    Gallery, 56*fig*, 57*fig*
Bourgeois, Léon, 58, 178*n82*
Bourgeois, Victor, 169*n14*, 170*n17*
Brangwyn, Frank, 52–53, 177*n68*
Braque, Georges, 48, 63, 65; *Violin
    and Palette*, 66*fig*
Breuer, Marcel, 160
Britton, Karla, 41
Brooks, Alan, 22
Building materials, indigenous, 36
Building setback regulations, 43

*C*ahiers d'aujourd'hui, 101–2
Carabin, Rupert, 182*n7*
Central Union of Fine Arts Applied
    to Industry, 49–50
Central Union of the Decorative
    Arts, 50, 52
Cercle des Artistes de Passy, 46
Cézanne, Paul, 60
Chagall, Marc, 48
Change, 4, 6

Chareau, Pierre: A Young Doctor's
    Consulting-Room and Bedroom,
    119*fig*; as *architect-décorateur*, 188*n6*;
    architecture's role in work of,
    143–47; ensembles, 99; first duty
    of architecture, 8, 162; French
    embassy interiors, 130, 132*fig*, 144;
    La Sarraz Declaration, 170*n17*;
    Maison de Verre, 144*fig*, 145*fig*;
    post-war design, 124, 129–30;
    role as modern architect, 191*n34*;
    Union des Artistes Modernes,
    131–32; Vicomte de Noailles villa,
    160; World War I, 117–18
Chavance, René, 92, 130, 185*n48*
Chez Francis Jourdain, 128
Choisy, Auguste, 25, 33, 35, 40
Cinqualbre, Olivier, 184*n47*
City of Tomorrow and Its Planning,
    (Le Corbusier), 8, 139
Clausen, Meredith, 22
Climate, 165
Clothing, 11–13
Cole, Henry, 49
Collages, 65, 173*n48*, 180*n107*, 191*n39*
Colomina, Beatriz, 21, 191*n34*
Color, 13
Coloristes: cubism and, 81, 183*n29*;
    ensembles as influenced by,
    183*n29*, 184*n39*, 186*n75*; Le Corbu-
    sier and, 102, 104, 192*n43*; in the
    post-war era, 189*n15*; at Salons
    d'Automne, 79–82, 91, 94–96
Common sense, 137–38, 152
Compagnie des Arts Français, 117
Compagnie des Chemins de Fer du
    Paris-Orléans, 130
Concrete: Duchamp-Villon's enthusi-
    asm for, 176*n52*; frames, 57; for
    habitability, 112, 115–16; Garnier's
    proposed use of, 35–40; mass-
    production of housing from,
    107–10; Perret as pioneer of use
    of, 40–41, 43–44, 176*n52*
Conder, Charles, 52, 177*n68*

Congrès Internationaux d'Architecture Moderne (CIAM), 10–11, 164–65

Constant, Caroline, 22, 149, 152

Constructeurs, 79, 98

Cottin, M., 51

Cottington, David, 22, 176*n*52

Courbet, Gustave, 60

Couyba, Charles, 182*n*7

Cubism: in architecture, 20, 22, 86, 87*fig*, 88; art as affected by, 24; collage, 173*n*48, 180*n*107, 191*n*39; and *coloristes*, 81, 183*n*29; French attitude toward, 91, 95; Puteaux group, 46, 65, 67, 183*n*29; Salon d'Automne, 59; use of banal objects, 63, 65

Cubism in the Shadow of War (Cottington), 22

Customs, 165–66

Dalbet, André, 146

Dalsace, Anna, 118, 146

Dalsace, Jean, 118, 146

Danto, Arthur, 21

Debussy, Claude, 24

Decoration, 62–63

Decorative art: architecture's rise over, 6, 120–21, 133, 142–43; competition between European powers, 24, 93; the end of, 133–34; French weakness in, 72; in Germany, 17–18, 93; as lesser form, 58; as pastiche, 90; Pavillon de l'Esprit Nouveau, 4, 7–8; perception over metaphysics in design of, 137–38; in the post-war era, 122

The Decorative Art of Today (Le Corbusier), 4, 8, 120, 122, 136, 138–40, 190*n*28

Degas, Edgar, 180*n*101

Delauney, Robert, 131

Denis, Maurice, 52, 60–61, 63; *April*, 64*fig*

Department stores, 189*n*15

Derain, André, 117

Deshairs, Léon, 161

Deshoulières, D., 22, 154

Design. *See* Decorative art; House design; Interior furnishings

Design journals, 175*n*23

Desvallières, Richard, 184*n*37

Deutscher Werkbund: development of, 16; exhibition (Stuttgart, *1927*), 8, 9*fig*, 10, 15, 19; focus of, 19, 136; foreign competition with, 93; offshoots from, 17, 106; production of interior furnishings, 68

Ditisheim, Ernst-Albert, 104

Ditisheim, Hermann, 104

Döcker, Richard, 169*n*14

Doesburg, Theo van, 160

Du Bois, Max, 107–8, 113

Dubief, Henri, 127, 188*n*10

Dubuffet, Jean, 44–45

Duchamp, Marcel, 89, 184*n*37, 191*n*39

Duchamp-Villon, Raymond, 86, 176*n*53; concrete and steel as used by, 176*n*52; entry portal of Un Salon Bourgeois, 86, 87*fig*; facade of Un Salon Bourgeois, 86, 87*fig*, 88–89

Dufrène, Maurice: artistic conservatism of, 79; cabinet and armchair, 78*fig*; department store sales by, 189*n*15; opulent interiors of, 122, 130; woman's bedroom, 121*fig*

Dutert, Ferdinand, 23, 27*fig*, 173*n*1

The Dwelling exhibition, 8, 15, 19, 164, 169*n*14

E.1027, 147–52

East Asia, 53

Ecole des Beaux-Arts, 56

Economies of scale, 112

Education, public, 35

Eiffel, Gustave, 23, 173*n*1

Eiffel tower, 23, 25–27, 29, 33, 124, 173*n*1

Eileen Gray (Constant), 22

Eliel, Carol S., 22

Engineered works, 23–25, 173*n*1

England: architecture in, 8, 17, 166; Arts and Crafts Movement, 68; German competition in crafts production, 93; interior furnishings, 48–49

Entry portals, 86, 87*fig*

Equipment, 109, 131, 134

Etude sur le mouvement d'art décoratif en Allemagne (Le Corbusier), 17–19, 105, 114

Exposition de la Cité Reconstituée (*1916*), 114–15

Exposition Internationale des Arts Décoratifs et Industriels Modernes, 6, 99, 127, 130, 140, 155–59

Exposition Universelle (Paris, *1855*), 28, 49

Exposition Universelle (Paris, *1878*), 28

Exposition Universelle (Paris, *1889*), 23, 27–29, 173*n*1; Chinese and Japanese houses, 28*fig*

Exposition Universelle (Paris, *1900*), 29–32; bedroom, 32*fig*; electrically lit night scene, 30*fig*; Le Chateau d'Eau, 30*fig*

Facades: in film sets, 157; free, 153; at Un Salon Bourgeois, 86, 87*fig*, 88–89, 93, 184*n*47; as urban art, 92

Fashion, 11–13, 123

Faure, Elie, 188*n*8

Fauves, 63, 180*n*101

Feminism, 13

Film sets, 154–55, 157–58, 185*n*47

Fine arts: domestic arts as inferior to, 58; domestic themes in, 59–67

Fixtures, 144

Flanders, 110–11, 113

Form, 164

Formalism, 164, 166

Frames, 57, 140

Frampton, Kenneth, 22, 41, 144, 146, 191*n*34

Frank, Josef, 169*n*14, 170*n*17

Frantz Jourdain and the Samaritaine (Clausen), 22

Free facades, 153

Free plans, 153

French Academy (Rome), 48

Freyssinet, Eugène, 173*n*46

Friedman, Alice, 13

Functionality, 194*n*15

Gaillard, Eugene, 79; bedroom, 32*fig*

Gallé, Emile, 52, 124

Gallerey, Thomas, 79

Gallery of Machines, 23, 25–27, 29, 33, 124, 173*n*1

Gampert, Jean-Louis, 184*n*37

Garnier, Catherine, 111

Garnier, Charles, 28–29, 33

Garnier, Tony: Academy of Fine Arts and, 48; architect's villa, 37–38, 39*fig*, 187*n*11; as innovator, 35–37; Le Corbusier and, 111–13, 187*n*11; as pre-war modern architect, 172*n*46; urban planning, 155; World War I, 114, 116, 118

Gaudet, Julien, 35, 40

Gauguin, Paul, 60

Geffroy, Gustave, 50, 188*n*8

Gender roles, 13–14

Genre painting, 60, 179*n*87

George, Waldemar, 130

Germany: architecture in, 8, 17, 166, 174*n*1; Bauhaus, 19, 136–37; competition with English crafts production, 93; decorative art, 17–18, 93; evaluating the arts of, 17–19, 70, 103; French competition with, 19–20, 67, 70–76, 83, 105–6, 113, 181*n*4; house design in, 16; influence on French design of, 184*n*39; La Sarraz declaration, 165; large-scale cooperation in design, 136–37; origins of industrial design

in, 181*n11*; production of interior
furnishings, 68–69; Salons d'Au-
tomne displays by, 72–77, 102
Gide, André, 176*n53*
Giedion, Sigfried, 10, 165, 173*n46*,
191*n34*
Gleizes, Albert, 89, 184*n37*
Golan, Romy, 22, 117, 121
Goldwater, Robert, 61
Goncourt, Edmund de, 52
Gordine, Dora, 47
Grand Palais, 3
Grasset, Eugene, 124
Gray, Eileen: architecture's role in
work of, 143, 147–53; bedroom,
E.1027, 148*fig*; E.1027, 147–52; exte-
rior of E.1027, 147*fig*; first duty of
architecture, 8, 162; Le Corbusier
compared to, 152–54; living room,
E.1027, 148*fig*; Mathieu-Lévy
apartment, 149–50; on modern
architecture, 166; post-war design,
124; role as modern architect,
191*n34*; standardization, 154;
Union des Artistes Modernes, 131;
Vicomte de Noailles villa, 160
Great Exhibition of the Works of
Industry of All Nations, 48–49
Gris, Juan, 125*fig*, 135–36
Gronberg, Tag, 13
Gropius, Walter, 12, 16, 169*n14*
Groult, André, 79; small salon, 75*fig*
Guévrékian, Gabriel, 160, 170*n17*
Guillemot, Maurice, 83
Guimard, Hector, 18

Habitability, 111–12, 115–16
Haefeli, Max Ernst, 170*n17*
Hallays, André, 29, 31–32
Hamilton, George Heard, 60
Häring, Hugo, 170*n17*
Herbert, Eugenia W., 178*n86*
Herbin, Auguste, 117
Hilberseimer, Ludwig, 169*n14*
Hitchcock, Henry-Russell, 163, 171*n30*

Home: A Short History of an Idea
(Rybczynski), 11
Horta, Victor, 53
Hoste, Huib, 170*n17*
Hour of architecture, 7, 136–43
Hourticq, Louis, 128
House design: as architecture, 68, 93;
Cubist influence, 59; feminism
and, 13; in Germany, 16; and
human needs, 23, 33–35; for low-
cost housing, 57–58, 106; mod-
ernism and, 10–11, 140; movable
partitions, 144; multipurpose/
living rooms, 99; redefining
rooms, 151; standardization in,
140–41, 154; for workers, 57, 83,
119*fig*, 158*fig*; World War I effect
on, 106, 116, 124, 188*n10*
Household goods. *See* Interior
furnishings
Housing. *See* House design
Huillard, Paul, 79
Human-limb object, 152
Huré, Marguerite, 47

Immeubles-villas, 4, 6*fig*, 126*fig*, 140,
188*n9*
Impressionism, 24, 60
*In Defiance of Painting: Cubism, Futur-
ism, and the Invention of Collage*
(Poggi), 21
Individual expression, 14
Individualism, 78, 90
Ingres, Jean-Auguste-Dominique,
179*n87*
Innovation (company), 128
Institut d'Art et d'Archéologie, 46
Integrated ensembles: costliness of,
129–30; French production of,
77–79; German displays of, 70–
75; as influenced by coloristes,
183*n29*, 184*n39*, 186*n75*; for multi-
purpose rooms, 99; in the Salons
d'Automne, 58–59
Interior finishing, 131

Interior furnishings: accommodation of human needs, 138; affordability of, 82, 128–30, 150; cubist influence, 65, 67; English, 48–49; as equipment, 109, 131, 134; foreign domination of French market in, 50; German, 68–69; individuality in design of, 78; mass production of, 27, 68–70, 91, 109, 110*fig*; as medium of individual expression, 135, 141–42; for the middle class, 50–52, 89, 92–106, 127; neoclassical, 79; nineteenth century, 48–49; painting and, 92; reversion to opulence in, 129–30. *See also* Integrated ensembles

International Exhibition (London, *1862*), 49

International Style architecture, 10, 163–66

The International Style (Hitchcock and Johnson), 163–64

Italy, 165

Jaeger, Henri, 177*n68*

Jallot, Léon, 79

Janneau, Guillaume, 188*n6*

Jaulmes, Gustave-Louis, 79, 95, 117

Jeanneau, H., 22, 154

Jeanneret, Charles-Edouard. *See* Le Corbusier

Jeanneret, Pierre: *The Dwelling* exhibition, 169*n14*; Equipment for Living display, 131; house of Ozenfant, 142*fig*; La Sarraz Declaration, 170*n17*; Maison Citrohan, 141*fig*; Pavillon de l'Esprit Nouveau, 4, 5*fig*, 7, 12*fig*, 125*fig*, 126*fig*

Johnson, Philip, 163, 171*n30*

Jourdain (Barré-Despond and Tise), 22

Jourdain, Francis: architecture's role in work of, 143; bedroom, 96, 97*fig*, 98; boutique for travel articles, 131*fig*; built-in cabinetry, 149; designing for the populace, 50, 99–100, 106, 111, 127, 129; end of decorative art, 134–35; first duty of architecture, 8, 162; French embassy interiors, 130; interior finishing, 131; Loos and, 100–102; mass-production of interior furnishings, 109, 110*fig*; post-war design, 124; rail-car interior, 130; role as modern architect, 191*n34*; salon/dining room, 97*fig*, 98–99; Vicomte de Noailles villa, 160; World War I, 114–15

Jourdain, Frantz: foreign influence on Un Salon Bourgeois, 91; German displays at Salon d'Automne, 72–73, 77, 102; introduction to *Une Cité Moderne*, 118; as reformer, 55–58; Vereinigte Werkstätten, 182*n7*

Julian, Philippe, 31

Kohn (furniture manufacturer), 135

Kostof, Spiro, 171*n30*

Kramer, Hilton, 171*n30*

La Chaux-de-Fonds, 102–3, 105–7, 109, 113, 135

La Cité Moderne (Lyon, *1914*), 115

La Fresnaye, Roger de: fireplaces, 89; mantelpiece, 80, 81*fig*; paintings by, 89; Un Salon Bourgeois, 184; World War I, 117

La Maison d'Art (Brussels), 53

La Sarraz Declaration (*1928*), 10, 165, 170*n17*

La Sizeranne, Robert de, 107

Lacambre, Geneviève, 60

Lalique, René, 52

Landscape, 116–17

L'Architecture vivante, 164, 192*n58*

Laurencin, Marie, 184*n37*

Le Corbusier: aesthetics minimized by, 163; architectural rules, 153; architecture's rise over decoration, 120, 142–43, 146–47; *coloristes*,

102, 104, 192*n43*; commercial glassware and crockery, 136*fig*; customs as factor in design, 165–66;
designing for the populace, 50,
127, 188*n8*, 188*n9*; dining room,
126*fig*; Ditisheim apartments,
104–5; as domestic designer, 16;
The Dwelling exhibition, 169*n14*;
end of decorative art, 133–35;
Equipment for Living display, 131;
evaluation of German arts, 17–19,
70, 103; first duty of architecture,
3, 8, 25, 161–62; French nationalism and, 113–14; Gray compared
to, 152–53; habitability, 116; house
of Ozenfant, 142*fig*; Jeanneret-
Perret residence, 103*fig*, 104; La
Sarraz Declaration, 170*n17*; living
room, 126*fig*; Maison Citrohan,
140–41; Maison Dom-ino interior,
113*fig*; mass-production housing
schemes, 107–12; "Milestones"
page, 123*fig*; modern architecture's advent, 124; paintings by,
125*fig*, 135–36, 138–39; Pavillon de
l'Esprit Nouveau, 4–8, 11–14,
125*fig*, 126*fig*, 127, 130; Perret's relationship with, 46, 103; post-war
design, 124; on the problem of
the house, 3, 6, 15, 169*n10*; production methods, 91; as Purist,
138–39; standardization, 154; as
teacher, 103–4; Tony Garnier and,
111–12, 187*n11*; urban planning,
155; visit to German interior furnishings factory, 69; World War I,
118, 120

*Le Corbusier before Le Corbusier: Applied
Arts, Architecture, Painting, Photog-
raphy, 1907–1922* (von Moos and
Rüegg), 22

Le goût das l'ameublement (de Noussane), 51*fig*

Léger, Fernand, 89, 117, 131, 135–36,
157, 184*n37*

L'Eplattenier, Charles, 17, 105–6

Les Ateliers Modernes, 98, 100, 111

Les mystères du Chateau de Dé, 154–55,
160

L'esprit nouveau, 7

*L'Esprit Nouveau: Purism in Paris, 1918–
1925* (Eliel), 22

Lethaby, W.R., 16–17

L'Herbier, Marcel, 159

Life, 164–67

L'inhumaine, 157, 159*fig*

Lipschitz, Jacques, 135–36

Living rooms, 185*n59*, 185*n60*

L'Oeuvre, 106, 113

L'Oeuvre: Association Suisse-
Romandede l'Art et l'Industrie,
106

"Logis d'ouvriers" (Guillemot), 83

Logue, William, 21, 35

Loos, Adolf: as domestic designer,
16, 192*n43*; Jourdain and, 100–102;
private nature of houses of, 12–13

Lorraine, 117

Louis, Michael, 157–58

Low-cost housing and furnishings,
57–58, 106, 129–30

Luggage, 128

Lurçat, Andre, 170*n17*

Magne, H. M., 128

Maison Citrohan, 140–41

Maison Cubiste. *See* Salon Bourgeois

Maison de Verre, 118, 144–46, 192*n53*

Maison Dom-ino, 107–10, 112–13, 116,
140

Majorelle, Louis, 79

Malancourt, 118*fig*

Male domination, 13

Mallarmé, Stéphane, 180*n101*

Mallet-Stevens, Robert: architecture's role in work of, 143; breadth
of work, 154–55; film sets, 154–55,
157–58, 185*n47*; first duty of architecture, 8, 162; French embassy
interiors, 130, 133*fig*; hall, 95*fig*, 96;

Mallet-Stevens, Robert (continued)
house design as architecture, 68,
93; music room, 96fig; post-war
design, 124; role as modern architect, 191n34; Salons d'Automne,
102; standardization, 154; Tourism
Pavilion, 130–31, 155, 156fig, 158–
59; Union des Artistes Modernes,
131; villa of Vicomte de Noailles,
158–61; worker's house, 119fig,
158fig; World War I, 118
Mare, André, 188n8; boudoir, 95;
designing for the populace, 50;
nationalism, 184n39; post-war
era, 118, 129, 189n17; as promoted
by Salon d'Automne, 79; Salon
d'Automne of 1911, 80–81, 89,
94, 162; study, 80fig, 81fig, 162;
Un Salon Bourgeois role of, 85–
86, 88–92; World War I, 117
Mariani, Ricardo, 38
Marinot, Maurice, 117, 184n37
Maschinenmöbel, 69
Mass-production housing schemes,
107–9
Mathieu-Lévy, Mme., 149–50
Matisse, Henri, 63; Harmony in Red,
64fig
May, Ernst, 170n17
Meier-Graefe, Julius, 177n71
Meissonier, Jean-Louis-Ernest,
60; The Laundresses in Antibes,
61fig
Mela Muter, Marie, 47
Mela Muter studio, 44–45, 46fig, 47
Melchior de Vogüé, Vicomte, 26
Mercadal, A. G., 170n17
Metzinger, Jean, 89, 117, 184n37
Meyer, Hannes, 170n17
Middle class: architecture's focus on,
92–100; designing for, 50, 99–100,
106, 111, 127; effect of war on, 127–
28; interior furnishings for, 50–52,
89, 92–106, 127

Mies van der Rohe, Ludwig, 8, 16,
169n14
Millet, Jean-François, 60; The Glean-
ers, 62fig
Model houses: Pavillon de l'Esprit
Nouveau, 3–8; of Tony Garnier,
37–40; at the Weissenhof housing
settlement, 8–10, 164
Modern Painting (Le Corbusier), 139
Modern style, 32, 99
Modernism, 10–11, 166
Modernism and the Decorative Arts:
Art Nouveau to Le Corbusier (Troy),
22
Modernity and Nostalgia (Golan), 22
Monet, Claude, 60, 180n101
Monod, François, 76
Moos, Stanislaus von, 22
Morice, Charles, 118
Morris, William, 178n82
Moser, W. M., 170n17
Motté (furniture manufacturer), 135
Mourey, Gabriel, 83, 100
Multipurpose rooms, 99, 185n60
Muthesius, Hermann, 12, 16, 181n1

Nabis, 24, 52, 60
Napoleon III, 31, 179n90
Nationalism, 184n39
Naturalism, 60
Netherlands, 8, 165–66
New liberalism, 21
Noailles, Charles de, 158–59, 160fig
Noailles, Marie-Laure de, 158
Nostalgia, 121–22
Not at Home: The Suppression of Domes-
ticity in Modern Art and Architec-
ture (Reed, ed.), 10–11
Noussane, Henri de, 51fig, 90

Oeuvre complete (Le Corbusier), 142,
186n2
Orloff, Chana, 47, 176n53
Ormo Corp., 136

"Ornament et crime" (Loos), 101
Oud, J. J. P., 9*fig*, 169*n14*
Ozenfant, Amédée, 135–36, 138, 176*n53*;
  Fugue, 139*fig*; house of, 142

Pach, Walter, 88
Painting: architecture and, 92; in
    Bing's L'Art Nouveau gallery, 52;
    challenge to academic styles, 60;
    composition of, 65; cubist, 63–65;
    as decoration, 63; domestic space
    and, 63; genre, 60, 179*n87*; by Le
    Corbusier, 125*fig*, 135–36, 138–39;
    in Le Corbusier's interiors, 104–
    5, 135–36, 142; in Mallet-Stevens's
    interiors, 131; in Mare's interiors,
    80, 81; and middle-class tastes,
    59, 63, 67; realism in, 60, 179*n90*;
    in the Salon d'Automn, 58–59;
    in Un Salon Bourgeois, 89
Palyart, Jacques, 94*fig*, 95–96
Partitions, 144
Paul, Bruno, 69–70, 79; small dining
    room, 71*fig*
Pavillon de l'Esprit Nouveau: absence
    of decorative art in, 134–35, 142;
    austerity of, 11–13, 127; as early
    example of modern architecture,
    3–8; as exemplar of new program
    for architectural design, 139–40,
    143, 162; progressive nature of,
    130; as synthesis of sensibilities,
    163; urban plans at, 14*fig*, 126*fig*;
    views of, 5*fig*, 125*fig*
Perception, 60
Pérez-Gómez, Alberto, 171*n30*
Perret, Auguste: Academy of Fine
    Arts and, 48; Champs-Elysées
    theater, 44; Chana Orloff studio,
    47*fig*; collaborators of, 46–48; con-
    crete and steel as used by, 40–41,
    43–44, 176*n52*; as innovator, 35;
    Le Corbusier's relationship with,
    46, 103; Mela Muter studio, 44–

45, 46*fig*; Notre Dame du Raincy
    church, 44; Pavillon de l'Esprit
    Nouveau, 7, 134; Ponthieu Garage,
    44; as pre-war modern architect,
    172*n46*; qualities of work of, 40–
    41; rue Franklin apartment, 41,
    42*fig*, 43, 44*fig*
Perriand, Charlotte, Union des Artistes
    Modernes, 131
Petite-genre scenes, 60
Peugeot cars, 136
Pevsner, Nicholas, 172*n46*
Philosophy as common sense, 24
Picasso, Pablo, 63, 65, 176*n53*; *Guitar
    and Wineglass*, 67*fig*
*Pierre Chareau: Architect and Crafts-
    man, 1883–1950* (Vellay and
    Frampton), 22
Pilotis, 153
Poelzig, Hans, 169*n14*
Poggi, Christine, 21, 65, 180*n107*
Poiret, Paul, 176*n53*
Political liberalization, 59
The Popular Culture of Modern Art
    (Weiss), 21
Post-war era, 118, 120–24, 189*n15*
*Privacy and Publicity: Modern Architec-
    ture as Mass Media* (Colomina), 21
Private spaces, 151
Problem of the house, 3, 6, 15, 167,
    169*n10*
Prouvé, Victor, 182*n7*
Public education, 35
Puteaux Cubists, 65, 67, 183*n29*

Quality of life, 25

Rading, Adolf, 169*n14*
Rambosson, Ivanhoë, 58, 129
Rational modernism, 38–39, 171*n30*
Rava, Carlo Enrico, 170*n17*
Ravel, Maurice, 24, 176*n53*
Ray, Man, 155, 160
Raymond, Emmeline, 90

Realism, 24, 60, 179*n90*

Reed, Christopher, 10–11

Regulating lines, 153

Rhulmann, Jacques, 189*n15*

Riemerschmid, Richard: corner of a
woman's room, 71*fig*; machine-
produced furniture, 69*fig*

Rietveld, Gerrit, 170*n17*

Rob Mallet-Stevens, Architecte (ed. by
Deshoulières and Jeanneau), 22

Rococo, 177*n64*

Rome Prize, 48

Roneo Corp., 136

Roof gardens, 153

Rowe, Colin, 65

Rüegg, Arthur, 22

Ruhlmann, Jacques-Emile, 130;
salon, 122*fig*

Ruskin, John, 124

Rybczynski, Witold, 11

Salon des Artistes Décorateurs, 128,
130, 154

Salon des Indépendants, 59

Salon des Refusés, 59

Salons d'Automne (Paris), 20, 58–59,
63, 67; *coloristes* at, 79–82, 91, 94–
96; *constructeurs* at, 79; Fauves at,
63; German displays at, 72–77, 102;
middle-class focus in *1913*, 92–100;
mobile fan partition in, 144; new
conceptions in architecture, 20,
58–59, 67; post-war, 118. *See also*
Un Salon Bourgeois

Sarazin, Charles, 57

Sartoris, Alberto, 170*n17*

Satie, Erik, 24

Saunier, Charles, 72–73, 76–77

Sauvage, Henri: house as anonymous
frame, 140; living rooms, 99;
modern architecture, 124, 127;
post-war design, 124; working-
class housing, 57

Scharoun, Hans, 169*n14*

Schmidt, Hans, 170*n17*

Schneck, Adolf G., 169*n14*

Schutz Group Photographers, 118*fig*

Schwartz, Frederic, 22

Screens, 144, 149

Second Empire (France), 59

Selmersheim, Pierre, 130

Selmersheim, Tony, 79

Sensuality, 166

Seurat, Georges, 180*n101*

Silver, Kenneth, 114

Silverman, Debora L., 22, 26, 50, 174*n11*

Slutzky, Robert, 65

Social criticism, 179*n90*

Société Anonyme de Pièces Détachées
pour Avions, 15

Société des Artistes Décorateurs, 72,
83, 130–32, 137

Société des Artistes Français, 57

Société du Nouveau Paris, 57

Société Française des Logements
Hygiéniques à Bon Marché, 57

Société Nationale des Beaux-Arts, 57

Solidarisme, 58

Spaces for living, 4, 63

Spain, 165

Stam, Mart, 169*n14*, 170*n17*

Standardization, 69, 110, 140–41, 154

Steel, 176*n52*

Steiger, Rudolf, 170*n17*

Steinberg, Leo, 63

Strip windows, 153

Structural rationalism, 24, 32–33, 46,
48

Suë, Louis, 79, 117, 129, 189*n17*;
boudoir, 94*fig*, 95–96

Switzerland, 17–18, 165

Symbolism, 24, 52, 60

Taut, Bruno, 169*n14*

Taut, Max, 169*n14*

Technology, 121–23

Third Republic (France), 21, 59, 127

Thonet, Michael, 125*fig*, 135–36, 142

Tiersten, Lisa, 35, 50–52, 90

Tiffany, Louis Comfort, 53, 177*n68*

Tise, Suzanne, 22, 101–2

Tools, 134

Toulouse-Lautrec, Henri de, 52, 63

Towards a New Architecture (Le Corbusier), 8, 139, 153

The Transfiguration of the Commonplace: A Philosophy of Art (Danto), 21

Troy, Nancy, 22, 183*n*29

"Type-Needs, Type-Furniture" (Le Corbusier), 138

Typenmöbel, 69

Type-objects, 138

Un Salon Bourgeois: catalog, 84*fig*; creation of, 47, 82; criticism of, 84, 90–91; as cubist work, 86, 88; entry of, 86, 87*fig*, 88–89; façade of, 86, 87*fig*, 88–89, 93; foreign influence on, 91; interior design, 89; interior layout, 84*fig*; legacy of, 92; Mare role in, 85–86, 88–92; mass-produced objects, 94. *See also* Salons d'Automne

Une Cité Industrielle (Garnier), 35–40, 111–13, 115–16; public area, 36*fig*; residential area, 38*fig*; standardization of living units, 140; transit station, 37*fig*

Une Cité Moderne (Mallet-Stevens), 118, 155, 157*fig*, 158*fig*

Une Ville Contemporaine, 149

Union des Artistes Modernes, 131, 137

Union Sacré, 114, 118

Universal Modernism, 166

Urban art, 92

Urban living, 4

Urban planning, 14*fig*, 38, 140, 155

Urbanisme (Le Corbusier), 8, 139

Urbanization, 27

Vaillat, Léandre, 79

Valéry, Paul, 176*n*53

Varenne, Gaston, 129–30, 133, 188*n*6

Vaudoyer, Jean-Louis, 129

Veil, Theodor, 74*fig*

Velde, Henri van de, 52, 177*n*68; dining room, 54*fig*; smoking room, 54*fig*

Vellay, Marc, 22, 144

Vera, Paul, 184*n*37

Vereinigte Werkstätten (Munich), 69–72, 93, 102, 182*n*7

Verne, Henri, 92, 185*n*48

Verneuill, M. P.: German vs. French artists, 75–76; on individualism, 78, 90; on salons, 73, 83–84, 92, 95–96; on stagnation of French architecture, 100

Villon, Jacques, 89, 184*n*37

Villon-Duchamp brothers, 46

Viollet-le-Duc, Eugène-Emmanuel, 23, 28; Academy of Fine Arts' as reactionary, 34; human needs and house design, 33–35; influences on, 40

Vlaminck, Maurice de, 117

Voisin cars, 136

Voisin Plan for Paris, 14*fig*, 140

Von der Mühll, Henri-Robert, 170*n*17

Von Moos, Stanislaus, 22

Vuillard, Edouard, 52, 63

W. E. Troutman, Inc., 116*fig*

Wagner, Otto, 16

War reconstruction: as French goal, 116–17; Garnier's role in, 114; Le Corbusier's proposals for, 110, 113; regional style of Flanders, 110–11, 113

Waring and Gillow, 117

Weimar School of Arts and Crafts, 137

Weisberg, Gabriel, 60

Weiss, Jeffrey, 21, 65, 173*n*48

Weissenhof housing settlement, 8*fig*, 9*fig*, 10

The Werkbund: Design Theory and Mass Culture before the First World War (Schwartz), 22

Werkstätten, 16, 68

Wiener Werkstätte, 17

Wigley, Mark, 11–13

Windows, 45, 110–11, 112, 151, 153

"Wohnhaus-Industry" (Gropius), 12

Women, 13

Women and the Making of the Modern House (Friedman), 13

Working class, 31, 57

World War I: architects' roles in, 114; casualties of, 117, 187n18; devastation from, 117, 118*fig*; disillusionment with technology as effect of, 121; effect on house design, 106, 116, 124, 188n10; effect on middle class, 127–28; soldiers as cave dwellers, 107; trenches, 116*fig*

Yosizaka, Takamasa, 190

Zavala, Juan de, 170n17

Zola, Emile, 26, 179n86

ILLUSTRATION CREDITS

Haven, Conn.: Yale University Press, 1996), **2.2**; Nan-Ching Tai, **1.15**, **1.17**; Nancy J. Troy, *Modernism and the Decorative Arts in France, Art Nouveau to Le Corbusier* (New Haven: Yale University Press, 1991), **1.7**, **1.20**, **2.3**, **2.5**, **2.6**, **2.7**, **2.8**, **2.16**, **4.1**; U.S. Library of Congress, **1.1**, **1.3**, **1.4**, **1.5**, **1.6**, **3.5**, **3.6**; Marc Vellay and Kenneth Frampton, *Pierre Chareau: Architect and Craftsman, 1883–1950* (New York: Rizzoli, 1984), **4.9**; Stanislaus Von Moos and Arthur Rüegg, eds., *Le Corbusier before Le Corbusier: Applied Arts, Architecture, Painting, Photography, 1907–1922* (New Haven, Conn.: Yale University Press, 2002), **2.24**; Gabriel P. Weisberg, *Art Nouveau Bing: Paris Style 1900* (New York: Harry N. Abrams, 1986), **1.21**.